A Bibliography of Ghana

A Bibliography
of Ghana   1930-1961

Compiled by
A. F. Johnson

Published for the
Ghana Library Board by
Longmans

1964

Longmans, Green & Co. Ltd.,
Industrial Estate, Ring Road South, Accra.
Associated companies, branches and
representatives throughout the world.

© Ghana Library Board 1964

First published 1964

Printed in Great Britain by
Spottiswoode, Ballantyne and Co Ltd
London and Colchester

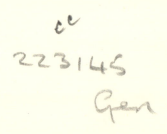

Contents

vi Contents

Introduction

The literature of the Gold Coast and Ghana is remarkably varied, and with the advent of independence in 1957 when the new state took the limelight in international news services, books and periodical articles appeared in many languages. Ghana became a topic for discussion and comment, not always well informed. Books of a scholarly nature on ethnology and native customs, linguistics and social studies have been a notable feature in writings on the Gold Coast, and these continue to appear. There are scientific studies in medicine, agriculture, botany and zoology, as well as the contributions of teachers, social workers and administrators. Much historical material needs to be rewritten by Africans, and there are numerous publications by the Pan-Africanists who seek to place a new interpretation on the forces that make up the new Africa. There are travel books and journalists' impressions, some well-informed and others prejudiced; and to balance these we have official reports and statistical summaries. In all fields of learning, including literature and the fine arts, we find that Ghana has a notable contribution to make.

This bibliography aims to cover the three decades from 1930 to 1961, and is in some respects a continuation of A.W. Cardinall's *A Bibliography of the Gold Coast* which appeared as a supplement to the Census Report of 1931. Cardinall's work is outstanding for its treatment of earlier historical documents and monographs from the arrival of the Europeans in West Africa to ultimate control of the Gold Coast under British administration. Cardinall carried out research into Portuguese, Danish, French and Dutch archives, resulting in a bibliography of unique interest to students of the Gold Coast.

In the same year that he issued his bibliography, Cardinall prepared a survey entitled *The Gold Coast, 1931*. To the observer of today this handbook of facts and figures as a comparison with the new Ghana illustrates the far-reaching changes that have taken place. It is opportune that Cardinall should have terminated his bibliography in the 1930's, for that decade was a turning point in the development of the first African state to achieve independence. The second World War was an upheaval that brought its effects to the west coast of Africa, and it was in the years immediately following the war that a new constitution was determined under the governor Sir Alan Burns. But the 1946 constitution was already outmoded and the disturbances which broke out in 1948 gave rise to the Watson Report and the formulation of a new constitution under J. Henley Coussey. The United Gold Coast Convention, led by Dr. J. B. Danquah was becoming more active in organising meetings with the programme of self-government. Dr. Kwame Nkrumah joined forces as organising secretary, but a rift took place when Dr. Danquah and other members of the U.G.C.C. took part in the deliberations of the Coussey Committee. Dr. Nkrumah wanted 'Self-Government Now'. He gained popular support and created his own party, the Convention People's Party in June 1949. Within two years Dr. Nkrumah was to lead his victorious party into power and was acclaimed Prime Minister in 1952. From 1952 to 1957 the Governor Sir Charles Arden-Clarke and Dr. Nkrumah were able to achieve the gradual transformation of the Gold Coast to independent Ghana and the new state was created on 6 March, 1957.

The years of consolidation which followed saw Ghana making immense strides in all aspects of social life, education and public services. The Ghana government had been planning for some years to create a new industrial community which would make the country less reliant upon cocoa, its basic export commodity. The Volta River Project was conceived as a means of using abundant supplies of bauxite for the manufacture of aluminium, and negotiations were made with overseas governments for the financing of the project. Already the port of Tema was nearing completion a few miles from Accra which was to serve as an outlet for the new industrial capacity resulting from the hydro-electric installations at Akosombo. The final agreement for the construction of the Volta River dam was signed in March 1962, and with this act of statesmanship the President made provision for future abundant supplies of power for the industrialisation of Ghana, with its attendant improvements in education, living standards, health and social welfare. The Gold Coast of 1931 was indeed a remote tropical dependency; the transformation was complete.

In this bibliography I have attempted to list all publications on the Gold Coast and Ghana during the formative years 1930–1961 with selected periodical articles. The list is intended to be comprehensive, including works of technical and scientific interest, translations and pure literature, but vernacular texts have been omitted. Information given in most entries consists of name of author, title, edition, publisher, date and pagination; price is given for some current publications and a brief note added when the title is insufficiently clear. Primary access to materials has been the aim for the majority of the items listed; in other cases secondary access has been possible through lists of books in periodicals and bibliographies. A classified arrangement is provided, based on broad subject groupings, with an alphabetical author index.

The improvement of bibliographical services in the African field is a matter of prime concern to research workers in African studies. Without bibliography the products of man's intellect would remain unchartered and unorganised, and this is particularly true of the new Africa where so many misconceptions and out-of-date assessments may arise. This was stressed by the President of Ghana in his speech at the opening of the Padmore Research Library in Accra: 'There is widespread misunderstanding and ignorance about the newly-developing independent nations of Africa. We are often misrepresented either because our critics do not take the trouble to check the facts or because they rely upon outdated and biased information.' African bibliography is still uncoordinated and uneven and many bibliographies are no longer obtainable. Such works are H. C. Luke's *Bibliography of Sierra Leone*[1], R. M. East's *Vernacular bibliography for the languages of Nigeria*[2], and A.W. Cardinall's *A Bibliography of the Gold Coast*[3]. Current national bibliographies exist only in the Union of South Africa[4] and in Nigeria[5]. Notable examples of bibliographies of individual areas are R. L. Hill's *Bibliography of the Anglo-Egyptian Sudan from the earliest times to 1937*[6], Ruth Perry's *A preliminary bibliography of the literature of nationalism in Nigeria*[7], and Evans Lewin's *Annotated bibliography of recent publications on Africa south of the Sahara*[8]. The bibliography of special subjects is also of interest to the research worker, examples being Howard Drake's *Bibliography of African education*[9], L. J. Ragatz's *Bibliography for the study of African history in the nineteenth and twentieth centuries*[10], I. Schapera's *Select bibliography of South African native life and problems*[11], and D. H. Varley's *African native music*[12].

Important bibliographical work is being carried out through the International African Institute in its *Africa Bibliography Series*, and the Library of Congress has issued a number of excellent bibliographies. Special libraries in the United States are active in this field, such as the Howard University Library, the African Department of Northwestern University, and the Schomburg Collection of New York Public Library. Publications of the Institut Français d'Afrique Noire in Dakar are also of special importance to research students.

The work of compilation of this bibliography would have been impossible without the valuable assistance of many persons both in Ghana and overseas. I wish to acknowledge the interest and advice of Professor G.W. Irwin, Department of History in the University of Ghana, Mr. K. E. Senanu and Mr. T. Stock. I was able to draw upon the resources of libraries of government Ministries and research institutes, notably those of the Ministry of Foreign Affairs (Mr. G. Eghan), Ministry of Agriculture (Mr. S. N. Tetteh), the Legislative Assembly (Mr. S. K. Kanda), the Central Office of Statistics (Mr. L. Agyei-Gyane,) the Medical Research Council (Mr. C. Tettey), the Ghana National Archives (Mr. J. M. Akita), the West African Cocoa Research Institute (Mr. T. W. Cochrane), and the West African Building Research Institute (Dr. Marion Petrie). The holdings of two important school and training college libraries were checked, and I should like to thank Mr. D. A. Chapman, Headmaster of Achimota School and the Rev. Noel Smith, Principal of the Presbyterian Training College, Akropong, for their valuable assistance. In addition I should mention the kindness of Mrs. J. B. Danquah in giving me access to her husband's personal library, and the guidance given by Mr. A. Ott, General Manager of the Presbyterian Book Depot whose private collection on the Gold Coast and Ghana is the most extensive I have seen. Acknowledgment must also be given to the Librarian and staff of the Balme Library for their unfailing help in checking some of the more rare and unusual items, and to the Ghana Library Board for placing at my disposal the Ghana Collection which forms the foundation of the newly established Padmore Research Library on African Affairs. The Padmore Librarian, Mr. S. A. Kotei, gave help from the inception of the work, and I am grateful for the encouragement of the Director of Library Services, Miss Evelyn J. A. Evans, C.B.E.

This record of thanks would not be complete without a note of overseas assistance. The Rev. Dr. Hans Debrunner offered his expert advice on selection of entries on Ethnology, Church Missions and Education. Miss Ruth Jones, Librarian of the International African Institute readily agreed to put the resources of her library at my disposal, but limitations of time and distance made this impossible. However, I am grateful for permission to include many references from the bibliography which appears in each issue of *Africa*, mostly of foreign language publications unobtainable in Ghana.

List of Abbreviations

Periodical reference	Full title
Advance	Advance (Accra)
Africa	Africa (London)
Afr. affairs	African affairs (London)
Afr. studies	African studies (Johannesburg)
Afr. world	African world (London)
Afrika	Afrika (Berlin)
Afr. u. Ubersee	Afrika und Ubersee (Hamburg)
Amer. anthropologist	American anthropologist (Wisconsin)
Amer. pol. sci. rev.	American political science review (Menasha, Wisconsin)
Ann. afr.	Annales africaines (Paris)
Ann. de géog.	Annales de géographie (Paris)
Ann. lateranensi	Annales lateranensi
Anthropos	Anthropos (Frieburg)
Atlantis	Atlantis
Bull. IFAN	Bulletin de l'Institut Français d'Afrique Noire (Dakar)
Bull. inter-Afr. Labour Inst.	Bulletin of the Inter-African Labour Institute (Brazzaville)
Bull. Sch. Orient. Afr. Studies	Bulletin of the School of Oriental and African Studies
Cah. Ét. afr.	Cahiers d'Études africaines (Paris)
Cah. int. soc.	Cahiers internationaux de sociologie
Community devel. bull.	Community development bulletin (London)
Die Erde	Die Erde (Berlin)

Econ. bull.	Economic bulletin (Accra)
Geog. J.	Geographical journal (London)
Ghana bull. theology	Ghana bulletin of theology (Accra)
Ghana teachers' J.	Ghana teachers' journal (Accra)
Gold Coast teachers' J.	Gold Coast teachers' journal (Accra)
Int. labour rev.	International labour review (Geneva)
Int. rev. missions	International review of missions (London)
J. Afr. admin.	Journal of African administration (London)
J. Afr. hist.	Journal of African history (London)
J. Afr. law	Journal of African law (London)
J. Hist. Soc. Nigeria	Journal of the Historical Society of Nigeria (Ibadan)
J. Roy. Afr. Soc.	Journal of the Royal African Society (London)
J. Roy. Anthrop. Inst.	Journal of the Royal Anthropological Institute (London)
J. Soc. Africanistes	Journal de la Société des Africanistes (Paris)
J. W. Afr. Science Assn.	Journal of the West African Science Association
Man	Man (London)
Mém. IFAN	Mémoires de l'Institut Français d'Afrique Noire (Dakar)
Mitt. Inst. f. Orient.	Mitteilungen des Instituts für Orientforschung
Nigerian field	Nigerian field (Ibadan)
Notes afr. IFAN	Notes africaines de l'Institut Français d'Afrique Noire (Dakar)
Oversea Educ.	Oversea education (London)
Présence afr.	Présence africaine (Paris)
S. A. J. Sci.	South African journal of science
S.-W. J. Anthrop.	Southwestern journal of anthropology (Albuquerque)
Soc. rev.	Sociological review
Soviet Etnogr.	Sovietskaya Etnografia (Moscow)

Trans. Gold Coast & Togoland Hist. Soc.	Transactions of the Gold Coast and Togoland Historical Society
Trans. Hist. Soc. Ghana	Transactions of the Historical Society of Ghana
Trans. Roy. Soc. Trop. Med. Hygiene	Transactions of the Royal Society of Tropical Medicine and Hygiene
Universitas	Universitas (Accra)
West Africa	West Africa (London)
W. Afr. J. Educ.	West African journal of education (London)
W. Afr. Med. J.	West African medical journal (Ibadan)
W. Afr. Rev.	West African review (Liverpool)
Zaire	Zaire (Brussels)
Z. f. Ethnol.	Zeitschrift für Ethnologie (Berlin)

References

1. OXFORD UNIVERSITY PRESS, 1925.
2. ZARIA, LITERATURE BUREAU, 1941.
3. ACCRA, GOVERNMENT PRINTER, 1931.
4. SOUTH AFRICAN CATALOGUE (of books). Complete edition, books published 1900–1942, with supplement of books published during 1943. Stellenbosch, 1943.
—— 3rd ed. 1900–1947.
—— 4th ed. 1900–1950. 2v.
Supplemented by monthly issues and annual cumulations.
5. NIGERIAN PUBLICATIONS. Ibadan, University College Library, 1950– A list of works received under the Publications Ordinance. Annual.
6. OXFORD UNIVERSITY PRESS, 1939.
7. IBADAN. Typescript, 1962.
8. ROYAL EMPIRE SOCIETY, 1943.
9. ABERDEEN, UNIVERSITY OF ABERDEEN ANTHROPOLOGICAL MUSEUM, 1942.
10. WASHINGTON, D.C., PEARLMAN, 1943.
11. OXFORD UNIVERSITY PRESS, 1941.
12. ROYAL EMPIRE SOCIETY, 1936.

Bibliographies

1 AMERICAN UNIVERSITIES FIELD STAFF. *A select bibliography: Asia, Africa, Eastern Europe, Latin America.* N.Y., 1960. 533 pp.

2 BANKS, A. *An Africa book list.* Edinburgh House Press, 1960. 35 pp.

3 BOSTON UNIVERSITY, CHENERY LIBRARY. *Catalog of African government documents and African area index.* Boston, Hall, 1960. 124 pp.

4 CARDINALL, ALLAN W. *A bibliography of the Gold Coast* [1496-1931] *issued as a companion volume to the census report of 1931.* Accra, Govt. Printer, [1932] xix, 384 pp.

5 COMMISSION FOR TECHNICAL CO-OPERATION IN AFRICA SOUTH OF THE SAHARA. *Inventory of economic studies concerning Africa south of the Sahara: an annotated reading list of books, articles, and official publications.* C.C.T.A., 1960. 310 pp.

6 DRAKE, HOWARD. *A bibliography of African education, south of the Sahara.* Aberdeen U.P., 1942. 97 pp.

7 EDINGTON, G. M., AND TETTEY, C. 'Survey of medical publications from the Gold Coast, 1953-54.' *W. Afr. Med. J.*, **6**, 1, 1957: 22-25.

8 GHANA. UNIVERSITY, BALME LIBRARY. *List of periodicals.* Legon, 1961. 168 pp.

9 GREAT BRITAIN, COLONIAL OFFICE. *Bibliography of land tenure in the Gold Coast.* [1947?] 16 pp. (Typescript.)

10 —— *Bibliography of published sources relating to African land tenure.* H.M.S.O., 1950. 156 pp.

11 HARRIS, F. C., AND TETTEY, C. 'Survey of medical publications from the Gold Coast (Ghana), 1955-56.' *W. Afr. Med. J.*, **6**, 3, 1957: 117-122.

12 HAZLEWOOD, ARTHUR. *Economics of underdeveloped areas: an annotated reading list of books, etc.* O.U.P., 1959, xii, 156 pp.

13 HEWITT, A. R. *Guide to resources for Commonwealth studies in London, Oxford and Cambridge, with bibliographical and other information.* Published for the Institute of Commonwealth Studies by the Athlone Press, 1957. 219 pp.

14   HEWITT, A. R. *Union list of Commonwealth newspapers in London, Oxford and Cambridge*. Published for the Institute of Commonwealth Studies by the Athlone Press, 1960. 101 pp.

15   HINTZE, URSULA. *Bibliographie der Kwa-Sprachen and der Sprachen der Togo-Restvölker*. Berlin, Akademie-Verlag, 1959. 102 pp.

16   HOLDSWORTH, MARY. *Soviet African studies, 1918–59: an annotated bibliography*. Royal Institute of International Affairs, 1961. 2 vols. (Chatham House memoranda.)

17   HOWARD UNIVERSITY. LIBRARY. *A catalogue of the African Collection in the Moorland Foundation, Howard University Library; edited by Dorothy B. Porter*. Washington, D.C., Howard U.P., 1958. 398 pp.

18   HUGHES, M. H., *comp. Medical bibliography of the Gold Coast, 1900–1951, with an index*. Accra, Govt. Printer, 1953. 30 pp. (Typescript).

19   INTERNATIONAL AFRICAN INSTITUTE. *Select annotated bibliography of tropical Africa*. N.Y., Twentieth Century Fund, 1956. [505] pp. Limited to material published before the end of 1954.

20   —— *West Africa: general, ethnography, sociology, linguistics*; compiled by RUTH JONES. 1958. 116 pp. (Africa bibliography series.)

21   ITALIAANDER, R. *Africana: selected bibliography of readings in African history and civilization*. Holland, Michigan, Hope College, 1961. 103 pp.

22   JOHNSON, A. F. *comp. Books about Ghana: a select reading list*. Accra, Ghana Library Board, 1961. 32 pp.

23   LEWIN, E. *Annotated bibliography of recent publications on Africa, south of the Sahara*. Royal Empire Society, 1943.

24   MAUNY, RAYMOND. 'Bibliographie de l'Empire du Mali.' *Notes afr. IFAN*, **82**, 1959: 55–56.

25   MEEK, C. K. *Colonial law: a bibliography with special reference to native African systems of law and land tenure*. O.U.P., 1948. 58 pp.

26   MERRIAM, ALAN P. 'An annotated bibliography of African and African-derived music since 1936.' *Africa*, **21**, 4, Oct. 1951: 319–329.

27   MORRELL, W. P. *British overseas expansion and the history of the Commonwealth: a select bibliography*. Historical Association, 1961. 40 pp.

28 MYLIUS, NORBERT. *Afrika Bibliographie, 1943–1951.* Wien, Verein Freunde der Völkerkunde, 1952. 237 pp.

29 PERHAM, MARGERY. *Colonial government: annotated reading list on British colonial government.* O.U.P., 1950. 80 pp.

30 PITCHER, GEORGE M. *Bibliography of Ghana, 1957–59.* Kumasi, College of Technology Library, 1960. 177 pp. (Typescript.)

31 RAGATZ, L. J. *Bibliography for the study of African history in the nineteenth and twentieth centuries.* Washington, D.C., 1943.

32 ROBERTS, H. *Foreign affairs bibliography, 1942–1952.* N.Y., 1955.

33 ROWLING, F., AND WILSON, C. E. *Bibliography of African Christian literature.* Conference of Missionary Societies of Great Britain and Ireland, 1923. 130 pp.

34 ROYAL EMPIRE SOCIETY. *Subject catalogue of the library of the Royal Empire Society, formerly Royal Colonial Institute,* by EVANS LEWIN. *Vol. 1: The British Empire generally, and Africa.* 1930. 700 pp.

35 RUTH SLOAN ASSOCIATES, WASHINGTON, D.C. *The press in Africa;* edited by HELEN KITCHEN. Washington, D.C., 1956. 96 pp.

36 SOUTH AFRICAN PUBLIC LIBRARY, CAPE TOWN. *A bibliography of African bibliographies, covering territories south of the Sahara.* 4th ed., revised to November 1960. Cape Town, 1961. iv, 79 pp. (Grey bibliographies, no. 7.)

37 TAIT, DAVID. 'David Tait, 1912–56: a bibliography.' *Trans. Hist. Soc. Ghana,* **3,** 2, 1957: 151.

38 TENRI. CENTRAL LIBRARY, JAPAN. *Africana: catalogue of books relating to Africa in the Tenri Central Library.* 1960. 431 pp.

39 U.S. LIBRARY OF CONGRESS. *Africa south of the Sahara; a selected, annotated list of writings, 1951–56;* compiled by HELEN F. CONOVER. 1957.

40 —— *Africa south of the Sahara: an introductory list of bibliographies;* compiled by HELEN F. CONOVER, Africana Section. 1961. 7 pp.

41 —— *African newspapers currently received in selected American libraries.* 1956. 16 pp.

42 —— *American doctoral dissertations concerned with Africa.* 1961.

43 —— *British West Africa: a selected list of references;* compiled by HELEN F. CONOVER. 1957.

44 —— *Introduction to Africa: a selective guide to background reading;* prepared by HELEN F. CONOVER. 1952. 237 pp.

4 Bibliographies

45 U.S. LIBRARY OF CONGRESS. *Non self-governing areas with special emphasis on Mandates and Trusteeships: a selected list of references.* 1947.

46 —— *Periodicals on Africa currently received in selected American libraries.* 1956. 34 pp.

47 —— *Research and information on Africa: continuing sources;* compiled by HELEN F. CONOVER. 1954. 70 pp.
A guide to publication programmes of universities, societies and research institutions throughout the world, relating to Africa.

48 —— *Serials for African studies;* compiled by HELEN F. CONOVER. 1961. viii, 163 pp.

49 WOLFSON, FREDA. 'Ghana in books.' *West Africa,* 1957, 2080–2083.

50 WOOLBERT, R. *Foreign affairs bibliography, 1932–1942.* N.Y., 1945.

51 WORK, M.T. *Bibliography of the Negro in Africa and America.* N.Y., 1928.

See also no. 246.

Periodicals

52   *Achimota Review*. Achimota College Press, 1927-1947.

53   *Advance*. Accra, Dept. of Social Welfare & Community Development. No. 1+ 1954+ Monthly.

54   *Africa:* Journal of the International African Institute. Vol. 1+ Jan. 1928+ Quarterly.
    Linguistic and ethnological studies, with bibliography of current publications.

55   *Africa*. Madrid, Instituto des Estudios Africanos, 1952+

56   *Africa Digest*. Africa Publication Trust. No. 1+ 1952+

57   *African Abstracts*. A quarterly review of ethnographic, social and linguistic studies appearing in current periodicals. International African Institute. Vol. 1+ Jan. 1950+
    Analyses over 150 current periodicals. Annual author and subject indexes.

58   *African Affairs*. Journal of the Royal African Society. Vol. 43+ 1944+
    Continuation of *Royal African Society. Journal*.

59   *African Eagle*. London, United Kingdom Branch, National Association of Socialist Students Organization. Vol. 1+ 1960+ 3 nos. per year.
    Convention People's Party, London Branch.

60   *African Music*. Journal of the African Music Society. Vol. 1, no. 1+ 1954+
    Continuation of *African Music Society. Newsletter*.

61   *African Music Society. Newsletter*. Vol. 1, nos. 3-6, 1950-1953.
    Continued as *African Music*.

62   *African Women*. London University, Institute of Education. Vol. 1+ 1954+

63   *African Worker*. Accra, T.U.C. Vol. 1+ 1961+
    Text in English and French.

64   *African World*. London, African Publications, Ltd., 1902+

6 Periodicals

65 *Africana.* The journal of the West African Society. Newcastle-upon-Tyne, 1948–50. Quarterly.
Ceased publication.

66 *Afrika.* Periodical on politics, economic affairs and culture in the new Africa. Munich, Federal Republic of Germany, 1959+

67 *Africa und Übersee.* Berlin, 1910+
Continuation of *Zeitschrift für kolonialsprachen.*

68 *Annales Africaines.* Université de Dakar, 1954+

69 *Anthropos.* International review of ethnology and linguistics. Vol. 1+ 1906+

70 *Auto Ghana.* Official journal of the Ghana Motor Club.

71 *Black Orpheus.* A journal of African and Afro-American literature. Vol. 1+ 1957+

72 *Cahiers d'Études Africaines.* No. 1+ 1960+

73 *Cahiers Internationaux de Sociologie.* t. 1+ 1946+

74 *Catholic Voice.* Cape Coast, Mfantsiman Press, 1927+ Weekly.

75 *Christian Messenger.* Accra, Presbyterian Press. Vol. 1+ 1960+ Monthly.
Published by the Basel Mission and the Presbyterian Church in Ghana.

76 *Cocoa Statistics.* Rome, F.A.O. Vol. 1, no. 1+ Jan. 1958+ Quarterly.

77 *Comité d'Études Historiques et Scientifiques de l'Afrique Occidentale Français.* Bulletin. 1923–38. Continued as *Institut Français d'Afrique Noire.* Bulletin.

78 *Cuadernos de Estudios Africanos.* Madrid, Instituto de Estudio Politkos, 1946+

79 *Economic Bulletin.* Accra, Guinea Press for the Economic Society of Ghana. Vol 1+ 1957+ Monthly.

80 *The Emancipator.* A nationalist magazine for the masses. Accra, C.P.P. No. 1+ April 1959+
Ceased publication.

81 *Estudos Ultramarinos.* Lisbon, Escola Superior de Ultramar, 1948+

82 *Ewe News-letter.* ed. by D. A. Chapman. Achimota Press. Nos. 1–15, 1945–1946.
Ceased publication.

83 *Ewe Studies.* ed. by D. A. Chapman. Achimota Press, Nos. 1 & 2, 1944.
Ceased publication.

84 *The Farmer.* Accra, United Farmers' Council, 1958+

85 *Ghana Builds.* Vol. 1, nos. 1 & 2, 1961.
Continued as *Ghana Reconstructs.*

86 *Ghana Bulletin of Theology.* Accra, University College. Vol. 1, no. 3+ 1957+ Bi-annual.
First printed issue.

87 *Ghana Co-operator.* No. 1+ 1952+
Continuation of *Gold Coast Co-operative News.*

88 *Ghana Farmer.* Accra, Ministry of Food and Agriculture. Vol. 1+ 1956+ Quarterly.
Vol. 1, nos. 1–3 were entitled *New Gold Coast Farmer.*

89 *Ghana Foreign Affairs.* Accra, Ministry of Foreign Affairs. Vol. 1+ Dec. 1960+
Ceased publication.

90 *Ghana Geographical Association.* Bulletin. Vol. 1+ 1956+

91 *Ghana Journal of Science.* University of Ghana, Ghana Science Association. Vol 1+ 1961+ Bi-annual.

92 *Ghana Labour News.* Accra, Ghana Trades Union Congress. No. 1+ 1957+
Continued as *Labour.*

93 *The Ghana Law Reports.* Accra, General Legal Council, 1959+

94 *Ghana Notes and Queries.* Accra, Historical Society of Ghana. Vol. 1+ 1961+

95 *Ghana Outlook.* Review of policy, economics, culture and information. Bonn, Embassy of the Republic of Ghana. Vol. 1+ 1960+
Text in English, French and German.

96 *Ghana Public Servant.* 1954–1957.
Nos. 1–5, 1954–1956 entitled *Gold Coast Public Servant.* Ceased publication at no. 1, 1957.

97 *Ghana Radio Review and TV Times.* Vol. 1+ 1960/1961+

98 *Ghana Reconstructs.* Accra, Ministry of Information. Vol. 1, no. 3+ Aug. 1961+ Monthly.
Continuation of *Ghana Builds.*

99 *Ghana Teacher.* Vol. 1, no. 1+ Dec. 1959+

100 *Ghana Teachers' Journal.* Published for the Ministry of Education, Ghana, by Nelson. Jan. 1958+ Quarterly.
1955–1957, no. 2 published as *Gold Coast Teachers' Journal.* Continuation of *Gold Coast Education.*

101 *Ghana through the World Press.* Accra, Ministry of Education and Information. Vol. 1, no. 1+ Dec. 1959+

102 *Ghana Today.* London, Office of the Ghana High Commissioner. Vol. 1+ 1956+
Vol. 1, 1956 entitled *Gold Coast Today.* Title changed, March 1957.

103 *Ghana Trade Journal.* No. 1+ 1959+

104 *Ghana Trade Review.* Vol. 1, nos. 1–4, 1959.
Ceased publication.

105 *Ghana Weekly Review.* Vol. 1, 6th March–16th Oct. 1957.
Continuation of *Gold Coast Weekly Review.*
Continued as *New Ghana.*

106 *Ghana World.* Accra, Ghana Graphic. Nos. 1–3, 1959.
Ceased publication.

107 *The Ghanaian.* Accra, Guinea Press. No. 1+ July 1958+ Monthly.

108 *Ghanaian Bulletin of Agricultural Economics.* Vol. 1, no. 1+ June 1961+

109 *The Ghanaian Woman.* Accra, Federation of Ghana Women. Vol. 1, no. 1+ Oct./Dec. 1958+
Ceased publication.

110 *Ghanaian Worker.* Official organ of the Ghana T.U.C. Vols. 1–3, Oct. 1958–May 1960.
Continued as *Labour.*

111 *Gold Coast and Togoland Historical Society. Transactions.* Vols. 1–2, 1952–1956.
Continued as *Historical Society of Ghana. Transactions.*

112 *Gold Coast Bulletin.* Vols. 1–6, 1946–1951.
Continued as *Gold Coast Weekly Review.*

113 *Gold Coast Education.* May 1952–1955.
Continued as *Gold Coast Teachers' Journal.*

114 *Gold Coast Farmer.* Vol. 1–Vol. 8, no. 9, 1932–1939.
Continued as *New Gold Coast Farmer.*

115　*Gold Coast Review.* Vols. 1–5, 1925–1929/31. Semi-annual.
　　Ceased publication.

116　*Gold Coast Teachers' Journal.* 1955–1957.
　　Continued as *Ghana Teachers' Journal.*

117　*Gold Coast Today.* Vol. 1, 1956+
　　Continued as *Ghana Today.*

118　*Gold Coast Weekly Review.* Vols. 1–7, 1951–1957.
　　Continuation of *Gold Coast Bulletin.*
　　Continued as *Ghana Weekly Review.*

119　*Historical Society of Ghana. Transactions.* Accra, University College
　　of Ghana. Vol. 1+ 1952+ Irregular.
　　Vols. 1–2, 1952–1956 published as *Gold Coast and Togoland
　　Historical Society. Transactions.*

120　*Historical Society of Nigeria.* Journal. Ibadan, 1956+ Irregular.

121　*Institut Français d'Afrique Noire.* Bulletin. Vols. 1–15, 1939–1953.
　　Continuation of *Comité d'Etudes Historiques et Scientifiques de
　　l'Afrique Occidentale Française.* Bulletin.

122　*Institut Français d'Afrique Noire.* Bulletin. Série A: Sciences natu-
　　relles. t. 16+ 1954+
　　Continuation of *Institut Français d'Afrique Noire.* Bulletin.

123　*Institut Français d'Afrique Noire.* Bulletin. Série B: Sciences hu-
　　maines. t. 16+ 1954+
　　Continuation of *Institut Français d'Afrique Noire.* Bulletin.

124　*Institut Français d'Afrique Noire.* Mémoires. No. 1+ 1940+

125　*Journal of African Administration.* Vol. 1+ 1949+

126　*Journal of African History.* Vol. 1+ 1960+

127　*Journal of African Law.* Vol. 1, no. 1+ Spring 1957+

128　*Journal of Local Administration Overseas.* Vol. 1, no. 1+ Jan. 1962+

129　*Journal of Management Studies.* Achimota, College of Administration,
　　1961+ Quarterly.

130　*Labour.* Official journal of the [Ghana] Trade Union Congress. Vol.
　　1+ 1960+

131　*London. University. School of Oriental and African studies.* Bulletin.
　　1920+

132　*Man.* A record of anthropological science. Vol. 1+ 1901+

133　*Modern Woman.* [Accra]. Vol. 1, no. 1+ Jan. 1961+

134   *Music in Ghana.* Accra, Ghana Music Society. Vol. 1+ 1958+

135   *New Ghana.* Accra, Ministry of Information. Vol. 1+ Oct. 1957+
Fortnightly.
Continuation of *Ghana Weekly Review.*

136   *New Gold Coast Farmer.* Vol. 1+ 1956+
Continued as *Ghana Farmer,* from Vol. 1, no. 4.

137   *The New Nation.* The Gold Coast new Christian monthly. Vol. 1,
no. 1+ Vol. 2, July 1955–1957.
Ceased publication.

138   *Nigerian Field.* Vol. 1+ 1930+

139   *Notes Africaines.* Dakar, Institut Français d'Afrique Noire. No. 1+
1939+

140   *Okyeame.* Accra, Ghana Society of Writers, P.O. Box M.15. No.
1+ 1960/61+

141   *One Africa.* Accra. All African People's Secretariat. Vol. 1+ Jan.
1961+
Ceased publication.

142   *Pan-African Sportsman.* Accra, Central Organisation of Sport. Vol. 1,
no. 1+ 1961+

143   *The Party.* Accra, Convention People's Party. Vol. 1+ 1960/61+
Monthly.

144   *Présence Africaine.* No. 1+ 1947+
English edition from no. 20.

145   *Royal African Society.* Journal. Vols. 1–42, 1901–1943.
Continued as *African Affairs.*

146   *Royal Anthropological Institute of Great Britain and Ireland.* Journal.
Vol. 1+ 1871+

147   *Société des Africanistes.* Journal. 1931+
Contains annual *Bibliographie africaniste,* compiled by PALAU
MARTI.

148   *Teacher's Journal* (Department of Education, Gold Coast). Vols.
1–11 1928–1939.
Ceased publication. Replaced by *Gold Coast Education,* 1952–
1955, and *Ghana Teachers' Journal.*

149   *Universitas.* Accra, University College of Ghana. Vol. 1, no. 1+
1953+

150 *Voice of Africa.* Accra, Bureau of African Affairs. Vol. 1+ 1960+

151 *WALA News.* Bulletin of the West African Library Association. Ibadan. No. 1+ 1954+

152 *West Africa.* No. 1+ 1917+

153 *West African Diplomatist.* Accra, Ghana Graphic. Vol. 1, nos. 1-4, 1958.
     Ceased publication.

154 *West African Journal of Education.* Vol. 1, no. 1+ Feb. 1957+

155 *West African Medical Journal.* New series. Ibadan University College. Vol. 1, no. 1+ March 1952+

156 *West African Review.* No. 1+ 1922+
     Continuation of *Elder Dempster Magazine.*

157 *West African Science Association.* Journal. Achimota, University College. Vol. 1+ Oct. 1954+

Newspapers

173 *Guinea Times.* Accra, Guinea Press.
   Continued as *The Ghana Times.*

174 *Northern Ghana Weekly.* Tamale, Govt. Printer.

175 *Sunday Mirror.* Accra, West African Graphic Co.

176 *Vox Populi.* 1917+
   Continuation of *Voice of the People.* Ceased publication 1939?

Directories

177 *Directory of the Republic of Ghana, including trade index & biographical section.* Diplomatic Press & Publishing Co., 1959+ Annual.

178 *Ghana. Ministry of Trade and Industry.* Handbook of commerce and industry. 2nd ed. Accra, Govt. Printer, 1959. 100 pp.
Appendices give lists of Government departments, air services, shipping lines, hotels, etc.

179 *Ghana Year Book.* Accra, Daily Graphic, 1957+

180 *Gold Coast Handbook.* Accra, West Africa Publicity Co., 1937. 442 pp.
General survey with estimated population in 1934.

181 *Gold Coast Year Book.* Accra, Daily Graphic, 1953+ Continued as *Ghana year book.*

182 *The "Sunlight" reference Almanac.* 1936. Compiled and edited by OHENEBA SAKYI DJAN. ABURI, 1936. 146 pp.

Geography

183 ACKAH, C. A. *West Africa: a School Certificate geography*. U.L.P., 1958. 208 pp.

184 ADAMS, DAVID THICKENS. *An elementary geography of the Gold Coast*. U.L.P., 1931. 240 pp.

185 —— *A Ghana geography*. New ed. U.L.P., 1960. 192 pp.
A revision of *A Gold Coast geography*, 1951.

186 ADAMS, DAVID THICKENS., AND HARMAN, H. A. *Ghana: a first geography reader*. 3rd ed. Longmans, 1958. 90 pp.
First published as *The Gold Coast: a first reader*, 1932.

187 ANANG, J. L., AND HAMPSHIRE, J. B. *Ghana for middle schools*. Evans, 1960. 106 pp.

188 —— *Ghana for primary schools*. Evans, 1960. 79 pp.

189 BOATENG, E. A. *A geography of Ghana*. C.U.P., 1959. 205 pp.
For School Certificate and University students.

190 —— *Tomorrow's map of West Africa*. Bureau of Current Affairs, 1952. 18 pp. (West African affairs pamphlets, no. 13.)

191 CHAPMAN, DANIEL A. *Our homeland: a regional geography. Book 1: South-east Gold Coast*. Achimota, Achimota Press, 1943. 124 pp.
No more published.

192 CHURCH, R. J. H. *West Africa: a study of the environment and of man's use of it*. 2nd ed. Longmans, 1960. 547 pp.
Physical, political and economic geography.

193 DALLIMORE, H. *A geography of West Africa*. 3rd ed., revised. Lutterworth Press, 1948. 113 pp.

194 FITZGERALD, WALTER. *Africa: a social, economic and political geography of its major regions*. 8th ed. revised by W. C. Brice. Methuen, 1955. xvi, 511 pp.

195 FORTES, MEYER. 'Human ecology in West Africa.' *Afr. affairs*, **44,** 174, Jan. 1945: 27–31.

196 GAUTIER, E. F. *L'Afrique noire occidentale: esquisse des cadres géographiques.* 2d. éd. Paris, Larose, 1943. viii, 188 pp.

197 —— 'Les cotes de l'Afrique occidentale au sud de Dakar.' *Ann. de Géog.*, **40**, 224, 15 mars 1931: 163–174.

198 GREAT BRITAIN. ADMIRALTY. HYDROGRAPHIC DEPT. *Africa pilot. Vol. I: West coast of Africa.* 11th ed. H.M.S.O., 1953. 515 pp.

199 HIGSON, F. G. *A certificate geography of West Africa.* Longmans, 1961. 223 pp.

200 JARRETT, H. R. *A geography of West Africa.* New ed. Dent, 1958. x, 148 pp.

201 —— *Physical geography for West Africa.* Longmans, 1959. 146 pp.

202 MELLOR, M. *A practical modern geography. Book 3: West Africa.* 4th ed. O.U.P., 1957. 120 pp.

203 NIVEN, C. R. *The land and the people of West Africa.* Black, 1958. 84 pp.

204 OBOLI, H. O. N. *An outline geography of West Africa.* Harrap, 1957. 224 pp.

205 PEDLER, F. J. *Economic geography of West Africa.* Longmans, 1955. 232 pp.

206 —— *West Africa.* 2nd ed. Methuen, 1959. 233 pp.

207 PUGH, J. C., AND PERRY, A. E. *A shorter geography of West Africa.* U.L.P., 1961. 288 pp.

208 SCHULTZE, J. H. *Beitrage zür Geographie Tropisch-Afrikas: Erläuterungen zu einer in der Beilage befindlichen Kartenserie von Guinea und Ostafrika.* Leipzig, Deutsches Institut für Länderkunde. Wissenschaftliche Veröffentlichungen, Neue Folge, 13/14, 1955. 137 pp.

209 STAMP, LAURENCE DUDLEY. *Africa: a study in tropical development.* Chapman & Hall, 1953. vii, 568 pp.

210 STEEL, ROBERT W. *The towns of Ashanti: a geographical study.* C. R. XVIe Congrès International de Géographie, Lisbonne, 1949: 81–93.

211 THOMPSON, V., AND ADLOFF, R. *French West Africa.* Allen & Unwin, 1958. 626 pp.

212 VARLEY, W. J., AND WHITE, H. P. *The geography of Ghana.* Longmans, 1958. 313 pp.

213 WISE, C. G. *Short notes on the major climatic regions of the world.* Achimota, College Press, 1935. 20 pp.

Maps

214 CHARTER, C. F. *Detailed soil map of the West African Cacao Research Institute station*. Scale 1:2,500. Tafo, the Institute, 1946.

215 GOLD COAST. COMMISSIONER OF LANDS. *Togoland, northern sphere,* 1949. Scale 1:50,000 and 1:100,000.
    8 sheets covering the Gold Coast–Togo frontier.

216 GOLD COAST. GEOLOGICAL SURVEY. *Geological map of the Gold Coast, southern sheet, showing positions of gold mines and prospects*. Scale 1-500,000. Accra, 1934.

217 —— *Geological map of the Gold Coast and Togoland under British trusteeship*. Scale 1:1m. Accra, 1955.

218 GOLD COAST. SURVEY DEPARTMENT. *Atlas of the Gold Coast*. 5th ed. Accra, 1949.
    A Portfolio of 12 Ghana maps was published in 1962.

219 —— *School atlas of the Gold Coast*. Accra, 1952. 16 pp.

220 —— *The Gold Coast: native states*. Scale 1:1 m. Accra, 1951.

221 —— *The Gold Coast: stock routes and veterinary sections*. Scale 1:1 m. Accra, 1952.

222 —— *Gold Coast survey: main framework diagram*. Scale 1:1 m. Accra, 1952.

223 —— *Magnetic observations in the Gold Coast*. Scale 1:1 m. Accra, 1932.

224 —— *Forts of Ghana*. Scale 1:1 m.

225 GHANA SURVEY DEPARTMENT. *Road map of Ghana: northern and southern sections*. 2 sheets. Accra, 1959. Scale 1:500,000.

226 —— *1:62,500 series*. 148 sheets covering the southern part of the country.

227 —— *1:125,000 series*. 54 sheets covering southern Ghana and part of the northern region.

228 —— *1:250,000 series*. 20 sheets covering the whole of Ghana.

229 —— *1:50,000 series*. 57 sheets covering part of southern Ghana.

230 STANFORD, E. publishers. *Map of the Gold Coast and part of Ashanti, showing the British Protectorate*. 1873. Scale: 9 miles to an inch.
    See also nos. 2601, 2602, 2603.

Geology and Climate

231 BRITISH WEST AFRICAN METEOROLOGICAL SERVICES. *Frequencies of temperature and dew point in specified ranges at airports in Nigeria, Gold Coast and Sierra Leone.* Lagos, Survey Dept., 1953.

232 CHANCELLOR, J. *West African weather patterns: a study of outstanding meteorological conditions in tropical Africa.* Chicago, 1946.

233 CROW, A. T. 'Geology and earthquakes in the Gold Coast.' *Nigerian field,* **21**, 2, 1956: 52–68.

234 FURON, RAYMOND. *Geologie de l'Afrique.* 2e éd. Paris, Payot, 1960. 400 pp.

235 GOLD COAST. GEOLOGICAL SURVEY DEPT. *Outlines of the mineral and water-power resources of the Gold Coast, British West Africa, with hints on prospecting,* by A. E. KITSON. Accra, 1925.

236 —— *Report on a rapid geological survey of the Gambia, British West Africa.* Accra, 1927.

237 —— *Microscopical features and chemical analyses of certain representative igneous rocks from the Gold Coast,* by N. R. JUNNER AND H. F. HARWOOD. Accra, 1928.

238 —— *References to occurrences of economic minerals in the Gold Coast, recorded in Annual Reports of the Director, Geological Survey,* by A. E. KITSON AND W. J. FELTON. Accra, 1930 (Bulletin no. 5.)

239 —— *Minerals of concentrates from stream-gravels, soils and crushed rocks of the Gold Coast,* by A. E. KITSON AND W. J. FELTON. Accra, 1930. (Bulletin no. 6.)

240 —— *Reports on the water supply of the coastal area of the Eastern Province of the Gold Coast Colony.* Accra, 1931.

241 —— *The geology of the Obuasi goldfield,* by N. R. JUNNER. Accra, 1932. 43 pp. (Memoir no. 2.)

242 —— *The geology of the Prestea goldfield,* by W. G. G. COOPER. Accra, 1934. 20 pp. (Memoir no. 3.)

243 —— *Gold in the Gold Coast,* by N. R. JUNNER, *with appendix: Gold Coast laws and their effect on mining,* by R. P. WILD. Accra, 1935. 76 pp. (Memoir no. 4.)

244 GOLD COAST. GEOLOGICAL SURVEY DEPT. *The bauxite deposits of the Gold Coast*, by W. G. G. COOPER. Accra, 1936. 35 pp. (Bulletin no. 7.)

245 —— *The geology of the Bosumtwi caldera and surrounding country*, by N. R. JUNNER. Accra, 1937. (Bulletin no. 8.)

246 —— *A bibliography of Gold Coast geology, mining and archaeology to March* 1937, by W. T. JAMES. Accra, 1937. (Bulletin no. 9.)

247 —— *The geology of the Tarkwa goldfield and adjacent country*, by T. HIRST. Accra, 1938. (Bulletin no. 10.)

248 —— *The geology and mineral resources of the Gold Coast*, by N. R. JUNNER. Accra, 1938. 112 pp.

249 —— *Geology of the Gold Coast and Western Togoland*. by N. R. JUNNER. Accra, 1940. 40 pp. (Bulletin no. 11.)

250 —— *The Accra earthquake of 22nd June, 1939*, by N. R. JUNNER, and *Reports on a seismological study of the earthquake*, by ERNEST TILLOTSON, and *The engineering aspects of the earthquake*, by C. S. DEAKIN. Accra, 1941. (Bulletin no. 13.)

251 —— *The Tarkwa gold field*, by N. R. JUNNER AND H. SERVICE. Accra, 1942. (Memoir no. 6.)

252 —— *The geology of the Konongo gold belt and surrounding country*, by T. HIRST. Accra, 1942. 27 pp. (Bulletin no. 14.)

253 —— *The geology of the Nsuta manganese ore deposits*, by H. SERVICE. Accra, 1943. 32 pp. (Memoir no. 5.)

254 —— *The diamond deposits of the Gold Coast, with notes on other diamond deposits in West Africa*, by N. R. JUNNER. Accra, 1943. (Bulletin no. 12.)

255 —— *Progress in geological and mineral investigations in the Gold Coast*, by N. R. JUNNER. Accra, 1946. 23 pp. (Bulletin no. 10.)

256 —— *Reports on the Bibiani goldfield*, by T. HIRST AND N. R. JUNNER. Accra, 1946.

257 —— *Chemical analyses of Gold Coast rocks, ores and minerals*, by N. R. JUNNER AND W. T. JAMES. Accra, 1947.

258 —— *Cretaceous and eocene fossils from the Gold Coast*, by L. R. COX. Accra, 1952. (Bulletin no. 6.)

259 —— *The rocks of the Sekondi series of the Gold Coast*, by A. T. CROW. Accra, 1952. (Bulletin no. 19.)

260 —— *The geology of the Bawku–Gambaga area*. Accra, 1956. (Bulletin no. 19.)

3

261 GOLD COAST. GEOLOGICAL SURVEY DEPT. *Some applications of geophysical methods to geological problems in the Gold Coast,* by L. O. GAY AND M. KOSTEN. Accra, 1956. (Bulletin no. 21.)

262 —— *The geology of the Bui Hydro-electric Project,* by L. O. GAY. Accra, 1956. (Bulletin no. 22.)

263 —— *General geological survey of development area in Krachi district, Trans-Volta Togoland.* 1956. 54 pp.

264 —— *Limestones of Ghana,* by J. MITCHELL. Accra, 1960. (Bulletin no. 23.)

265 GREAT BRITAIN. METEOROLOGICAL OFFICE. *A pilot's primer of the West African weather.* 1944.

266 —— *Weather on the West Coast of tropical Africa.* H.M.S.O., 1949. 281 pp.

267 KOMIATCHKY, N. *Géologie du territoire du Togo.* Paris, Bull. Com. d'ét. Hist. Sci., A.O.F. 16, 4, Oct–Dec 1933: 493–629

268 KRENKEL, E. *Geologie von Afrika.* 2 vols. Berlin, 1928.

269 WHITELAW, O. A. L. 'Drilling on the Gold Coast.' *Oil news,* **26,** 1929.

See also nos. 216, 217, 2039, 2045, 2052, 2274, 2309.

Botany

270 ADAMS, C. D., 'Activities of Danish botanists in Guinea, 1783–1850.' *Trans. Hist. Soc. Ghana*, **3**, 1957: 30–46.

271 ADAMS, C. D., AND ALSTON, A. H. G. 'A list of the Gold Coast pteridophyta.' *Bull. of the British Museum (Natural history), Botany*, **1**, 6, 1955: 143–185.

272 ADRIAN, JEAN., AND SAYERSE, C. *Les plantes alimentaires de l'Ouest africain*. Dakar, Dir. Gén. de la Santé Publique, 1955. 167 pp.

273 ALSTON, A. H. G. *The ferns and fern allies of west tropical Africa*. Crown Agents, 1959. 89 pp.

274 ANINAKWA, P. K. *Guide to Aburi Botanic Gardens*. (Typescript.)

275 ANSA, C. A. *The teaching of nature study in African primary schools*. Accra, Scottish Mission Book Depot, [1953 ?]. 44 pp.

276 AUBREVILLE, A. *Les forêts du Dahomey et Togo*. Paris, 1937.

277 BEGUE, L. *Contribution à l'étude de la vegetation forestière de la Haute Côte d'Ivoire*. Paris, Comité d' Etudes Historiques et Scientifiques de l'A.O.F., 1937.

278 BRUGGEMAN, L. *Tropical plants and their cultivation*. Thames & Hudson, 1957. 228 pp.
　　Many coloured plates and extensive notes. A good general introduction.

279 CARPENTER, A. J. *A West African nature study*. 4th ed. Longmans, 1953. 348 pp.

280 DALZIEL, J. M. 'The useful plants of west tropical Africa.' being an appendix to *The Flora of west tropical Africa*, by HUTCHINSON AND DALZIEL. Crown Agents, 1937. 612 pp.

281 GITHENS, THOMAS S. *Drug plants of Africa*. Philadelphia, Pennsylvania U.P.; O.U.P., 1948. 125 pp.

282 GOLD COAST. DEPT. OF AGRICULTURE. *Aburi Botanic Gardens: handbook and guide*. Accra, Govt. Printer, 1935.

283   HUGHES, S. J. *Fungi from the Gold Coast.* Accra, University College, 1952–3. 2 vols.

284   HUTCHINSON, J., AND DALZIEL, J. M. *Flora of west tropical Africa.* 2nd ed. revised by R.W. J. Keay. Crown Agents, 1954– .
Published on behalf of the governments of Nigeria, Ghana, Sierra Leone and the Gambia. Issued in parts: Vol. 1, part 1, Vol. 1, part 2.

285   IRVINE, FREDERICK ROBERT. *Botany and medicine in West Africa.* Ibadan, University Press, 1955. 10 pp.

286   —— *Flowerless plants.* Accra, Govt. Printer, 1932. 11 pp.

287   —— *Plants of the Gold Coast.* O.U.P., 1930. 521 pp.

288   —— *West African botany.* 2nd ed. O.U.P., 1952–203 pp.
First published 1931.

289   —— *Woody plants of Ghana, with special reference to their uses.* O.U.P., 1961. 868 pp.
Revision of *Plants of the Gold Coast*, 1930.

290   MORTON, J. K. *West African lilies and orchids.* Longmans, 1961. 71 pp.

291   SAUNDERS, H. N. *A handbook of West African flowers.* O.U.P., 1959. 124 pp.

292   TAYLOR, C. J. *Synecology and silviculture in Ghana.* Published on behalf of the University of Ghana, by Nelson, 1960. 418 pp.
Author is Lecturer, Dept. of Forestry, University of Edinburgh, and was formerly Conservator of Forests, Ghana. Records the tree seedlings of all species found in Ghana.

See also nos. 597, 720.

Zoology

293 BANNERMAN, D. A. *The birds of tropical West Africa.* Crown Agents, 1930–51. 8 vols.

294 —— *The birds of west and equatorial Africa.* Oliver and Boyd, 1953. 2 vols.
An abridgment of the previous work.

295 —— *Larger birds of West Africa.* Penguin Books, 1958. 195 pp.

296 BATES, G. L. *Handbook of the birds of West Africa.* John Bale Sons and Danielsson, 1930. 572 pp.

297 BOETTGER, CAESAR R. *Die Haustiere Afrikas: ihre Herkunft, Bedeutung und Aussichten bei der weiteren wirtschaftlichen Erschliebung des Kontinents.* Jena, Fischer Verlag, 1958. x, 314 pp.

298 BOOTH, A. H. *Small mammals of West Africa.* Longmans, 1960. 68 pp.

299 CANSDALE, G. S. *Animals of West Africa.* 3rd ed. Longmans, 1960. 124 pp.
Of Ghana, specifically. A useful introduction.

300 —— *Provisional check list of Gold Coast mammals.* Accra, Govt. Printer, 1948. 16 pp.
Land mammals only, giving zoological and Twi names with brief descriptions.

301 —— *Reptiles of West Africa.* Penguin Books, 1955. 104 pp. (Penguin West African series.)

302 —— *West African snakes.* Longmans, 1961. 74 pp.

303 ELGOOD, J. H. *Birds of the West African town and garden.* Longmans, 1960. 66 pp.

304 FAIRBAIRN, W. A. *Some common birds of West Africa.* Lagos, Church Missionary Society Bookshop, 1933.

305 —— *Some game birds of West Africa.* Oliver and Boyd, 1952. 92 pp.

306 GASS, M. D. I. 'Some migrant birds of Ghana.' *Nigerian field,* **22**, 4, 1957: 166–168.

307 LEESON, F. *Gold Coast snakes.* Revised ed. Accra, Govt. Printer, 1946. 26 pp.

308 —— *Identification of snakes of the Gold Coast.* Crown Agents, 1950. 142 pp.

309 —— *Key to Gold Coast snakes.* Accra, Govt. Printer, 1945.

310 TEBBLE, N. 'The polychaete fauna of the Gold Coast.' Bull. of the British Museum (Natural History), *Zoology*, 1955.

311 VILLIERS, A. *Les serpents de l'Ouest africain.* Dakar, IFAN, 1950. 148 pp.

312 WEBB, G. C., AND WEBB, J. E. *A guide to West African mammals.* Ibadan, University Press, 1957. 40 pp.

Missions and Churches

313 ALEXANDRE, P. 'L'Afrique noire et l'expansion de l'Islam.' *Le Monde Non-Chrétien*, **36**, 1955: 315–334.

314 ALLEYNE, CAMERON C. *Gold Coast at a glance: specially adapted to missions study classes.* N.Y., Hunt Printing Co., 1931. 143 pp.

315 ANNAN, J. S. '"European" marriage at the Gold Coast—and home life in Great Britain.' *W. Afr. Rev.*, **14**, 186, 1943: 15–17.

316 ANSAH, J. K. *The centenary history of the Larteh Presbyterian Church, 1853–1953.* Larteh, Presbyterian Church, 1955. 111 pp.

317 ANSTEIN, H. *Nicht durch Heer oder Kraft: 125 Jahre Basel Mission, 1815–1940.* Basel, Basel Mission, 1940.

318 ASHANIN, C. B. 'The social significance of religious studies in West Africa.' *Universitas*, **4**, 1, Dec. 1959: 9–11.

319 BAETA, CHRISTIAN GONÇALVES KWAMI. 'New nations in a new world.' *Ecumenical review*, **8**, 4, 1956: 369–372.

320 —— *Prophetism in Ghana.* [Unpublished thesis, University of London, 1959. 382 pp.]

321 —— *Report of Rev. C. G. Baeta on his tour of the Gold Coast, July–September, 1938, at the meeting of the Council held on 21st October 1938.* Accra, Christian Council of the Gold Coast, 1939.

322 BANE, MARTIN J. *Catholic pioneers in West Africa.* Dublin, Clonmore & Reynolds, 1956. 220 pp.

323 *Basel Evangelical Mission on the Gold Coast, Western Africa from 1828–1893.* Basel, Basel Mission, 1894.

324 *The Basel Mission centenary, 1828–1928.* Accra, Scottish Mission, 1928. 27 pp.

325 BELLON, IMMANUEL. 'Kulturgeschichtliche Wanderung durch die Goldküste.' *Evang. Missionsmag.*, **75**, 12, 1931: 356–365.

326 BELSHAW, HARRY. 'Church and state in Ashanti.' *Int. rev. missions*, **35**, 140, Oct. 1946: 408–415.

327 BELSHAW, HARRY. *Facing the future in West Africa.* Cargate Press, 1951. 128 pp.

328 BIELBY, M. R. *Alone to the City of Blood.* [Kumasi.] Edinburgh House Press, 1941. 32 pp. (Eagle books.)

329 BLUMER, R. C. *The reason for monogamy.* Achimota, Achimota Press, [1933] 16 pp.

330 BOUCHARD, JOSEPH, *L'église en Afrique noire.* Paris, La Palatine, 1958.

331 *Brief history of the Methodist Church, Winneba, 1899–1959.* Cape Coast, Mfantsiman Press, 1959. [15] pp.

332 BROKENSHA, DAVID W. *Christianity and change.* Pittsburg, Duquesne U.P., 1961. 8 pp. (Institute of African Affairs pamphlet, no. 8.)
The story of the introduction of Christianity to Larteh, by a Canadian social anthropologist.

333 BRUCE, ERNEST. *Rural echoes, 1, being sermons preached on various occasions in towns and country places.* Koforidua, the author, 1958. 90 pp.

334 BUHL, C. *Die Basler Mission auf der Goldküste.* Basel, Basel Mission, 1882.

335 CATHOLIC CHURCH, ACCRA. *Following the Mass through the psalms.* Accra, Catholic Press, 1957.

336 CHRISTIAN COUNCIL OF THE GOLD COAST. *Christianity and African culture: the proceedings of a conference held at Accra, Gold Coast, May 2nd–6th, 1955, under the auspices of the Christian Council.* Accra, the Council, 1955. 80 pp.

337 —— *The Church in the town: addresses given at a conference in Accra, Gold Coast, May 15th–18th, 1951.* Accra, Christian Council, 1951. 63 pp.
Theme of the conference was to consider the social breakdown revealed in K. A. Busia's Report on a social survey of Sekondi-Takoradi, 1950.

338 —— *Silver Jubilee, 1954: handbook and directory.* Accra, 1954. 31 pp.

339 CHURCH OF SCOTLAND. FOREIGN MISSION COMMITTEE. *The Gold Coast.* [1944?] 43 pp.

340 COLLETT, M. *Accra.* S.P.G., 1928. 80 pp.

341 COOKSEY, J. J., AND MCLEISH, A. *Religion and civilization in West Africa: a missionary survey of French, British, Spanish and Portuguese West Africa, with Liberia.* World Dominion Press, 1931. 277 pp.

342 DEBRUNNER, HANS, AND OTHERS. Early Fante Islam. *Ghana bull. theology*, I, 7, Dec. 1959 23–33.

343 —— Notable Danish chaplains on the Gold Coast. *Trans. Gold Coast & Togoland Hist. Soc.*, 2, 1956: 13–29.

344 —— *Pioneers of church and education in Ghana: Danish chaplains to Guinea, 1661–1850.* Kirkehistoriske Samlinger, 1962: 373–425.

345 DELANO, I. O. *An African looks at marriage.* Lutterworth Press, 1945. 47 pp.

346 DOVLO, CHRISTIAN K. *Africa awakes: some of the problems facing Africa today as seen from the Christian point of view.* Accra, Scottish Mission Book Depot, 1952. 77 pp.

347 —— The Gold Coast Church. *Africana*, I, 2, April 1949: 12–13.

348 FENTON, THOMAS. *Black harvest.* Cargate Press, [195–?] 160 pp.
Christian missions on the Ivory Coast.

349 FIELD, MARGARET JOYCE. *The cure for some present-day ills: a sermon delivered at Achimota, 14th May, 1933.* Achimota, College Press, 1933. 12 pp. (Achimota pamphlets, no. 11.)

350 FISHER, HUMPHREY. 'Planting Ahmadiyya in Ghana.' [Moslem faith] *West Africa*, 2226, Jan. 1960: 121.

351 GOUILLY, ALPHONSE. *L'Islam dans l'Afrique occidentale française.* Paris, Larose, 1952.

352 GROVES, C. P. *The planting of Christianity in Africa.* Lutterworth Press, 1948–58. 4 vols.

353 HARRIS, E. BERYL. *Studying the Bible together.* Accra, Scottish Mission Book Depot. 1954. 47 pp.

354 HARTENSTEIN, K. *Anibue: die "Neue Zeit" auf der Goldküste und unsere Missionsausgabe.* Basel, Evang. Missionsverlag, 1932.

355 —— *Anibue: de "Niewe Tijd" op de Goudkust en onze Zendingstaak.* Culemborg, 1933. 175 pp.
Dutch translation of the German edition.

356 HEMAN-ACKAH, DAVID. *Marriage problems in Ghana.* [Revised ed.] Accra, the author, 1961. 127 pp.
First published 1938.

357 HENKING, H. *Durch Nacht zum Licht: 125 Jahre Basler Missionsarbeit auf der Goldküste.* Basel, Basel Mission, 1953. 63 pp.

358 HUPPENBAUER, HANS. *Keine rechten Europaer.* Stuttgart, Evang. Missionsverlag, 1958. 16 pp.
Missionary work in north Togo.

359 HUPPENBAUER, HANS. *Wie ich den Dagomba die Weihnachtsgeschichte erzählte.* Stuttgart, Evang. Missionsverlag, 1956. 16 pp.

360 INTERNATIONAL MISSIONARY COUNCIL. *The Ghana Assembly of the International Missionary Council, 28th December, 1957 to 8th January, 1958: selected papers.* Edinburgh House Press, 1958. 240 pp.

361 Islam in the Gold Coast. *West Africa*, 18/25, Dec. 1954: 1188, 1203.

362 JEHLE, A. *Köstlicher denn das vergängliche Gold: 100 Jahre Basler Missionsarbeit auf der Goldküste.* Basel, Basel Mission, 1928. 87 pp.

363 JONES, A. GORDON. *Bridge of friendship.* Cargate Press, (1946?) 95 pp. Methodist Church in the Gold Coast.

364 KITTLER, GLENN D. *The White Fathers.* W. H. Allen, 1957. 319 pp. Northern Ghana.

365 LAING, GEORGE E. F. *Dom Bernard Clements in Africa.* S.C.M. Press, 1944. 56 pp. Missions in Ashanti.

366 ——— *A king for Africa.* United Society for Christian Literature, 1945. 63 pp.

367 LE COEUR, C. *Le culte de la génération et l'évolution religieuse et sociale en Guinée.* Paris, Leroux, 1932. 146 pp.

368 MAUNY, RAYMOND. 'Le judaisme, les juifs et l'Afrique occidentale.' Bull. *IFAN*, 11, 3/4, juil-oct. 1949: 354–378.

369 MAXWELL-LAWFORD, F. *Catholics at Achimota: an account of the first six years.* Achimota, College Press, 1933. 25, xv pp. [Privately printed.]

370 MENSAH, ANNAN ATTAH. 'The Akan church lyric.' *Int. rev. missions*, 49, 194, April 1960: 183–188.

371 METHODIST CHURCH, GOLD COAST. '*I will build my Church': the report of the Commission appointed by the Synod of the Methodist Church, Gold Coast, to consider the life of the Church.* [Accra, Methodist Church] 1948. 171 pp.

372 MONTEIL, VINCENT. 'Problèmes du Soudan occidental: juifs et judaïses.' *Hesperis*, 38, 3/4, 1951: 265–298.

373 MORGAN, DEWI. 'We espied the coast of Barbary.' *W. Afr. Rev.*, May 1951: 472–473. Christian missions in the Gold Coast.

374 NIMAKO, S. GYASI. *The Christian and funerals.* Cape Coast, Methodist Book Depot, 1954. 94 pp.

375 NKRUMAH, KWAME. *Address to the International Missionary Assembly at Accra, 28th December, 1957.* Accra, Govt. Printer, 1958. 3 pp.

376 NORTEY, KOBINA. *The responsibility of Africans as a race.* [Glasgow, Maclellan, 1957] 16 pp.

377 OELSCHNER, WALTER. *Landung in Osu: das Leben des Andreas Riis für Westafrika.* Stuttgart, Evang. Missionsverlag, 1959.
Adaptation of *En Stjerne i Natten* by Christian Christensen.

378 OFORI ATTA I (NANA). *Memorandum to the Synod of the Presbyterian Church of the Gold Coast, by the State Council of Aykem Abuakwa, 1941.*

379 OFORI ATTA II (NANA). *Address of welcome to the Synod Committee of the Presbyterian Church of the Gold Coast.* Accra, [1954]. 15 pp

380 OSEKRE, BOSS ADJEI. *Genealogy of morals among the Ghana peoples: religion in transition: ancient Ghana—Gold Coast—Ghana.* Cape Coast, Mfantsiman Press, 1958. 11 pp.

381 PARRINDER, E. GEOFFREY. *African traditional religion.* Hutchinson, 1954. v, 160 pp.

382 —— *West African religion: illustrated from the beliefs and practices of the Yoruba, Ewe, Akan and kindred peoples.* Epworth Press, 1949. 223 pp.

383 PLATT, WILLIAM J. *From fetish to faith.* Livingstone Press, 1935. 159 pp.
Church history in West Africa.

384 *Prelude to Ghana: the Churches' part.* Edinburgh House Press, 1957. 16 pp.

385 PRESBYTERIAN CHURCH OF THE GOLD COAST. *The Church in the State: the reply of the Presbyterian Church of the Gold Coast to a memorandum presented by the State Council of Akim Abuakwa.* Accra, Scottish Mission Book Depot, 1942. 42 pp.
See also no. 378.

386 —— *Regulations, practice and procedure.* Revised ed. Accra, Scottish Mission Book Depot, 1953. 48 pp.

387 PRESBYTERIAN CHURCH OF GHANA. *Comments on the White Paper on marriage, divorce & inheritance.* Accra, Presbyterian Press, 1961. 14 pp. [Private circulation.]
See also no. 2556.

388 PRESBYTERIAN TRAINING COLLEGE. AKROPONG. *A hundred years, 1848–1948*. Akropong, the College, [1949]. 55 pp.

389 RINGWALD, WALTER. *Die Religion der Akanstämme und das Problem ihrer Bekehrung*. Stuttgart, Evang. Missionsverlag, 1952. 358 pp.

390 —— *Stafette in Afrika: der Weg einer Jungen Kirche in Ghana*. Stuttgart, Evang. Missionsverlag, 1957. 92 pp.

391 SCHRENK, ELIAS. *Ein Leben im Kampf um Gott*. Stuttgart, Evang. Missionsverlag, 1936.

392 —— 'What shall become of the Gold Coast?' *Evang. Missions-Magazin*, Feb. 1958.
Refers to a report submitted by the Basel Mission to a Parliamentary Commission, May 1865, on the future of the Gold Coast.

393 SMITH, EDWIN WILLIAM. *African beliefs and Christian faith*. Lutterworth Press, 1944.

394 —— *African ideas of God*: a symposium; editor and contributor, Edwin W. Smith. 2nd ed. revised and edited by E. G. Parrinder. Edinburgh House Press, 1961. x, 308 pp.

395 —— 'Religious beliefs of the Akan.' *Africa*, **15**, 1, 1945: 23–29.

396 SMITH, NOEL J. *The Presbyterian Church of Ghana, 1835–1960: a younger church in a changing society*. (Unpublished thesis, Edinburgh University, 1962.)

397 SOUTHON, A. E. *Gold Coast Methodism: the first hundred years, 1835–1935*. Accra, Methodist Book Depot; Cargate Press, 1934. 158 pp.
Beginning with the arrival of Joseph Dunwell at Cape Coast on New Year's Day, 1835, the story of Methodist missionaries includes that of Thomas Birch Freeman and Dr. Aggrey.

398 *Spiritual issues of the war: being a series of talks broadcast from Accra in March and April, 1941*. Accra, Govt. Printer, 1941. 16 pp.

399 STÖCKLE, JOHANNES, 'Die ursprünglichen religiösen Vorstellungen und die Entwicklung des Christentums in Ghana.' *Mitt. Inst. Auslandsbeziehungen*, **9**, 4, Oct.–Dec. 1959: 247–257.

400 TILDSLEY, ALFRED. *The remarkable work achieved by Rev. Dr. Mark C. Hayford in promotion of the spiritual and material welfare of the natives of West Africa, and proposed developments*. Morgan & Scott, 1926. 36 pp.

401 TRIMINGHAM, J. S. *The Christian Church and Islam in West Africa*. S.C.M. Press, 1956. 64 pp. (I.M.C. research pamphlets, no. 3.)

402 TRIMINGHAM J. S. *Islam in West Africa*. O.U.P., 1959. 262 pp.
Author is Secretary of the Church Mission Society in the
Sudan.

403 'White Fathers of the N.T.s.' [Society of Missionaries of Africa.]
W. Afr. Rev., March 1954: 210–213.

404 WILLIAMSON, S. G. *Christ or Muhammad?* Cape Coast, Methodist
Book Depot, [1953 ?]. 64 pp.

405 —— 'The lyric in the Fante Methodist Church.' *Africa*, **28**, 2,
April 1958: 126–133.

406 WILLIAMSON, S. G., AND BARDSLEY, J. *The Gold Coast: what of the
Church?* Edinburgh House Press, 1953. 24 pp.

407 WILSON, J. MICHAEL. *Christian marriage*. [New ed.] Accra, Presbyterian Book Depot, 1961. 32 pp.

408 WILTGEN, R. M. *Gold Coast mission history, 1471–1880*. Illinois,
Divine Word Publications, 1956. 181 pp.
The spread of Catholicism from the arrival of the Portuguese to
the founding of the Society of African Missions.

409 WRONG, MARGARET. *West African journey*. Edinburgh House Press,
1946. 80 pp.
Margaret Wrong (1887–1948) was Secretary of the International
Committee on Christian Literature in Africa.

See also nos. 33, 420, 425.

Education

410 ABEDI-BOAFO, J. *Modern problems in Gold Coast elementary schools.* Mampong Akwapim, the author, 1951. 53 pp.

411 ACHIMOTA. COLLEGE. *Achimota in 1932: report on Achimota College.* Achimota, College Press, 1933.

412 —— *Notes of lectures given at the Teachers' Refresher Course, July 8th to 21st, 1926.* Achimota, Training College, 1926. 60 pp.

413 *Achimota.* Reprinted from *The round table,* Dec. 1925. 16 pp.

414 ADALI-MORTTY, GEORMBEEYI. 'Adult education and international understanding.' *Adult education,* **28**, 1, summer 1955: 29–37.

415 *Adult education in the Gold Coast: a report for the year 1948–49 by the Resident Tutor.* O.U.P., 1949. 27 pp.

416 AKUFFO, F.W.K. *Youth leaders' handbook: for the use of pastors, teachers, catechists and youth leaders who are engaged in youth work.* Accra, Presbyterian Church of Accra, [1959] 22 pp.

417 ASAMOA, E. A. 'The problem of language in education in the Gold Coast.' *Africa,* **25**, 1, Jan. 1955: 60–78.

418 BALME, D. M. 'University aims in the Gold Coast.' *Universitas,* **I**, 3, 1954: 13–15.

419 BARNARD, G. L. 'Gold Coast children out of school.' *Oversea education,* **28**, 4, Jan. 1957: 163–172.

420 BARTELS, F. L. '. . . *The beginning of Africanisation . . .*' *The dawn of the missionary motive in Gold Coast education: Rev. Thomas Thompson.* Cape Coast, Methodist Book Depot, 1951. 12 pp.

421 —— 'Education in the Gold Coast.' *Afr. affairs,* **48**, 193, Oct. 1949: 300–309.

422 —— 'The Gold Coast: educational problems.' *Year Book of Education,* 1949: 348–358.

423 BARTON, OWEN. 'Mass education teams in the Gold Coast.' *Oversea education,* **21**, 2, Jan. 1950: 1022–1024.

424   BARTON, T. *Education in the Gold Coast*. Nelson, 1954.

425   BELSHAW, HARRY. 'Religious education in the Gold Coast.' *Int. rev. missions*, **34**, 135, July 1945: 267–272.

426   BLUMER, R. C. *The aim of the curriculum*. Achimota, College Press, 1931. 26 pp. (Achimota pamphlets, no. 1.)

427   —— *The case for Achimota*. Achimota, Achimota Press, [1933] 19 pp.

428   —— *List of theorems in a school geometry course*. Achimota, Achimota Press, 1938. 26 pp.

429   BOTSIO, KOJO. *Plan for mass literacy and mass education*. Accra, Dept. of Social Welfare, 1951. 44 pp.

430   —— *Progress in education in the Gold Coast*. Accra, Govt. Printer, 1953. 20 pp.

431   BOWDEN, B. V. 'Universities' task in Ghana: urgent need for technologists.' *Guardian*, 9, 10 March 1960.

432   BROWN, E. J. P. *Gold Coast and Ashanti reader*. Accra, 1929. 2 vols.

433   BUSIA, KOFI ABREFA. *Education for citizenship*. Bureau of Current Affairs, 1950. 16 pp. (West African affairs pamphlets, no. 1.)

434   CARMAN, B. E. 'Teachers of the Gold Coast.' *Advance*, **8**, Oct. 1955: 1–5.

435   CHAPMAN, DANIEL A. 'Achimota College, Gold Coast.' *Scottish Geographical Magazine*, **60**, 1, June 1944: 12–14.

436   CONTON, WILLIAM F. 'History in the classroom.' *Trans. Hist. Soc. Ghana*, **3**, 1957: 157–168.

437   CRANSTON, T. D. *A few practical hints to young teachers in the Gold Coast*. Accra, 1925. 34 pp.

438   CROOKALL, R. E. *Handbook for history teachers in West Africa*. Evans, 1960. 270 pp.

439   DAVIS, JACKSON, AND OTHERS. *Africa advancing: a study of rural education and agriculture in West Africa and the Belgian Congo*. International Committee for Christian Literature for Africa, 1945.

440   DE GRAFT JOHNSON, J. C. 'African traditional education.' *Présence afr.*, **7**, avr.–mai 1956: 51–55.

441   EDU, JOHN E. *Dangerous delays in Gold Coast mass education*. Accra, 1949.

442   EDU, JOHN E. 'Plan for mass literacy and mass education, Gold Coast: report on the 1952 literacy drive.' *Community devel. bull.*, **4**, 1, Dec. 1952: 13–14.

443   *Education in Trans-Volta Togoland.* [Accra, Govt. Printer, 1955?] 16 pp.

444   FRASER, ALEXANDER G. *Achimota: comments on the inspectors' report.* Achimota, Prince of Wales' School Press, 1932. (Achimota pamphlets, no. 8.)

445   —— 'My education policy.' *Oversea education*, **29**, 4, 1958: 145–151.

446   GHANA. MINISTER OF EDUCATION (C. T. NYLANDER). *Education in Ghana: text of speech given in the Ghana Parliament June 13, 1957.* Washington, D.C., Information Office, Embassy of Ghana, 1957. 10 pp.

447   GHANA. MINISTRY OF EDUCATION. *First seminar on the writing of school textbooks for Ghana: the background papers.* Accra, Bureau of Ghana Languages, 1959. 64 pp.

448   —— *Music syllabus for primary schools.* Accra, Govt. Printer, 1959. 12 pp.

449   'Ghana's two Universities.' *New Commonwealth*, July 1961: 467–468.

450   GOLD COAST. DEPT. OF SOCIAL WELFARE AND COMMUNITY DEVELOPMENT. *Literacy campaign.* Accra, West African Graphic Co., 1952. 52 pp.

451   GOLD COAST GOVERNMENT. *Report of the committee appointed in 1932 by the Governor of the Gold Coast Colony to inspect the Prince of Wales's College and School, Achimota.* Crown Agents, 1932. 82 pp.

452   —— *Report of the committee appointed by the Governor to inspect the Prince of Wales's College, Achimota.* Crown Agents, 1939.

453   —— *Further proposals for the development of education in the Gold Coast.* Accra, Govt. Printer, 1945. 3 pp.

454   —— *Accelerated development plan for education.* Accra, Govt. Printer, 1951. 23 pp.

455   —— *Report upon Achimota School, 1952, by Inspectors appointed by the Governor.* Accra, Govt. Printer, 1953. 71 pp. (Chairman, J. J. Robertson.)

456   GOLD COAST. MINISTRY OF EDUCATION. *Nature study: a pamphlet for teachers.* Accra, Govt. Printer, 1930. 34 pp.

457 GOLD COAST, MINISTRY OF EDUCATION. *A plan in action.* Accra, Govt. Printer, 1955. 22 pp.

458 —— *Report on research into the teaching and learning of English in the Gold Coast,* by P. GURREY. Accra, Govt. Printer, 1953.

459 —— *Primary school language syllabus.* Nelson, 1953.

460 GOLD COAST. UNIVERSITY COLLEGE. *The University College of the Gold Coast, 1948–1952: report by the Principal* (D. M. Balme). Nelson, 1953. 71 pp.

461 GUGGISBERG, SIR FREDERICK GORDON. *The keystone: education is the keystone of progress.* 1924. 59 pp.

462 GUGGISBERG, SIR FREDERICK GORDON, AND FRASER, ALEXANDER G. *The future of the Negro: some chapters in the development of a race.* S.C.M. Press, 1929. 152 pp.

463 GURREY, P. *On the study and discipline of literature: an inaugural lecture delivered before the University College of the Gold Coast on 21st November, 1950.* 1952. 17 pp.

464 —— *The teaching of English literature in West Africa.* Achimota, University College of the Gold Coast, 1949.

465 HEMINGFORD, DENNIS GEORGE RUDDOCK HERBERT, 2ND BARON. *Achimota: the eighth annual Vaughan Memorial Lecture, delivered at Doncaster Grammar School on 27th June, 1960.* Doncaster, Doncaster Grammar School, [1962]. 14 pp.

466 HERBERT, A. 'Co-operation in West Africa's Universities.' *W. Afr. Rev.,* **33**, 411, March 1962: 12–13.

467 HILLIARD F. H. *A short history of education in British West Africa.* Nelson, 1957. 186 pp.

468 HODGE, P. 'Work with youth in the towns of Ghana.' *W. Afr. J. Educ.,* **2**, 3, 1958: 96–100.

469 HODGKIN, THOMAS. 'Adult and workers' education in the Gold Coast and Nigeria.' *Fundamental & Adult Education,* **5**, 1, Jan. 1953: 28–32.

470 IFATUROTI, M. A. 'Patterns of education in the West.' *W. Afr. Rev.,* **32**, 402, June 1961: 43–47.

471 INTERNATIONAL FEDERATION OF WORKERS' EDUCATIONAL ASSOCIATIONS. *Adult education in a changing Africa: a report on an International African Seminar held in the Gold Coast from December 10–23, 1954;* edited by DAVID AND HELEN KIMBLE. Leicester, Gee, 1955.

472   JAHODA, GUSTAV. 'The social background of a West African student population: 1, [University College of the Gold Coast].' *British J. of Soc.*, **5**, 4, Dec. 1954: 355–365.

473   JONES-QUARTEY, K. A. B. 'Our language and literature problem.' *Africana*, **1**, 3, 1949: 23–24.

474   KAYE, BARRINGTON. *Bringing up children in Ghana*. Allen & Unwin, 1962.

475   —— *Child training in Ghana: an impressionistic survey*. Legon, University of Ghana, Institute of Education, 1960. 686 pp. (Institute of Education child development monographs, no. 1.) (Typescript.)

476   KIMBLE, DAVID. *Outlook for adult education*. Bureau of Current Affairs, [1954?]. (West African affairs pamphlets, no. 4.)

477   —— *Progress in adult education*. Accra, University College of the Gold Coast, 1950.

478   LE CORRE, Y. J. 'Aspects of teacher-training for technical and vocational instructors in Ghana and its applications to accelerated teaching.' *Bull. inter-Afr. Labour Inst.*, **6**, 2, March 1959: 34–45.

479   LEWIS, L. J. *Educational policy and practice in British tropical areas*. Nelson, 1954. 141 pp.

480   —— *Education and social growth*. Nelson, for the University College of the Gold Coast, 1957. 18 pp.

481   —— 'Ghana teacher training: a scheme of directed studies for tutors.' *Oversea education*, **30**, 4, Jan. 1959: 170–173.

482   —— *An outline chronological table of the development of education in British West Africa*. Nelson, 1953. 21 pp.

483   —— *Perspectives in mass education and community development*. Nelson, [1955]. 101 pp.

484   —— 'Technological change and the curriculum in Ghana.' *Yearbook of Education*, 1958: 421–425.

485   'Trends in West African education.' *W. Afr. Rev.*, **31**, 383, Aug. 1960: 49–51.

486   LYSTAD, MARY H. 'Paintings of Ghanaian children.' *Africa*, **30**, 3, July 1960: 238–242.

487   MCWILLIAM, H. O. A. *The development of education in Ghana: an outline*. Longmans, 1959. xiii, 114 pp.

A brief outline of educational progress from the first European settlements to 1957.

488 MAIR, W. H. 'Education in the Royal West African Frontier Force.' *Gold Coast teachers' J.*, **3**, Dec. 1955: 44–50.

489 MARTEI, S. *The advance general intelligence book; compiled for students and the general public.* Cape Coast, the author, [1957]. 47 pp.

490 MENSAH, GODWIN. 'Adisadel: a vivacious educational establishment.' [Cape Coast] *W. Afr. Rev.*, Dec. 1951: 1435–1437.

491 MILBURN, S. *The growing cost of education.* Bureau of Current Affairs, [195-]. (West African affairs pamphlets, no. 14.)

492 MOORE, J. W. 'School-leavers in the Gold Coast.' *Oversea education*, **19**, 4, July 1948: 747–748.

493 NEWEY, H. N. 'Educating an army.' [West African School of Infantry and Education, Teshie] *W. Afr. Rev.*, **22**, 280, Jan. 1951: 75–78.

494 NKETIA, J. H. KWABENA. 'Progress in Gold Coast education.' *Trans. Gold Coast & Togoland Hist. Soc.*, **1**, 1953: 63–71.

495 NKRUMAH, KWAME. *Flower of learning: some reflections on African learning, ancient and modern, contained in two speeches on his installation as Chancellor of the University of Ghana, Legon, and of the University of Science and Technology at Kumasi.* Accra, Govt. Printer, 1962. 16 pp.

496 —— *The noble task of teaching: an address to the Conference of Teachers Associations on 6th April, 1961.* Accra, Govt. Printer, 1961. 4 pp.

497 ODOI, N. A. *Facts to remember.* Accra, Presbyterian Book Depot, [1962] 151 pp.
    Essential facts in nature study, hygiene, history and geography.

498 OSEKRE, BOSS ADJEI. *Educational problems and philosophy of Ghana.* Amsterdam, Duwaer, 1957. 12 pp.

499 OWIREDU, P. A. *Some reflections on education in the Gold Coast.* Cape Coast, the author, 1955. 56 pp.

500 OWUSU, C. A. P. 'Nursery schools in tropical countries—Ghana.' *African women*, **3**, 2, June 1959: 26–28.

501 PHELPS-STOKES FUND. *A university comes of age: excerpts from parliamentary debates and other statements dealing with the University of Ghana, 1961.* N.Y., Phelps-Stokes Fund, 1961. 19 pp. (Typescript.)

502   PICKARD-CAMBRIDGE, A. W. *The place of Achimota in West African education.* Oxford, Blackwell, 1944. 10 pp.
Reprint from the Journal of the Royal African Society, April 1940.

503   PICKERING, A. K. 'Village drama in Ghana.' *Fundamental & Adult education,* **9,** 4, 1957: 178–183.

504   PRATT, SYDNEY A. *Le petit Kofi.* C.U.P., 1961. 74 pp.
French exercises by the Senior French Master, Achimota school.

505   —— *La vie de Kofi.* C.U.P., 1961. 2 vols.

506   PROSSER, A. R. G. 'Progress in literacy through mass education.' *Advance,* **8,** Oct. 1955: 6–7.

507   PWAMANG, R. L. *A guide for primary and middle school teachers.* Accra, Catholic Press, 1960. 58 pp.

508   REYNOLDS-AFARI, E. W. 'Gold Coast technical education: Kumasi College's contribution to the country's development. *Afr. world,* Oct. 1953: 14.

509   RIGNELL, J. H., AND BENZIES, D. *Notes on physical training.* Accra, Govt. Printer, 1930. 15 pp.

510   ROBERTS, E. D. 'Emergency teacher training in the Gold Coast.' *Oversea education,* **28,** 2, July 1956: 75–84.

511   SENOO, C. Y. 'The People's Educational Association of the Gold Coast.' *Gold Coast Teachers' J.,* **2,** April 1957: 27–30.

512   SMITH, D. A. 'Progress and problems in secondary education in Ghana.' *W. Afr. J. Educ.,* **1,** 3, Oct. 1957: 72–73.

513   STAMFORD-BEWLAY, P. 'The role of government technical institutes in Ghana.' *Ghana Teachers' J.,* **1,** Jan. 1958: 30–35.

514   STOPFORD, R. W. *What is and what might be.* Achimota, Achimota Press [1941]. 13 pp.

515   STRATMON, DAVID L. 'The Ghana educational system.' *J. Negro Education,* **28,** fall 1959: 394–404.

516   *The University College of the Gold Coast.* Achimota, Achimota Press, 1950.

517   'Vocational training for boys.' *Advance,* **6,** April 1955: 7–9.

518   WALTON, G. *English studies in the University of Ghana: a public lecture delivered in Commonwealth Hall on 19 May, 1959.* Nelson, 1960. 15 pp.

519 WARD, BARBARA. *Five ideas that changed the world.* Published for the University College of Ghana by H. Hamilton, 1959. 143 pp. (Aggrey-Fraser-Guggisberg lectures.)

520 WISE, COLIN G. 'Finding the correct ages of Gold Coast secondary school candidates.' *Oversea education,* **23,** 2, Jan. 1952: 227–234.

521 —— *History of education in British West Africa.* Longmans, 1956. 134 pp.

522 WORLD UNIVERSITY SERVICE OF CANADA. *Africa and tomorrow: reports on the International Seminar sponsored jointly with W.U.S. of Ghana held at the University College of Ghana, June 17 to July 7, 1957.* Toronto, W.U.S., 1957. 45 pp.

523 YANKAH, J. T. N. 'The Gold Coast Teachers' Union.' *Gold Coast teachers' J.,* **3,** Dec. 1955: 18–23.

See also nos. 6, 1116, 1119, 2254, 2283, 2302, 2320, 2337, 2373, 2382, 2384, 2403, 2420, 2424, 2559, 2560, 2581.

Community Development

524 'Aids in the cocoa campaign.' *Advance*, **12**, Oct. 1956: 10-14.
Mass education projects in the cocoa growing regions.

525 CHADWICK, E. R. *Community development.* Bureau of Current Affairs, [1954?] (West African affairs pamphlets, no. 6.)

526 'The cocoa campaign.' *Advance*, **7**, July 1955: 1-8.

527 DICKSON, A. 'Training community leaders in the Gold Coast.' *Oversea education*, **22**, 1, Oct. 1950: 8-21.

528 DU SAUTOY, PETER. 'Casework.' *Advance*, **26**, April 1960: 1-25.

529 —— *Community development in Ghana.* O.U.P., 1958. 209 pp.

530 —— 'The community goes ahead in Ghana.' *Corona*, **9**, 12, Dec. 1957: 461-462.

531 —— 'Lessons from mass education in the Gold Coast.' *Corona*, **6**, 8, Aug. 1954: 289-291.

532 —— 'Technical equipment for village development.' *Community devel. bull.*, **6**, 4, Sept. 1955: 91-93.

533 'Fort William Youth Centre, Anomabu.' *Advance*, **6**, April 1955: 2-6.

534 GARDINER, R. K., AND JUDD, H. O. *The development of social administration.* 2nd ed. O.U.P., 1959. 208 pp.
First published, 1954.

535 GHANA. DEPT. OF SOCIAL WELFARE & COMMUNITY DEVELOPMENT. *Community development in Ghana.* Accra, Govt. Printer, 1959. 20 pp.

536 GREEN, L. G. 'Voluntary work-camps and their contribution to education.' *W. Afr. J. Educ.*, **2**, Feb. 1958: 26-30.

537 HARRIS, B. 'Women's training centre, Kwadaso.' *Community devel. bull.*, **4**, 2, March 1953: 35-36.
Methodist training centre near Kumasi.

538 'The history and growth of case-work in Ghana,' by J.D.A.E. *Advance*, **26,** April 1960: 1–3.

539 HODGE, P. 'Community development in towns.' *Community devel. bull.*, **10,** 2, March 1959: 26–30.

540 KODZO, J. W. 'Fighting mass apathy through band music.' *Community devel. bull.*, **4,** 2, March 1953: 33–35.

541 LEWIS, L. J. 'Community development and university training.' *Advance*, **10,** April 1956: 23.

542 PROSSER, A. R. G. 'An experiment in community development.' [Gold Coast Film Unit.] *Community devel. bull.*, **2,** 3, June 1951: 52–53.

543 SHIRER, W. L., AND PICKERING, A. K. 'The potentialities of Disney health films in mass education in the Gold Coast.' *Fundamental & adult education*, **6,** 3, July 1954: 109–120.

544 'Training in casework.' *Advance*, **10,** April 1956: 12–14.

545 'The use of visual aids in the Frafra resettlement scheme.' *Advance*,· **14,** April 1957: 13–15.

Libraries

546 ACHIMOTA. COLLEGE. LIBRARY. *Achimota library catalogue.* Achimota, Achimota Press, 1935. 264 pp.

547 CORNELIUS, DAVID. 'On trek with the mobile library in Ghana.' *Unesco Bull. for Libraries*, **12**, Aug.-Sept. 1958: 206–207.

548 CROOKALL, R. E. *School libraries in West Africa.* U.L.P., 1961. 128 pp.

549 DOPSON, LAURENCE. 'The medical libraries of West Africa.' *W. Afr. Rev.*, Oct. 1953: 1050–1052.

550 EVANS, EVELYN J. A. *The development of public library services in the Gold Coast.* Library Association, 1956. 32 pp.

551 —— 'Library service in British West Africa.' *Fundamental education*, **3**, 1, Jan. 1951: 28–33.

552 GRIFFIN, ELLA. *A study of the reading habits of adults in Ashanti, southern Ghana and Trans-Volta Togoland.* Accra, Bureau of Ghana Languages, [1958 ?]. 95 pp.

553 KENWORTHY, L. S. 'Library progress in Ghana.' *Wilson Library Bull.*, **34**, 1959: 267–268.

554 KIMBLE, HELEN. 'A reading survey in Accra.' *Universitas*, **2**, 3, 1956: 77–81.

555 LANCOUR, HAROLD. *Libraries in British West Africa: a report of a survey for the Carnegie Corporation of New York, October–November, 1958* [i.e. 1957]. University of Illinois Library School, 1958. 32 pp. (Occasional papers, no. 53.)

556 MASON, I. 'Notes on book distribution.' *Books for Africa*, **21**, 1, Jan. 1951: 9–11.
     Bookselling in the Gold Coast.

557 MIDDLEMAST, KENNETH. 'The Gold Coast Library Board and its contribution to literacy, particularly in the rural areas.' *Advance*, **8**, Oct. 1955: 13–14.

558 —— 'Public Libraries in Ghana.' *Library Journal*, **82**, 20, 1957: 2871–2873.

559 MIDDLEMAST, KENNETH. 'A tropical regional library.' [Sekondi]. *Library Association Record*, **58**, 1, Jan. 1956: 9–11.

560 PERRY, RUTH. 'Libraries in West Africa.' *W. Afr. Rev.*, Sept. 1955: 827–831.

561 PLUMBE, WILFRED J., ED. 'Current trends in newly developing countries'. *Library Trends*, Oct. 1959.

562 RYDINGS, H. ANTHONY. 'Libraries and scientific progress in West Africa.' *WALA news*, **3**, 3, June 1959: 109–116.

563 SPAULDING, WILLIAM E., AND SMITH, DATUS C. *Books for Ghana and Nigeria*. N.Y., Franklin Publications, 1962. 33 pp. A survey of the book trade.

564 STRICKLAND, JOHN T. 'Patterns of library service in Africa.' *Library Trends*, Oct. 1959: 163–191.

565 TETTEH, S. N. 'Library provision in the Gold Coast.' *Library Association Record*, **53**, 6, June 1951: 191–193.

566 WALKER, ELISE. 'The University College of the Gold Coast library.' *Library Association Record*, **56**, 5, May 1954: 166–170.

Agriculture

567 ANYANE, S. LA. *Aweso: a Manya Krobo huza.* Accra, Division of Agriculture, 1958. (Typescript.)
Land purchase in the Akwapim area.

568 —— 'A strip system of farming in Ghana.' *Econ. Bull.*, **4**, 1, Jan. 1960: 12.

569 AYIVOR, V. F. K., AND HELLINS, C. E. K. *Poultry keeping in the tropics.* 2nd ed. O.U.P., 1960. 58 pp.
A revision of C.E.K. Hellins's Elementary lessons in poultry keeping, Achimota Press, 1933. Previous ed. 1953.

570 BAKER, E. M. *African fruits.* U.L.P., 1949. 48 pp.

571 BOX, H. E. *Citrus moths investigations: report.* Achimota, Achimota Press, 1942. 88 pp.

572 COLLINS, W. B. 'Preserving Ghana's game.' *W. Afr. Rev.*, Nov. 1960: 55–57.

573 COX, R. 'Expanding Ghana's agriculture.' *West Africa*, 2264, 1960: 1201.

574 FAULKNER, O. T., AND MACKIE, J. R. *West African agriculture.* C.U.P., 1933. 168 pp.

575 GOLD COAST. AGRICULTURAL DEVELOPMENT CORPORATION. *Mensah the oil palm farmer.* Accra, Dept. of Information Services, 1956. 39 pp.

576 GOLD COAST. DEPT OF AGRICULTURE. *Cassava mosaic*, by H. A. DADE. Accra, Govt. Printer, 1930.

577 —— *Root-rot of coco-yams*, by J. WRIGHT. Accra, Govt. Printer, 1930. (Bulletin no. 23.)

578 —— *Recommendations concerning agricultural development and policy. Part A: Administration; Part B: Crops.* Accra, 1932. (Bulletin nos. 24–25.)

579 —— *Lessons in elementary book-keeping for co-operative workers* by D. T. ACKAH. Accra, 1934. (Bulletin no. 29.)

580 GOLD COAST. DEPT. OF AGRICULTURE. *Report on a visit to Northern Nigeria to study mixed farming*, by C. W. LYNN. Accra, 1937. (Bulletin no. 33.)

581 —— *Agriculture in north Mamprusi*, by C. W. LYNN. Accra, 1937. (Bulletin no. 34.)

582 —— *War-time cookery book: methods of utilizing Gold Coast produce in place of imported provisions*. Accra, [194–]. 20 pp. (Booklet no. 1.) (Typescript.)

583 —— *How to make sugar: methods of using sugar-cane to make sugar*. Accra, [194–]. 4 pp. (Booklet no. 3.)

584 —— *Preparation of fruits and vegetables for market*. Accra, [194–]. 12 pp. (Booklet no. 4.)

585 —— *Rubber: methods of tapping Funtumia, Para and rubber vines, and simple methods of preparing the rubber*. Accra, [194–]. 6 pp. (Booklet no. 5.)

586 —— *Vegetable growing*. Accra, 1942. 19 pp. (Booklet no. 6.)

587 —— *Better methods of preparing and serving fresh vegetables*. Accra, 1942. 9 pp. (Booklet no. 7.)

588 —— *Sheep: methods of managing, housing and feeding sheep in the Gold Coast*. Accra, 1942. 8 pp. (Booklet no. 8.)

589 —— *Rubbers: methods of tapping, preparing, curing and packing for export*. Accra, 1944. 30 pp. (Booklet no. 9.)

590 —— *Rabbits: methods of housing, feeding and managing tame rabbits in the Gold Coast*. Accra, 1944. 8 pp. (Booklet no. 10.)

591 —— *Vegetable growing*. Accra, 1946. 42 pp. (Booklet no. 11.)

592 —— *Sheep feeding, housing and management of sheep in the southern parts of the Gold Coast*. Accra, 1953. 8 pp.

593 GHANA. MINISTRY OF AGRICULTURE. *Diseases of economic plants in Ghana, other than cacao*, by R. I. LEATHER. Accra, Govt. Printer, 1959. vii, 42 pp. (Bulletin no. 1.)

594 —— *Miscellaneous information*, 1960–61. Accra, 1961. 225 pp.

595 —— *[Report of the] First Grassland Symposium, 7th–9th December, 1960*. Accra, 1961. 119 pp.

596 —— *Conquering the Accra plains: Dawhwenya Dam Project for irrigation and livestock development*. Accra, 1961. 20 pp. (South Eastern coastal savannah development projects, Accra Plains, Project no. 1.)

597 GHANA MINISTRY OF AGRICULTURE. *A check list of fungi recorded from Ghana*, by L. J. PIENING. Accra, Govt. Printer, 1962. 130 pp. (Bulletin no. 2.)

598 HALL, D. W. *Report on food storage in the Gold Coast.* Colonial Office, 1955.

599 HELLINS, CONSTANCE E. K. *Elementary lessons in practical agriculture. Part 1: Poultry keeping.* Achimota, College Press, 1933. 25 pp.

600 —— *Elementary lessons in practical agriculture. Part 2: Vegetable gardening.* Achimota, College Press, 1934. 33 pp.

601 —— *Elementary lessons in practical agriculture. Part 3: Livestock.* Achimota, College Press, 1935. 27 pp.

602 HILTON, THOMAS ERIC. 'Land planning and resettlement in northern Ghana.' *Geography*, **44,** 4, Nov. 1959: 227–240.

603 IRVINE, FREDERICK ROBERT. *A textbook of West African agriculture, soils and crops.* 2nd ed. O.U.P., 1953.

604 JONES, G. HOWARD. *The earth goddess: a study of native farming on the West African coast.* Longmans, 1936. 205 pp.

605 MANSHARD, WALTHER. 'Agrarische Organisationsformen für den Binnenmarkt bestimmter Kulturen in Waldgürtel Ghanas.' *Erdkunde*, **11**, 3, Aug. 1957: 215–224.

606 —— *Die geographischen Grundlagen der Wirtschaft Ghanas unter besonderer Berücksichtigung der agrarischen Entwicklung.* Koln, 1959.

607 ——*Die geographischen Grundlagen der Wirtschaft Ghanas.* Wiesbaden, Steiner, 1961. 308 pp.

608 MASON, I. L. *The Classification of West African livestock.* Commonwealth Agriculture Bureaux, 1951. 39 pp.

609 MILLER, W. C. *Report on animal health and husbandry in the Gold Coast Colony.* Accra, Govt. Printer, 1947.

610 ORGANISATION FOR EUROPEAN ECONOMIC CO-OPERATION. *The cultivation of groundnuts in West Africa.* Paris, O.E.E.C., 1953. 54 pp.

611 PHILLIPS, T. A. *Farm managment in West Africa.* Longmans, 1961. 150 pp.

612 PIM, SIR ALAN WILLIAM. *Colonial agricultural production.* O.U.P., 1946. ix, 190 pp.

613 RAE, C.J. *Preliminary report on the possibility of agricultural development by land drainage, irrigation or reclamation in the Gold Coast Colony.* Accra, Dept. of Agriculture, 1943. 19 pp. (Typescript.)

614   RAMSAY, J. M. 'Land planning in the Northern Territories.' *Gold Coast Teachers' J.*, **2**, April 1957: 20–26.

615   ROWE, JAMES E. *Elementary lessons in practical agriculture. Part 4: Decorative gardening.* Achimota, College Press, 1935. 35 pp.

616   SMITH A. *Agricultural problems, 1: Growing more food.* Bureau of Current Affairs, [195–]. (West African affairs pamphlets, no. 16.)

617   —— *Agricultural problems, 2: Cash crops.* Bureau of Current Affairs, [195–]. (West African affairs pamphlets, no. 17.)

618   STEWART, J. L., AND JEFFREYS, M.D.W. *The cattle of the Gold Coast.* Revised ed. Accra, Govt. Printer, 1956. 48 pp.

619   TETE-ANSA, WINIFRED. *Africa at work.* [193–] 95 pp.

620   TORTO, J. O. 'The cultivation of yams in the Gold Coast.' *New Gold Coast farmer*, **1**, 1, 1956: 6–8.

621   WATERS, H. B. 'Agriculture in the Gold Coast.' *Empire J. of Experimental Agriculture*, **12**, 46, April 1944: 83–102.

622   WHITE, H. P. 'Environment and land utilization on the Accra Plains.' *J.W. Afr. Science Association*, **1**, 1, Oct. 1954: 46–62.

623   WILLS, J. B., ED. *Agriculture and land use in Ghana.* Published for the Ghana Ministry of Food & Agriculture by O.U.P., 1962: 504 pp.
  An authoritative survey, with many illustrations, maps and bibliography.

See also nos. 221, 272, 439, 855, 2255, 2261, 2275, 2288, 2327, 2331, 2336, 2586, 2587.

Soil Surveys

624 ADU, S. V. *Report on the detailed soil survey of the central agricultural station, Nyankpala, Dagomba District, Northern Region.* Kumasi, Dept. of Soil & Land-Use Survey, 1957. 27 pp. (Technical report, no. 28.) (Typescript.)

625 BRAMMER, H. *Detailed soil survey of the Kpong pilot irrigation area.* Kumasi, Dept. of Soil & Land-Use Survey, 1955. 102 pp.

626 —— *The soils of the Lawra District Agricultural Station, Babile.* Kumasi, Dept. of Soil & Land-Use Survey, 1956. 9 pp. (Technical report, no. 17.) (Typescript.)

627 —— *Visit to Haute-Volta, 30th January–3rd March, 1955.* Kumasi, Dept. of Soil & Land-Use Survey, 1955. 50 pp. (Technical report, no. 9.)

628 BRAMMER, H., AND ENDREDY, A. S. DE. *The tropical grey earths of the Accra Plains, Gold Coast.* Kumasi, Dept. of Soil & Land-Use Survey, 1956. 6 pp.

629 CHARTER, C. F. *Cocoa soils good and bad: an introduction to the soils of the forest regions of West Africa.* Tafo, W.A.C.R.I., 1948. 125 pp. (Typescript.)

630 —— *Soils and fertilisers: the nutrient status of Gold Coast forest soils with special reference to manuring of cocoa.* Kumasi, Dept. of Soil & Land-Use Survey, 1955. 18 pp.

631 CLACEY, J. L., AND RAMSAY, J. M. 'Land use, soil and water conservation in the Northern Territories of the Gold Coast.' *African soils,* **3,** 3, 1955: 338–353.

632 CROSBIE, A. J. *Peneplain remnants in the Kumasi region, Gold Coast.* Kumasi, Dept. of Soil & Land-Use Survey, 1956. 8 pp.

633 ENDREDY, A. S. DE, AND MONTGOMERY, C. W. *Some aspects of cation exchange in Gold Coast forest soils.* Kumasi, Dept. of Soil & Land-Use Survey, 1956. 11 pp.

634 ENDREDY, A. S. DE, AND QUAGRAINE, K. A. *Total phosphorus in Gold Coast soils.* Kumasi, Dept. of Soil & Land-Use Survey, 1956. 6 pp.

635   GOLD COAST. DEPT. OF SOIL & LAND-USE SURVEY. *The soil survey report: a description of the contents of memoirs giving the results of detailed preliminary surveys.* Kumasi, Dept. of Soil & Land-Use Survey, 1955. 14 pp. (Bulletin, no. 2.)

636   GHANA. MINISTRY OF FOOD AND AGRICULTURE. *Report of the semi-detailed soil survey of Pong Tamale Veterinary Station, Dagomba District, Northern Ghana,* by A. R. STOBBS. Kumasi, Dept. of Soil & Land-Use Survey, 1960. 150 pp.

637   —— *Soils of the lower Tano basin, south-western Ghana,* by P. M. AHN. Crown Agents, 1960.

638   HOTSON, J. M. *Method of detailed survey, Western Region.* Kumasi, Dept. of Soil & Land-Use Survey, 1956. 16 pp. (Bulletin, no. 3.)

639   —— *Some little known soils of the closed forest zone of the Gold Coast.* Kumasi, Dept. of Soil & Land-Use Survey, 1956.

640   OBENG, H. B. *The major soils of the Seilo-Tuni land planning area, north-western Ghana.* Kumasi, Division of Agriculture, Soil & Land-Use Branch, 1959.

641   PURNELL, M. F. *Detailed soil survey of Ohawu Agricultural Station, Keta District, Trans-Volta Togoland.* Kumasi, Dept. of Soil & Land-Use Survey, 1956. 31 pp. (Technical report, no. 18.)

642   —— *Report on a semi-detailed survey of the proposed Dumbai Agricultural Station.* Kumasi, Division of Agriculture, Soil & Land-Use Branch, 1957. 14 pp. (Technical report, no. 23.) (Typescript.)

643   —— *Report on a survey of Princes Coconut Station, Ahanta-Nzima District, Western Region, Kumasi.* Kumasi, Dept. of Soil & Land-Use Survey, 1957. 21 pp. (Technical report, no. 22.)

644   RADWANSKI, S. A. *Soils associated with the late tertiary peneplain and its erosion in the upper Tano drainage basin of the Gold Coast.* Kumasi, Dept. of Soil & Land-Use Survey, 1956. 9 pp.

645   —— *Soils developed over ancient drifts in the forest zone of the Gold Coast with particular reference to the upper Tano drainage basin.* Kumasi, Dept. of Soil & Land-Use Survey, 1956. 7 pp.

646   WILLS, J. B. *The application of the World Land Use Survey Scheme in the Gold Coast.* Kumasi, Dept. of Soil & Land-Use Survey, 1955. 31 pp.

See also nos. 214, 623.

Cocoa

647 BAREAU, P. *Cocoa: a crop with a future.* Bournville, Cadbury Bros., 1953. 39 pp.

648 BECKETT, W. H. *Akokoaso: a survey of a Gold Coast village.* Lund, Humphries, for the London School of Economics, 1944. 95 pp.
Cocoa production in a rural community.

649 —— *Koransang: a Gold Coast cocoa farm.* Accra, Govt. Printer, 1945. 24 pp.

650 BOOKER, H. S. 'Debt in Africa.' *Afr. affairs,* **48,** 191, April 1949: 141–149.
Income and expenditure at Akokoaso. *See also* no. 648.

651 BRAY, F. R. *Cocoa development in Ahafo, west Ashanti.* Achimota, 1959. 83 pp. (Typescript.)

652 BROATCH, J. D. 'Problems of cocoa growing in the Gold Coast.' *New Gold Coast Farmer,* **I,** 1, 1956: 2–5; **I,** 2, 42–44.

653 BYLES, L. A. *Trends in the production and consumption of raw cocoa.* Cocoa Conference, 1951.

654 CADBURY BROTHERS, LTD. *Mission to Ghana: the good-will tour by Cadbury scholarship holders.* Bournville, Cadbury Bros., [1958] 12 pp.

655 —— *Our 50 years in the Gold Coast and Ghana, 1907–1957.* Bournville, Cadbury Bros., [1958]. 38 pp.

656 GOLD COAST. COCOA MARKETING BOARD. *Kofi the good farmer.* Accra, the Board, 1950. 50 pp.

657 —— *The Gold Coast Cocoa Marketing Board: what it is and what it does.* Accra, the Board, [1952?]. 8 pp.

658 —— *The Gold Coast Cocoa Marketing Board at work.* Accra, the Board, 1956. 20 pp.

659 GHANA. COCOA MARKETING BOARD. *Ghana cocoa.* Accra, the Board, [1959]. 12 pp.

660 GHANA. COCOA MARKETING BOARD. *The Ghana Cocoa Marketing Board at work.* 3rd ed. Accra, the Board, 1959. 20 pp.

661 —— *Hints to cocoa farmers.* Accra, the Board, [1959] 40 pp. In English, Ashanti-Twi, Akwapim-Twi, Fante and Ewe.

662 GOLD COAST. DEPT. OF AGRICULTURE. *Further observations on cacao pod diseases in the Gold Coast,* by H. A. DADE. Accra, Govt. Printer, 1930. (Bulletin, no. 23.)

663 —— *Infestation of stored cocoa by weevil and moth,* by G. S. COTTERELL. Accra, Govt. Printer, 1934. (Bulletin, no. 28.)

664 —— *Household uses for cocoa.* Accra, [194–]. 8 pp. (Booklet no. 2.)

665 GOLD COAST. INFORMATION SERVICES. *Golden harvest: the story of the Gold Coast cocoa industry.* Accra, 1953. 56 pp.

666 GREENWOOD, M. *Report on the Central Cocoa Research Station, Tafo, 1938–42.* Accra, Govt. Printer, 1943. 63 pp.

667 HAMMOND, P. S. 'Capsid control on mature cocoa.' *New Gold Coast farmer,* **1,** 3, 1957: 109–115.

668 HANNA, A. D., AND OTHERS. 'Systematic insecticides for the control of insects transmitting swollenshoot virus disease of cacao in the Gold Coast.' *Bull. Entomological Res.,* **46,** 3, 1955: 669–710.

669 HILL, POLLY. *Cocoa research series, 11–14.* Accra, University College of Ghana, 1958.
Author is Research Fellow, Dept. of Economics, university of Ghana.

670 —— *The Gold Coast cocoa farmer: a preliminary survey.* O.U.P., 1956. 139 pp.

671 —— 'The history of the migration of Ghana cocoa farmers.' *Trans. Hist. Soc. Ghana,* **4,** 1959: 14–28.

672 —— 'The migrant cocoa farmers of southern Ghana.' *Africa,* **31,** 3, 1961: 209–230.

673 —— 'Women cocoa farmers.' *Econ. bull.,* **2,** 6, June 1958: 3–5.

674 HILL, POLLY, AND MCGLADE, CELIA. '"Companies" and cocoa growing in Akim Abuakwa.' *Universitas,* **2,** 4, 1956: 109–111.

675 MILSOME, J. R. 'Cadburys and Ghana.' *W. Afr. Rev.,* Oct. 1961: 31–35.

676 PREISWERK, MAX. *Documentary evidence of the pioneer work for the cultivation of cocoa in Ghana carried out by the Basel Mission at Akropong Agricultural Station, 1857–1868.* [1957.] 7 pp. (Typescript.)

677 TANBURN, E. *Intensive survey of the cocoa-producing areas of the Gold Coast and trends in potential production.* Accra, Dept. of Agriculture, 1955. 63 pp.

678 'Tetteh Quarshie and the cocoa industry.' *W. Afr. Rev.*, July 1951: 744–755.
Tetteh Quarshie first introduced the cocoa plant to the Gold Coast in 1879, after his return from the Portuguese island of Fernando Po.

679 THE TIMES. 'Production of raw cocoa: West Africa, the world's largest supplier.' *Times Rev. Brit. Col.*, 5, Spring 1952: 11–14.

680 UNITED AFRICA COMPANY. 'What cocoa means to the economy of the Gold Coast.' *Statistical & Economic Rev.*, **2**, Sept. 1948: 1–28.

681 URQUHART, DUNCAN HECTOR. *Cocoa.* 2nd ed. Longmans, 1961. 293 pp. (Tropical agriculture series.)

682 —— *Report on the cocoa industry in Sierra Leone and notes on the cocoa industry of the Gold Coast.* Bournville, Cadbury Bros., 1955. 43 pp.

683 VOELCKER, O. J. 'The West African Cacao Research Institute.' *Nature*, **161**, 4082, 24 Jan. 1948: 117–119.

684 WEST AFRICAN CACAO RESEARCH INSTITUTE. TAFO. *A summary of the results of capsid research in the Gold Coast,* by D. J. TAYLOR. 1954. 20 pp. (Technical bulletin, no. 1.)

685 —— *Capsids and capsid control in the Belgian Congo, with special reference to Lukolela Plantations,* by J. NICOL AND D. J. TAYLOR. 1954. 10 pp. (Technical bulletin, no. 2.)

686 —— *The propagation of cacao by cuttings,* by J. F. ARCHIBALD. 1955. 7 pp. (Technical bulletin, no. 3.)

687 —— *The control of cacao swollen shoot disease in West Africa: a review of the present situation,* by J. M. THRESH. 1958. 36 pp. (Technical bulletin, no. 4.)

688 —— *The spread of virus disease in cacao,* by J. M. THRESH. 1958. 36 pp. (Technical bulletin, no. 5.)

689 —— *A review of the use of shade and fertilizer in the culture of cocoa,* by R. K. CUNNINGHAM. 1959. 15 pp. (Technical bulletin, no. 6.)

690 WEST AFRICAN CACAO RESEARCH INSTITUTE. TAFO. *The viruses of cacao*, by J. M. THRESH AND T. W. TINSLEY 1959. 32 pp. (Technical bulletin, no. 7.)

691 —— *Die-back of cocoa*, by D. KAY. 1961. 20 pp. (Technical bulletin, no. 8.)

692 —— *Report upon a visit to French Togo, Dahomey, Nigeria and the Cameroons during the dry season, December 1943 to March 1944*, by HAROLD E. BOX. 1944. 69 pp.

693 —— *W.A.C.R.I., 1944–1949.* Tafo, 1950.

694 —— *W.A.C.R.I. and the cocoa farmer.* Lagos, Nigerian Information Service, [1960?]. 23 pp.

See also nos. 214, 2270, 2282, 2315, 2316, 2340, 2347, 2399, 2400, 2438, 2489, 2577, 2580, 2582, 2590.

Forestry

695   BROOKS, R. L. *West African forestry.* Nelson, 1949. 70 pp.

696   COLLINS, W. B. *The perpetual forest.* Staples Press, 1958. 272 pp.

697   —— *They went to bush.* MacGibbon & Kee, 1961. 231 pp.
Experiences of a forestry officer in Ghana.

698   —— 'The tropical forest: an animal and plant association.'
Nigerian field, **21,** 1, 1956: 4–27.

699   GOLD COAST. FORESTRY DEPT. *The vegetation zones of the Gold Coast,*
by C. J. TAYLOR. Accra, Govt. Printer, 1952. (Bulletin no. 4.)

700   —— *Gold Coast timbers.* Accra, Govt. Printer, 1949. 37 pp.

701   —— *Silvicultural notes on some of the more important Gold Coast
trees,* compiled by D. KINLOCH. Accra, Govt. Printer, 1945. 70 pp.
A supplement to *Gold Coast timbers.*

702   —— *Gold Coast timber industry: report of a fact finding committee.*
Accra, Govt. Printer, 1951. 69 pp.

703   —— *Empire forests and the war.* Accra, Govt. Printer, 1947. 49 pp.

704   GOLD COAST. PUBLIC RELATIONS DEPT. *Wealth in wood: a brief
description of forestry and the timber industry in the Gold Coast.* Accra,
Govt. Printer, 1950. 24 pp.

705   GHANA. DEPT. OF AGRICULTURE. *The principal areas of remaining
original forest in western Ghana, and their agricultural potential,* by
PETER M. ANN. Accra, Govt. Printer, 1959. 10 pp.

706   LOGAN, W. M. 'The Gold Coast Forestry Department, 1908–1945.'
Empire Forestry Rev., **25,** 1, 1946: 52–59.

707   —— 'Some effects of mining on the forest of Tarkwa District.'
Farm & Forest, **7,** 1, June 1946: 45–50.

708   SELLIER, R. *Twin-brother hell.* Hutchinson, 1960. 208 pp.
Sawmilling operations in Ghana.

709   STEBBING, E. P. *The forests of West Africa and the Sahara: a study of
modern conditions.* Chambers, 1937. viii, 245 pp.

710   WILLS, J. A. 'Kumasi Timber Producers' Co-operative Society.'
Farm & Forest, **5,** 4, Dec. 1944: 169–170.
See also nos. 276, 277, 292, 2314, 2364, 2372.

Fisheries

711   BOTSIO, KOJO. *The opening of Tema fishing harbour: a speech.* Accra, Govt. Printer, 1961. 6 pp.

712   COLLINS, W. B. 'The sea is their hunting ground: the romance of the Gold Coast fishing industry.' *W. Afr. Rev.*, July 1955: 589–594.

713   HILTON, THOMAS ERIC. 'The fisheries of the Volta system of Ghana.' *Oriental Geog.* [*Dacca*]. **5,** 1, 1961: 21–34.

714   IRVINE, FREDERICK ROBERT. *The fishes and fisheries of the Gold Coast.* Crown Agents, 1947. 352 pp.

715   —— *Gold Coast crabs and lobsters.* Accra, Govt. Printer, 1932. 20 pp.

716   LAWSON, ROWENA M. 'The structure, migration, and resettlement of Ewe fishing units.' *Afr. Stud.*, **17,** 1, 1958: 21–27.

717   MANSHARD, WALTHER. 'Die Küsten- und Fluss- fischerei Ghanas.' *Die Erde,* **89,** 1, 1958: 21–33.

See also nos. 802, 2363.

Medicine, Food and Health

718   AJOSE, OLADELE ADEBAYO. *Public health in tropical countries.* Churchill, 1958. 198 pp.

719   ARMATTOE, RAPHAEL ERNEST GRAIL. 'A dental survey of the British Isles.' *Nature,* **152,** 1953: 630. (Reprint.)

720   —— *Materia medica: a study of over three hundred medicinal plants in all parts of the world.* Londonderry, Lomeshire Research Institute, [1946?]. 280 pp.

721   —— 'The pattern of youth: an interim report.' *Nature,* **152,** 1943: 217. (Reprint.)
      Effects of war on the relative stature and weight of adolescents.

722   —— *Personal recollections of the Nobel Laureation Festival of 1947.* Londonderry, Lomeshire Research Institute, [1948]. 62 pp.

723   —— 'A racial survey of the British people.' *Londonderry Sentinel,* 4 April, 1944. (Reprint).

724   —— *Select correspondence of interest to men of science.* [Londonderry, Lomeshire Research Institute, 1950?] 20 pp.

725   —— *The Swiss contribution to western civilisation; with a foreword by Professor Julian S. Huxley.* Dundalk, Dundalgan Press, 1944. 91 pp.

726   AYLWARD, F. *Interim report to the Government of Ghana on foods and nutrition.* Rome, FAO, 1961. 76 pp. (Typescript.)

727   BROWNE, M.P., AND WADDY, B. B. *Report on outbreak of cerebro-spinal meningitis in the western Northern Territories, 1st January–21st March, 1945.* Accra, Govt. Printer, 1946.

728   COLBOURNE, M. J. 'The effect of malaria suppression in a group of Accra schoolchildren.' *Trans. Roy. Soc. Trop. Med. Hygiene,* **49,** 4, 1955: 356–369.

729   —— 'Malaria in Gold Coast students on their return from the United Kingdom.' *Trans. Roy. Soc. Trop. Med. Hygiene,* **49,** 5, 1955: 483–487.

730 COLBOURNE, M.J. 'A medical survey in a Gold Coast village.' [Kwansakrom.] *Trans. Roy. Soc. Trop. Med. Hygiene*, **44**, 3, Dec. 1950: 271–290.

731 COLBOURNE, M. J., AND HAMILTON, J. A. *Health in the village: the story of Kwansakrome*. Bureau of Current Affairs, 1951. 16 pp. (West African affairs pamphlets, no. 7.)

732 COLBOURNE, M. J., AND WRIGHT, F. N. 'Malaria in the Gold Coast.' *W. Afr. Med. J.*, **4**, 4, 1955: 161–174.

733 CRISP, G. *Simulium and onchoceriasis in the Northern Territories of the Gold Coast*. Published for the British Empire Society for the Blind, by H. K. Lewis, 1957. 171 pp.

734 DAVEY, THOMAS HERBERT. *Disease and population pressure in the tropics*. Ibadan U.P., 1958. 22 pp.

735 —— *Trypanosomiasis in British West Africa*. H.M.S.O., 1948. 15 pp.

736 DAWSON, J., AND OTHERS. 'A note on vitamin B complex deficiency states among Africans in the Gold Coast.' *Trans. Roy. Soc. Trop. Med. Hygiene*, **42**, 3, Nov. 1948: 277–282.

737 DUFF, D. *Yellow fever and its prevention*. Achimota, Achimota Press, [1937]. 6 pp.

738 DU SAUTOY, MARJORIE. *Some Gold Coast foods, or, what to eat for a balanced diet*. Accra, Govt. Printer, 1953. 20 pp.

739 EDWARDS, E. E. 'Human onchoceriasis in West Africa with special reference to the Gold Coast.' *J. W. Afr. Science Association*, **2**, 1, 1956: 1–35.

740 FIAWOO, F. KWASI. 'Health and diet of the African child.' *Afr. affairs*, 1947: 243.

741 FIELD, MARGARET JOYCE. *Gold Coast food*. Achimota, Achimota Press, 1951.

742 GOLD COAST. INFORMATION SERVICES. *Nurses in training: a noble career for Gold Coast girls*. Accra, 1952. 24 pp.

743 GOLD COAST. TSETSE CONTROL DEPT. *Annual reports, 1949–1957*. Accra, Govt. Printer.

744 GHANA. DEPT. OF SOCIAL WELFARE AND COMMUNITY DEVELOPMENT. *Good food for good health: mass education project guide*. Revised and edited by ELLA GRIFFIN. Accra, Bureau of Ghana Languages, 1959. [50] pp.

745 GHANA. MINISTRY OF HEALTH. *Report of the proceedings of a conference of health inspectors and health superintendents held in Accra, Ghana, 16th–18th November, 1956*. Accra, Govt. Printer, 1957.

746   GHANA. NATIONAL FOOD AND NUTRITION BOARD. *Healthy homes for healthy families.* 1: *Suitable dishes for weaning;* 2: *Planning of meals.* Accra, Catholic Press, 1962. 20 pp.

747   *Ghana nutrition and cookery.* Nelson, 1960. 347 pp.
    Hints on planning meals, diet and recipes based on West African food. Compiled with the co-operation of the Ghana Medical and Education Departments. Previous edition entitled *Gold Coast nutrition,* 1953.

748   GRANT, FAYE W. 'Diet in Gold Coast villages'. *West Africa,* 1863, Nov. 1952: 1039–1040.

749   —— *The nutrition and health of children in the Gold Coast.* Chicago U.P., 1955. 67 pp. (University of Chicago. Committee on Home Economics. Publications.)

750   —— 'Nutrition and health of Gold Coast children.' *J. Amer. Dietetic Association,* **31,** 7, 1955: 685–702.

751   HACKETT, C. J. *An international nomenclature of yaws lesions . . . in co-operation with an international group of experts on yaws, and participants at the International Conference on Yaws Control, Enugu, Nigeria, 1955.* Geneva, World Health Organisation, 1957. 103 pp. (Monograph series, no. 36.)

752   'Health services in Ghana: encouraging progress of campaigns against disease and malnutrition.' *Afr. world,* May 1961: 10–12.

753   HUGHES, M. H. 'Bacillary dysentery in Accra, Gold Coast.' *W. Afr. Med. J.,* **4,** 2, 1955: 73–77.

754   —— 'Enteric fevers and normal salmonella agglutinins in the Gold Coast.' *J. Hygiene,* **53,** 3, 1955: 368–378.

755   MILLER, M. J. 'Suppression of malaria by monthly drug administration.' *Amer. J. trop. med. hygiene,* **4,** 5, 1955: 790–799.

756   MILLS, JOHN TAYLER. 'Three men died: tales of the Gold Coast.' *W. Afr. Rev.,* Aug. 1950: 961–963.
    Yellow fever research at Korle Bu Hospital, Accra.

757   MORRIS, K. R. S. *Fighting a fly: the story of the campaign against the tsetse in the Gold Coast.* Accra, Public Relations Dept., 1950. 24 pp.

758   —— 'A large-scale experiment in the eradication of tsetse (*Glossina palpalis* and *G. tachinoides*).' *Farm and forest,* **5,** 4, Dec. 1944: 149–156.

759 MURRAY, A. J., AND CROCKET, J. A. *Report on silicosis and tuberculosis among mine workers in the Gold Coast.* Accra, Govt. Printer, 1947.

760 NASH, T. A. M. *Tsetse flies in British West Africa.* H.M.S.O., 1948. 77 pp.

761 OFORI-ATTA, SUSAN B. G. 'Nutritional deficiencies and maternal and child health in Africa.' *J. Nat. Med. Association* [*Tuskegee, Ala.*], **52,** Jan. 1960: 41–46.

762 ONABAMIRO, S. D. *Food and health.* Penguin Books, 1954. 121 pp. (Penguin West African series.)

763 ——*Why our children die: the causes, and suggestions for prevention of infant mortality in West Africa.* Methuen, 1949. xi, 196 pp.

764 PURCELL, F. M. *Diet and ill health in the forest country of the Gold Coast.* H. K. Lewis, 1939. 77 pp.

765 RODGER, F. C. 'Onchocerciasis in the northern Gold Coast.' *Nigerian field,* **20,** 4, 1955: 161–165.

766 SAUNDERS, GEORGE F. T. 'Sleeping sickness campaign in the Gold Coast.' *Farm and forest,* **5,** 3, Sept. 1944: 138–140.

767 SUSMAN, I. A. *The true facts about leprosy: prepared primarily for use in schools.* Accra, Govt. Printer, [1960]. 25 pp.

768 TAIT, DAVID. 'Food in the Northern Territories.' *Universitas,* **2,** 3, 1956: 76–77.

769 TETTEY, CHARLES. 'A brief history of the Medical Research Institute and laboratory service of the Gold Coast, 1908–1957.' *W. Afr. Med. J.,* **9,** 2, 1957: 73–85.

770 *They that walk in darkness: the cure and prevention of leprosy in the Gold Coast, by a Doctor.* Accra, Society of Friends of Lepers, [195–?]. 23 pp.

771 TOOTH, GEOFFREY. *Studies in mental illness in the Gold Coast.* H.M.S.O., 1950. 72 pp. (Colonial research publications.)
    Published under the auspices of the Colonial Social Science Research Council.

772 WILSON, J. MICHAEL. *Health talks, by a Radio Doctor (J. Michael Wilson).* Accra, Scottish Mission Book Depot, [195–]. 49 pp.

See also nos. 7, 11, 18, 281, 285, 795, 797, 1036, 2267, 2268, 2277, 2329, 2352, 2377, 2381, 2390, 2452, 2453, 2521.

Ethnology

General

773 AGBLEY, SETH. 'The origin of idols.' *Ghana bull. theology*, **1**, 7, Dec. 1959: 3–6.

774 ALICOE, T. 'The evolution of Gold Coast chiefship.' *Sheffield Telegraph & Star*, [1952]. 102 pp.

775 AMAMOO, J. G. 'The position of chiefs in Gold Coast society.' *Afr. world*, March 1954: 9.

776 ARMITAGE, CECIL H. *The tribal markings and marks of adornment of the natives of the Northern Territories of the Gold Coast Colony.* Harrison 1924. viii, 22 pp.

777 BASCOM, WILLIAM R. 'West Africa and the complexity of primitive cultures.' *Amer. anthropologist*, n.s. **50**, 1, 1, Jan.–March 1948: 18–23.

778 BASCOM, WILLIAM R., AND HERSKOVITS, M. J. *Continuity and change in African cultures.* Chicago U.P., 1959. 309 pp.

779 BAUMANN, H., AND WESTERMANN, DIEDRICH HERMANN. *Les peuples et les civilisations de l'Afrique.* Paris, Payot, 1948.

780 BOLINDER, GUSTAF. *Svarta folk i Vestafrika.* Köbenhavn, Bonnier, 1931. 221 pp.

781 BRIGGS, L. CABOT. 'A review of the physical anthropology of the Sahara and its prehistoric implication.' *Man*, Feb. 1957.

782 —— *Tribes of the Sahara.* Harvard U.P.; O.U.P., 1960. 295 pp.

783 BROWN, PAULA. 'Patterns of authority in West Africa.' *Africa*, **21**, 4, Oct. 1951: 261–278.

784 BUELL, R. *The native problem in Africa.* N.Y., 1931. 2 vols.

785 BUSIA, KOFI ABREFA. *The place of the chief in the Gold Coast.* Achimota, Achimota Press, 1949. 10 pp.

786 BUTT-THOMPSON, F. W. *West African secret societies: their organisations, officials and teaching.* Witherby, 1929. 320 pp.

787 BUXTON, L. H. DUDLEY, ED. *Custom is king: essays presented to R. R. Marett.* Hutchinson, 1935.

788 CARDINALL, ALLAN W. *The natives of the Northern Territories of the Gold Coast, their customs, religion and folklore.* Routledge, 1920. 158 pp.

789 CHAMPAGNE, P. E. 'Traits de la vie payenne dans la préfecture apostolique de Navrongo.' *Ann. lateranensi,* **8,** 1944: 147–154.

790 CHRISTIAN COUNCIL OF THE GOLD COAST. *Report on common beliefs with regard to witchcraft.* Accra, Scottish Mission Book Depot, 1932. 8 pp.

791 DEBRUNNER, HANS. 'Note sur les "Azongu" de Half-Assini en Gold Coast.' *Notes afr. IFAN,* **60,** 1953.

792 DELAFOSSE, M. *The negroes of Africa.* Washington, D. C., Associated Publishers, 1931.

793 DEMAISON, ANDRÉ. *La vie des noirs d'Afrique du Sénégal au Congo.* Paris, Bourrelier, 1950. 128 pp.

794 DENNETT, R. E. *At the back of the black man's mind, or, notes on the kingly office in West Africa.* Macmillan, 1906. xv, 288 pp.

795 FIELD, MARGARET JOYCE. 'Mental disorder in rural Ghana.' *J. mental science,* **104,** 437, Oct. 1958: 1043–1051.

796 —— 'The *otutu* and the *hionte* of West Africa.' *Man,* **43,** 18, March–April 1943: 36–37.
      Relics of burial grounds in the Gold Coast.

797 —— *Search for security: an ethno-psychiatric study of rural Ghana.* Faber, 1960. 478 pp.

798 —— 'Some new shrines of the Gold Coast and their significance.' *Africa,* **13,** 2, 1940: 138–149.

799 —— 'Witchcraft as a primitive interpretation of mental disorder.' *J. mental science,* **101,** 425, Oct. 1955: 826–833.

800 FORDE, DARYLL, ED. *African worlds.* O.U.P., 1954. 243 pp.

801 —— 'The cultural map of West Africa: successive adaptations to tropical forests and grasslands.' *Trans. N.Y. Acad. Science,* ser. 2, **15,** 1953: 206–219.

802 FORTES, MEYER. 'Communal fishing and fishing magic in the Northern Territories of the Gold Coast.' *J. Roy. Anthrop. Inst.,* **67,** 1937: 131–142.

803 FORTES, MEYER. *Social structure: studies presented to A. R. Radcliffe-Brown.* O.U.P., 1949. 232 pp.

804 FORTES, MEYER, AND EVANS-PRITCHARD, E. E., Eds. *African political systems.* O.U.P., 1940. xxiii, 302 pp.

805 FRANKFORT, H. *Kingship and the Gods.* Chicago U.P., 1948. Traces cultural similarities in West Africa and Egypt.

806 FRAZER, SIR J. G. *Totemism and exogamy.* Macmillan, 1910. 4 vols. Supplementary vol., 1937.

807 'Ghana's talking drums.' *W. Afr. Rev.*, May 1959: 357–359.

808 GLUCKMAN, MAX. *Custom and conflict in Africa.* Oxford, Blackwell, 1955. ix, 173 pp.

809 GOODY, JACK. *The ethnography of the Northern Territories of the Gold Coast, west of the White Volta.* Colonial Office, 1954. 59 pp. (Typescript.)

810 GORER, G. *Africa dances.* 2nd ed. Lehmann, 1949.

811 GOUZY, RENÉ. *Visages de l'Afrique: Soudan, Niger, Dahomey et Côte de Guinée.* Paris, Neuchatel, 1940. 177 pp.

812 HAITZ, LINN. *Juju gods of West Africa.* St. Louis, Concordia Publishing House, 1961. 113 pp.

813 HILTON, THOMAS ERIC. 'Bawku.' *Universitas,* **3,** 4, 1958: 108–109.

814 JAHODA, GUSTAV. 'Boys' images of marriage partners and girls' self-images in Ghana.' *Sociologus,* **8,** 2, 1958: 155–169.

815 JOHODA, GUSTAV. 'Love, marriage, and social change: letters to the advice column of a West African newspaper.' [Accra] *Africa,* **29,** 2, April 1959: 177–189.

816 LABOURET, HENRI. *Histoire des noirs d'Afrique.* Paris, Presses Universitaires de France, (194–). 128 pp.

817 —— *Paysans d'Afrique occidentale.* Paris, Gallimard, 1941. 308 pp.

818 LITTLE, KENNETH L. 'The study of 'social change' in British West Africa.' *Africa,* **23,** 4, Oct. 1953: 274–284.

819 LYSTAD, MARY H. 'Traditional values of Ghanaian children.' *Amer. anthropologist,* **62,** 3, June 1960: 454–464.

820 MACALL, DANIEL F. 'Koforidua: a West African town.' *J. human relations,* **8,** 3/4, 1960: 419–436.

821 MANOUKIAN, MADELINE. *Tribes of the Northern Territories of the Gold Coast.* International African Institute, 1951. 101 pp. (Ethnographic survey of Africa, Western Africa, Part 5.)

822 MAUPOIL, BERNARD. *La géomancie à l'ancienne Côte des Esclaves.* Paris, Institut d'Ethnologie, 1943. xxvii, 690 pp.

823 MIDDLETON, JOHN, AND TAIT, DAVID Eds. *Tribes without rulers: studies in African segmentary systems.* Routledge, 1958. xi, 234 pp.

824 MOUEZY, H. *Assinie et le royaume de Krinjabo: histoires et coutumes.* Paris, Larose, 1942. 225 pp.

825 NICOLAS, FRANÇOIS J. 'Les notions d'âme et de divinité en Afrique occidentale.' *Anthropos*, **51**, 3/4, 1956: 551–594.

826 OLDEROGGE, DMITRII ALEKSEEVICH, AND POTEKHIN, I. I. *Narody Afriki.* [The peoples of Africa] Moscow, Institut Etnografii, 1954. 732 pp.

827 —— *Die Völker Afrikas: ihre Vergangenheit und Gegenwart.* Berlin, Deutscher Verlag, 1961. 2 vols.
    German translation of the Russian text.

828 ONWONA-OSAFO, F. 'Talking drums in the Gold Coast.' *Gold Coast teachers' J.*, **2**, April 1957: 9–12.

829 OTTENBERG, SIMON, AND OTTENBERG, PHOEBE, Eds. *Cultures and societies of Africa.* N.Y., Random House, 1960. 614 pp.

830 OWIREDU, P. A. 'The changing role of chiefs in Ghana.' *W. Afr. Rev.*, Sept. 1959: 579–581.

831 PARRINDER, E. GEOFFREY. *West African psychology: a comparative study of psychological and religious thought.* Lutterworth Press, 1951. 229 pp.

832 —— *Witchcraft: a critical study of the belief in witchcraft from the records of witch hunting in Europe yesterday and Africa to-day.* Penguin Books, 1958. 208 pp.

833 POTEKHIN, I. I. *Afrikanski etnograficheski sbornik.* [African ethnographic collection.] Moscow, Akademia Nauk S.S.S.R., 1956. 286 pp.
    Four studies, including *The Ewe*, by V. N. Vologdina.

834 —— 'Ethnographic observations in Ghana.' *Soviet Etnogr.*, **3**, 1958: 142–154.

835 —— 'Etnickeski i klassovoi sostav naselenia Zoltogo Berega.' [The ethnic and class composition of the population of the Gold Coast.] *Soviet Etnogr.*, **3**, 1953: 112–133.

836   POTEKHIN, I. I. 'Professor Potekhin reports.' [Abbreviated from: 'Ethnographic observations in Ghana.' *Soviet Etnogr.*, **3**, 1958] *West Africa*, **2169**, Nov. 1958: 1061–1062.

837   PRICE, J. H. 'A *bori* dance in Accra.' *W. Afr. Rev.*, **28**, 352, Jan. 1957: 20–24.

838   RADCLIFFE-BROWN, A. R., AND FORDE, DARYLL, EDS. *African systems of kinship and marriage.* O.U.P., 1951. 391. pp.

839   RATTON, CHARLES. 'L'or fétiche.' *Présence Afr.*, **10/11**, 1951: 136–155.

840   RATTRAY, ROBERT SUTHERLAND. 'Totemism and blood groups in West Africa' (*in* BUXTON, L. H. D., *Custom is king*, 1935).

841   RINGWALD, WALTER. 'Häuptlingswesen und indirekte Verwaltung auf der Goldküste.' *Arch. f. Anthrop.*, Neue Folge, **28**, 1/2, 1942: 1–30.

842   ROUCH, JEAN. 'Migrations au Ghana.' *J. Soc. Africanistes*, **26**, 1/2 1956: 33–196.

843   —— *Notes sur les migrations en Gold Coast: premier rapport de la mission effectuée en Gold Coast de mars à déc., 1954.* Accra, 1954. 103 pp.

844   —— 'Second generation migrants in Ghana and the Ivory Coast' (in SOUTHALL, A., ED., *Social change in modern Africa*, 1961).

845   SELIGMAN, C. G. *Races of Africa.* 3rd ed. O.U.P., 1957. 236 pp.

846   SHAW, C. THURSTAN. 'Bread-making with a bow-drill in the Gold Coast.' *J. Roy. Anthrop. Inst.*, **75**, 1/2, 1945: 45–50.

847   SMITH, EDWIN W. *The secret of the African.* 2nd ed. S.C.M., 1930. 142 pp.

848   SOUTHALL, AIDAN, ED. *Social change in modern Africa.* Published for the International African Institute by O.U.P., 1961. 337 pp.

849   STAPLETON, G. BRIAN. 'Nigerians in Ghana.' *West Africa*, **2184**, Feb. 1959: 175.

850   SUTHERLAND, D. A. *State emblems of the Gold Coast.* 2nd ed. Accra, Govt. Printer, 1956. 80 pp.

851   TRANAKIDES, G. 'Observations on the history of some Gold Coast peoples.' *Trans. Gold Coast & Togoland Hist. Soc.*, **I**, 1953: 33–44.

852   WESTERMANN, DIEDRICH HERMANN. *The African today and tomorrow.* O.U.P., 1949.

853 WILKS, IVOR. 'Tribal history and myth.' *Universitas*, **2**, 3, 1956: 84–86; **2**, 4, 116–118.

854 WILLIAMS, J. 'Africa's Gods: 1, Gold Coast and its hinterland.' Boston College Graduate School, *Anthrolopogical series*, **1**, 1936: 1–81.

Adangme (Krobo)

855 FIELD, MARGARET JOYCE. 'The agricultural system of the Manya-Krobo of the Gold Coast.' *Africa*, **14**, 1, 1943: 54–65.

856 HALLERAN, T. 'Krobo marriage customs.' *Anthropos*, **46**, 5/6, Sept.– Dec. 1951: 996–997.

857 HUBER, HUGO. 'Adangme purification and pacification rituals.' *Anthropos*, **53**, 1/2 1958: 161–191.

858 —— 'Representations of figures in the roof decoration of the Krobo and their symbolism.' *Anthropos*, **55**, 3/4, 1960: 578–580.

859 —— 'Ritual oaths as instruments of coercion and self-defence among the Adangme of Ghana.' *Africa*, **29**, 1, Jan. 1959: 41–49.

860 MATE KOLE, NENE AZZU. 'The historical background of Krobo customs.' *Trans. Gold Coast & Togoland Hist. Soc.*, **1**, 1954: 133–140.

861 RAPP, EUGEN LUDWIG. 'The African explains witchcraft: Adangme.' *Africa*, **8**, 4, 1935: 554–555.
See also nos. 567, 882, 2142, 2156.

Ahanta

862 WELMAN, C. W. *The native states of the Gold Coast: history and constitution. 2: Ahanta.* Crown Agents, 1930. 88 pp.

863 WESTERMANN, DIEDRICH HERMANN. 'Jan Cuny.' *Afrika*, **2**, 1, 1943: 1–3.

Akan

864 ADU, A. L. *The role of chiefs in the Akan social structure: an essay.* Accra, Govt. Printer, 1949. 18 pp.

865 AMOO, J. W. A. 'The effect of western influence on Akan marriage.' *Africa*, **16**, 4, Oct. 1946: 228–237.

866 BALMER, W. T. *A history of the Akan peoples of the Gold Coast.* Atlanta Press. [1925]. 208 pp.

867   DANQUAH, JOSEPH BOAKYE. *The Akan doctrine of God: a fragment of Gold Coast ethics and religion; with 9 illustrations by Kofi Antubam.* Lutterworth Press, 1944. xx, 206 pp.

868   —— *Akan laws and customs and the Akim Abuakwa constitution.* Routledge, 1928. x, 272 pp.

869   —— *The Akim Abuakwa handbook.* Forster, Groom, 1928. 128 pp.

870   —— *Ancestors, heroes and God: the principles of Akan-Ashanti ancestor-worship.* Kibi, George Boakie, 1938. 46 pp.

871   —— 'The culture of the Akan.' *Africa,* **22,** 4 Oct. 1952: 360–366. Review of *The sacred state of the Akan,* by E. L. R. Meyerowitz.

872   —— *The Gold Coast Akan.* United Society for Christian Literature, Lutterworth Press, 1945. 62 pp. (Africa's own library series, no. 11.)

873   —— 'Notes on "Oburoni" and "Buronya".' *Trans. Gold Coast & Togoland Hist. Soc.,* **2,** 1956: 71–72.

874   —— *An objectified history of Akim-Abuakwa: a lecture.* Kibi, 1938. 27 pp.

875   —— *Obligation in Akan society.* Bureau of Current Affairs, 1951. 16 pp. (West African affairs pamphlets, no. 8.) Cover title: *Akan society.*

876   DANQUAH, JOSEPH BOAKYE, ed. *Cases in Akan law delivered by the Hon. Nana Sir Ofori Atta.* [Paramount Chief of Akim Abuakwa.] Edited with introduction, synopses and notes by J. B. Danquah. Routledge, 1928. 26 pp.

877   DEBRUNNER, HANS. *Witchcraft in Ghana: a study on the belief in destructive witches and its effects on the Akan tribes.* Kumasi, Presbyterian Book Depot, 1959. 210 pp.

878   DE GRAFT JOHNSON, J. W. 'Akan land tenure.' *Trans. Gold Coast & Togoland Hist. soc.,* **1,** 1954: 99–103.

879   EVANS, H. ST. JOHN T. 'The Akan doctrine of God' (*in* SMITH, E. W., *African ideas of God,* 1950: 241–259).

880   GOODY, JACK. 'Ethnohistory and the Akan of Ghana.' *Africa,* **29,** 1, 1959: 67–81.

881   HANNIGAN, A. ST. J. J. 'The present system of succession amongst the Akan people of the Gold Coast.' *J. Afr. admin.,* **6,** 4, Oct. 1954: 166–171.

882 MANOUKIAN, MADELINE. *The Akan and Ga-Adangme peoples of the Gold Coast.* International African Institute, 1950. 112 pp. (Ethnographic survey of Africa, Western Africa, Part 1.)

883 MEYEROWITZ, EVA L. R. 'The Akan and Ghana.' *Man,* **52,** 99, June 1957: 83–88.

884 —— *The Akan of Ghana: their ancient beliefs.* Faber, 1958. 164 pp.
Religious beliefs and customs of the Asanti, Fante and other tribes who comprise the Akan group.

885 —— *Akan traditions of origin.* Faber, 1952. 149 pp.
Historical traditions in the regions south of the Sudanese Kingdoms of Ghana, Mali and Songhai.

886 —— 'Concepts of the soul among the Akan of the Gold Coast.' *Africa,* **21,** 1, Jan. 1951: 24–31.

887 —— *The divine kingship in Ghana and Ancient Egypt.* Faber, 1960. 260 pp.
Attempts to trace the cults of the Pharaohs in present day Akan.

888 —— 'Gold and the Akan of Ghana.' *Africa South,* **3,** 1, 1958: 103–108.

889 —— *The sacred state of the Akan.* Faber, 1951. 222 pp.
Ceremonial life among the Akan peoples and their religious symbolism. *See also* 872.

890 NKETIA, J. H. KWABENA. *Funeral dirges of the Akan people.* Accra, University College of the Gold Coast, 1955. 296 pp.
A linguistic, literary and musical study of the dirges of the Twi and Fante speaking peoples.

891 OWIREDU, P. A. 'The Akan system of inheritance today and tomorrow.' *Afr. affairs,* **58,** 231, April 1959: 161–165.

892 TAUXIER, LOUIS. *Religion, moeurs et coutumes des Agnis de la Côte d'Ivoire.* Paris, Geuthner, 1932. 255 pp. (Etudes soudanaises.)

893 WILKS, IVOR. 'Akwamu and Otublohum: an eighteenth-century Akan marriage arrangement.' *Africa,* **29,** 4, Oct. 1959: 391–403.

See also nos. 382, 389, 395, 932, 2158, 2163.

Akim

894 AKYEAMPONG, H. K. *The Akim Abuakwa crisis: with a foreword by Dr. J. B. Danquah.* Accra, the author, [1958]. 63 pp.

6

895 DANQUAH, JOSEPH BOAKYE. *An epistle to the educated young man in Akim Abuakwa.* Accra, Palladium Press, [192–?]. 57 pp.

896 FIELD, MARGARET JOYCE. *Akim-Kotoku: an oman of the Gold Coast.* Crown Agents, 1948. 197 pp.
An ethnographic and political study of western Akim.

897 FRIMPONG, KWAME. 'The final obsequies of the late Nana Sir Ofori Atta, K. B. E., Abuakwahene.' *Africa,* **15,** 2, April 1945: 80–86.

Ashanti (Jamasi)

898 'The *adae-kesie* festival.' [Ashanti.] *W. Afr. Rev.,* March 1957: 178–179.

899 AGYEMAN-DUAH, J. 'Mampong, Ashanti: a traditional history to the reign of Nana Safo Kantanka.' *Trans. Hist. Soc. Ghana,* **4,** 2, 1960: 21–25.

900 AKESSON, SAM K. 'The secret of Akom.' [Rites of fetish priests.] *Afr. affairs,* **49,** 196 July 1950: 237–246; Oct. 1950: 325–333.

901 [APPIAH, J. W. K.] *Report on the observances of the funeral custom of the late Kumasihene.* Accra, Govt. Printer, 1933. 9 pp.
Nana Edward Agyeman Prempeh I, Kumasihene, died in 1931.

902 ARMATTOE, RAPHAEL ERNEST GRAIL. 'Akwasidae.' [Kumasi festival.] *Afr. affairs,* **50,** 198, Jan. 1951: 61–63.

903 ARYEE, R. T. *A short history of Okomfo Anokye, 1660–1740.* Accra, Catholic Press, 1962. 8 pp.

904 BEART, C. 'Les poupés *akua ba* du Ghana.' *Notes afr. IFAN,* **78,** 37, avr. 1958.

905 'Bosomtwe: Ashanti's sacred lake.' *W. Afr. Rev.,* Feb. 1962: 29–30.

906 BREFFIT, G. V. 'Ashanti's living legend: the history of the sacred stool of Ashanti.' *W. Afr. Rev.,* Nov. 1960: 40–43.

907 BUSIA, KOFI ABREFA. 'Ashanti: land of the Golden Stool.' *Times Brit. Col. Rev.,* **24,** 1956: 23.

908 —— 'The Ashanti of the Gold Coast' (in FORDE, D. *African worlds,* 1954.)

909 —— *The position of the chief in the modern political system of Ashanti.* O.U.P., 1951. xii, 233 pp.
A standard work on the traditional status and functions of the chief.

910 CANHAM, PETER. 'An Ashanti case-history.' *Africa*, **17**, 1, Jan. 1947: 35–40.

911 CARDINALL, ALLAN W. *In Ashanti and beyond*. Seeley, Service, 1927. 288 pp.

912 CLARKE, E. 'The sociological significance of ancestor-worship in Ashanti.' *Africa*, **3**, 4, 1930: 431–471.

913 DELANGE, JACQUELINE. 'The El Dorado ruled by the Ashanti kings.' *Unesco Courier*, Oct. 1959.

914 FIELD, MARGARET JOYCE. 'Ashanti and Hebrew shamanism.' *Man*, **58**, 14, 1958.

915 FORTES, MEYER. 'The Ashanti social survey: a preliminary report.' *Human problems in Brit. Cent. Afr.* [Livingstone] **6**, 1948: 1–36.

916 —— 'Ashanti survey, 1945–46: an experiment in social research.' *Geog. J.*, **110**, 4/6, Oct.–Dec. 1947: 149–179.

917 —— 'Time and social structure: an Ashanti case study' (in FORTES, M., *Social structure*, 1949: 54–84).

918 —— 'Kinship and marriage among the Ashanti' (in RADCLIFFE-BROWN, A. R., AND FORDE, D., Eds., *African systems of kinship and marriage*, 1950: 252–284).

919 GOODY, JACK. 'Anomie in Ashanti?' *Africa*, **27**, 4, Oct. 1957: 356–363.
    Witchcraft.

920 GORDON, J. 'Some oral traditions of Denkyira.' *Trans. Gold Coast & Togoland Hist. Soc.*, **1**, 3, 1953: 27–33.

921 HALBFASS, W. 'Der Bosumtwi-See in Ashanti.' *Petermanns geog. Mitt.*, **84**, 4, 1939: 128.

922 HALL, W. M. *The great drama of Kumasi*. Putnam, 1939. 369 pp.

923 HENNESSY, M. N. 'Warriors of Ashanti.' *W. Afr. Rev.*, Jan. 1950: 11; Feb. 1950: 134.

924 HERSKOVITS, MELVILLE J. 'The Ashanti *Ntoro*: a re-examination.' *J. Roy. Anthrop. Inst.*, **67**, 2, July–Dec. 1937: 287–296.

925 LYSTAD, R. A. *The Ashanti: a proud people*. New Brunswick, Rutgers U.P., 1958. 212 pp.
    An American appraisement of Ashanti culture and traditions.

926 MATSON, J. N. *A digest of the minutes of the Ashanti Confederacy Council, 1935–49, and a revised edition of Warrington's notes on*

Ashanti custom, prepared for the use of District Commissioners. Cape Coast, Prospect Printing Press, [1951]. 76 pp.

927 —— 'Testate succession in Ashanti.' *Africa,* **23,** 3, July 1953: 224–232.

928 MEYEROWITZ, EVA L. R. 'A note on the early history of the Jamasi people.' *Trans. Gold Coast & Togoland Hist. Soc.,* **1,** 1954: 141–143.

929 OSEI, K. O. 'The great Golden Stool of Ashanti.' *W. Afr. Rev., Sept.* 1950: 1039.

930 PARRINDER, E. GEOFFREY. 'Divine kingship in West Africa.' *Numen,* **3,** 2, 1956: 111–121.

931 PATON, J. C. M. *The worship of the Tano fetish.* Accra, Govt. Printer, 1948. 11 pp.

932 RATTRAY, ROBERT SUTHERLAND. *Akan-Äshanti folk tales . . . illustrated by Africans of the Gold Coast Colony.* Oxford, Clarendon Press, 1930. 275 pp.

933 —— *Ashanti.* Oxford, Clarendon Press, 1923. 348 pp. [Reprinted 1955].

934 —— *Ashanti law and constitution.* O.U.P., 1929. xx, 420 pp. [Reprinted 1956.]

935 —— *Ashanti proverbs: the primitive ethics of a savage people; translated from the original with grammatical and anthropological notes.* O.U.P., 1961. 190 pp.

936 —— *Religion and art in Ashanti.* O.U.P., 1927. 414 pp. [Reprinted 1954.]

937 —— 'The tribes of the Ashanti hinterland.' *J. Roy. Afr. Soc.,* **30,** 118, Jan. 1931: 40–57.

938 —— *Tribes of the Ashanti hinterland.* Oxford, Clarendon Press, 1932. 2 vols.

939 RINGWALD, WALTER. 'Züge aus dem sozialen Leben in Asante.' *Afrikanistische Studien,* ed. J. Lukas, 1955: 205–219.

940 ROHLEDER, H. P. T. 'Lake Bosumtwi, Ashanti.' *Geog. J.,* **87,** 1, 1936; 51–65.

941 SMITH, EDWIN W. *The Golden Stool.* Holborn Publishing House, 1927.

942 WARD, BARBARA E. 'Some observations on religious cults in Ashanti.' *Africa,* **26,** 1, Jan. 1956: 47–61.

943 WILD, ROBERT P. 'The inhabitants of the Gold Coast and Ashanti before the Akan invasion.' *Teachers' J.*, **6**, 3, 1934: 195–201.

See also nos. 210, 326, 328, 1857, 1869, 2104, 2107, 2117, 2118, 2119, 2123, 2127, 2128, 2133, 2134.

Avatime

944 WARD, BARBARA E. 'An analysis of the distribution of population in a town in British Togoland.' *Man*, **55**, 43, March 1955: 35–39.

Brong

945 ARTHUR, JOHN. *Brong Ahafo handbook.* Accra, Graphic Press, [1960]. 143 pp.

946 'The Ashanti-Brong dispute'. *West Africa*, 25 June–10 Sept. 1955.

947 'A Chief of the Brongs.' *W. Afr. Rev.*, **1778**. March 1951: 245–246.

948 MEYEROWITZ, EVA L. R. 'Bono-Mansu: the earliest centre of civilisation in the Gold Coast.' *3rd Int. W. Afr. Conf*, 1949: 118–120.

Dagari (LoDagaa, LoWiili)

949 GOODY, JACK. 'Death and social control among the LoDagaa.' *Man*, **59**, 204, Aug. 1959: 134–138.

950 —— *Death, property and the ancestors: a study of the mortuary institutions of the LoDagaa of West Africa.*
Forthcoming.

951 —— 'Fields of social control among the LoDagaa.' *J. Roy. Anthrop. Inst.*, **87**, 1, Jan.–June 1957: 75–104.

952 —— 'The mother's brother and the sister's son in West Africa.' *J. Roy. Anthrop. Inst.*, **89**, 1, Jan.–June 1959: 61–86.
A study of the LoWiili and LoDagaa communities of northern Ghana.

953 —— *The social organisation of the LoWiili.* H.M.S.O., 1956. 119 pp. (Colonial research studies, no. 19.)

954 HOLAS, BOHUMIL. 'Le divorce chez les Dagari.' [Haute Volta] *Notes afr. IFAN*, juil. 1948: 1–2.

955 LESOURD, JEAN. *En Afrique occidentale française: les Dagaris.* Paris, Pères Blancs, 1939. 34 pp.

956   PATERNOT, MARCEL. *Lumière sur la Volta, chez les Dagari.* Paris, Association des Missionaires d'Afrique, 1953. 254 pp.

Dagomba

957   DUNCAN-JOHNSTON, A., AND BLAIR, H. A. *Enquiry into the constitution and organization of the Dabgon kingdom.* Accra, Govt. Printer, 1932. 68 pp.

958   GILL, J. WITHERS. *A short history of the Dagomba tribe; translated from a Hausa manuscript in the Library of the School of Oriental Studies.* [London University.] Accra, Govt. Printer, [192–]. 16 pp.

959   TAMAKLOE, E. FORSTER. *A brief history of the Dagbamba people.* Accra, Govt. Printer, 1931. 76 pp.

960   —— 'Mythical and traditional history of Dagomba.' (in CARDINALL, A. W. *Tales told in Togoland*, 1931: 230–279).

961   'The Tolon Na.' *West Africa*, **2083**, 16 March 1957: 245. Portrait of a Dagomba chief.

See also no. 359.

Dogon

962   CALAME-GRIAULE, GENEVIÈVE. 'Diversité linguistique et organisation sociale chez les Dogon du Soudan français.' *Notes afr. IFAN*, **55**, juil. 1952: 77–79.

963   CHELHOD, J. 'Le monde mythique arabe: examiné à la lumière d'un mythe africain.' *J. Soc. Africanistes*, **24**, 1, 1954: 49–61.

964   CLAMENS, GABRIEL. 'Rapprochements Senoufo-Dogon.' *Notes afr. IFAN*, **58**, Janv. 1953: 15.

965   DIETERLEN, GERMAINE. *Les âmes des Dogons.* Paris, Institut d'Ethnologie, 1941. viii, 272 pp.

966   —— 'Parenté et mariage chez les Dogon.' *Africa*, **26**, 2, April 1956: 107–148.

967   —— 'La personalité chez les Dogons: autels individuels. *Anthropologie*, **49**, 6, 1939–40.

968   GANAY, SOLANGE DE. *Les devises des Dogons.* Paris, Institut d'Ethnologie, 1941. viii, 14 pp.

969   —— 'Instruments aratoires et herminettes Dogon.' *Notes afr. IFAN*, **60**, oct. 1953: 113–115.

970 GRIAULE, MARCEL. *Jeux dogons*. Paris, Institut d'Ethnologie, 1938. vii, 291 pp.

971 —— *Masques dogons*. Paris, Institut d'Ethnologie, 1938. xi, 896 pp.

972 —— 'Notes complémentaires sur les masques dogons.' *J. Soc. Africanistes*, **10**, 1940: 79–85.

973 —— 'Remarques sur le mécanisme du sacrifice dogon.' *J. Soc. Africanistes*, **10**, 1940: 127–129.

974 GRIAULE, MARCEL, AND DIETERLEN, GERMAINE. 'The Dogon' (in FORDE, D. *African worlds*, 1954: 83–110).

975 PAULME, D. *Organisation sociale des Dogon*. Paris, Ed. Domat-Montchrestien, 1940. 603 pp.

976 PIAZZINI, GUY. *Horizons noirs*. [Dogon et Lobi.] Paris, Ed. Toison d'or, 1954. 217 pp.

977 TAIT, DAVID. 'An analytical commentary on the social structure of the Dogon.' *Africa*, **20**, 3, July 1950: 175–198.

978 —— 'Language and social symbiosis among the Dogon of Sanga.' *Bull. IFAN*, **17**, (B), 3/4, juil.–oct. 1955: 525–527.

Ewe (Peki)

979 ADAM, LEONHARD, *Het eenheidsstreven der Ewe*. Leiden, Afrika-Instituut, 1952. 26 pp.

980 AGBLEMAGNON, F. N'SOUGAN. 'Le concept de crise appliqué à une société africaine: les Ewés.' *Cah. int. soc.*, **23**, 1957: 157–166.

981 AGBLEY, SETH. 'The origin of idols.' [Ewe.] *Ghana bull. theology*, **1**, 7, Dec. 1959: 3–11.

982 ARMATTOE, RAPAEL ERNEST GRAIL. 'Epe-Ekpe.' [New Year cult of the Glidji Ewe] *Afr. affairs*, **50**, 201, Oct. 1951: 326–331.

983 —— *The golden age of West African civilization*. Londonderry, Published for the Lomeshire Research Centre by "The London-derry Sentinel", 1946. 116 pp.

984 —— *Moeurs et coutumes Ewé*. Paris, 1939.

985 CARDINALL, ALLAN W. *Tales told in Togoland*. O.U.P., 1931. 290 pp.

986 CHARDEY, F. 'Résurrection d'un mort et apparitions de morts chez les Ewe.' *Anthropos*, **46**, 5/6, Sept.–Dec. 1951: 1005–1006.

987 FIAWOO, D. K. *The influence of contemporary social changes in the magico-religious concepts and organisation of the southern Ewe-Speaking*

peoples of Ghana. (Unpublished thesis, Edinburgh University, 1959.)

988 GARNIER, CHRISTINE, AND FRALON, JEAN. *Le fétichisme en Afrique noire* [Togo-Cameroun]. Paris, Payot, 1951. 213 pp.

989 HAERTTER, G. 'Das Gottesgericht bei den Ewe.' *Z. f. Ethnol.,* **69,** 1/3, 1937: 63–72.

990 HEPP, M. 'Le problème Ewé.' *Bull. d'Information de la France d'Outre-mer,* **134,** mai 1950: 3–6.

991 HERSKOVITS, MELVILLE J. *Dahomey: an ancient West African kingdom.* N.Y., Augustin, 1938. 2 vols.
Includes references to the Ewe.

992 HUBER, HUGO. 'Schwangerschaft, Geburt und frühe Kindheit im Brauchtum der Bata-Ewe.' *Ann. lateranensi,* **21,** 1957: 230–244.

993 JOHNSON, G. KUAWOVI. 'Sur la patronymie Ge ou Guin (Mina) et Ewe du Bas-Togo.' *Notes afr. IFAN,* **47,** juil. 1950: 97–98.

994 KWAKUMÉ, HENRI. 'Notes sur les peuples de race éwé.' *Echo Missions afr. Lyon,* fév. 1935: 20–22; avr. 1935: 71–73.

995 —— *Précis d'histoire du peuple éwé (évhé).* Lomé, [Mission Catholique] 1948, 39 pp.

996 LEVY-ERELL, L. 'Die Ewe, ein Negerstamm der Goldküste.' *Atlantis,* **6,** 2, 1930: 348–356.

997 MANOUKIAN, MADELINE. *The Ewe-speaking people of Togoland and the Gold Coast.* International African Institute, 1952. 63 pp. (Ethnographic survey of Africa, Western Africa, Part 6.)

998 MEYEROWITZ, EVA L. R. 'Snake-vessels of the Gold Coast.' *Man,* **40,** 59, 1940: 48.

999 MONOD, D. Sokpé, pierres de foudre.' *Notes afr. IFAN,* juil. 1945: 21–22.

1000 PARRINDER, E. GEOFFREY. 'Theistic beliefs of the Yoruba and Ewe peoples of West Africa' (in SMITH, E. W. *African ideas of God,* 1950: 224–240).

1001 PAUVERT, JEAN-CLAUDE. *L'étude des migrations au Togo.* Lomé, Institut de Recherche du Togo, 1956.

1002 —— 'L'évolution politique des Ewe.' *Cah. ét. afr.,* **2,** mai 1960: 161–192.

1003 SENAYAH, EMMANUEL. 'African marriage customs: Ewe traditions.' *W. Afr. Rev.*, March 1953: 277–279.

1004 SOSSAH, C. 'L'anneau royal et Sa Majesté Eklou Folikpo-V.P.' *Liaison*, **45**, 1955: 38–46.

1005 VOLOGDINA, V. N. 'The Ewe.' *Inst. Etnogr. Akad. Nauk SSSR, Kratkiye soobshcheniye*, **2**, 1954.

1006 —— 'Narod Ewe.' (in POTEKHIN, I. I. *Afrikanski etnograficheski sbornik*, 1956: 69–118).

1007 WARD, BARBARA E. 'An example of a 'mixed' system of descent and inheritance.' [Ewe] *Man*, **55**, 2, Jan. 1955: 3–5.

1008 —— *The social organisation of the Ewe-speaking people.* (Unpublished thesis, University of London, 1949. 73 pp.)

1009 —— 'Some notes on migration from Togoland.' *Afr. affairs*, **49**, 195, April 1950: 129–135.

1010 WELMAN, C. W. *The native states of the Gold Coast: 1, Peki.* London, 1924.

1011 WESTERMANN, DIEDRICH HERMANN. 'The African explains witchcraft: Ewe.' *Africa*, **8**, 4, 1935: 548–550.

1012 —— 'The African explains witchcraft: Glidyi Ewe.' *Africa*, **8**, 4, 1935: 550–552.

1013 —— 'The chameleon and the sun-god Lisa on the West African slave-coast' [Translation of an Ewe text by B. Foli] (in BUXTON, L. H. D., ed. *Custom is king*, 1935: 143–153.)

1014 —— *Die Glidyi-Ewe in Togo.* Berlin, de Gruyter, 1935. xv, 320 pp.

1015 —— 'So, der Gewittergott der Ewe.' *Z. f. Ethnol.*, **70**, 3/5 1939: 152–159.

1016 —— 'Texte in der Ge-Mundart des Ewe.' *Afrika und Übersee*, **39**, 1, Dez. 1954: 1–5; Sept. 1955: 119–127. Ewe folk tales.

1017 —— *Volkwerdung und Evangelium unter den Ewe.* Bremen, Norddeutsche Missions-Gesellschaft, 1936. 20 pp.

See also nos. 382, 2145, 2146, 2150.

Fante

1018 ACQUAH, G. A. *The Fantse of Ghana.* [Accra, the author, 1957?] 63 pp. [Printed in East Germany.]

1019 AIKINS, L. S. 'The Nkusukum state.' *Ghana Teachers' J.*, **3**, July 1960: 8–13.

1020 CHRISTENSEN, JAMES BOYD. *Double descent among the Fanti*. New Haven, Human Relations Area Files, 1954. 145 pp.

1021 ——— 'Marketing and exchange in a West African tribe.' [Fanti.] *S.–W. J. Anthrop.*, **17**, 2, summer 1961: 124–139.

1022 ——— 'The Tigari cult of West Africa.' Papers of the Michigan Academy of Science, *Arts & Letters*, **39**, 1954: 389–398.

1023 CHRISTIAN COUNCIL OF THE GOLD COAST. *Tigare: a report*. Accra, Scottish Mission Book Depot, 1947. 8 pp.
An account of the Tigare fetish.

1024 DE GRAFT JOHNSON, J. C. 'The Fanti Asafu.' *Africa*, **5**, 3, 1932: 307–322.

1025 DUNN, J. S. 'Fante star lore.' *Nigerian field*, **25**, 2, April 1960: 52–64.

1026 LANTIS, MARGARET. 'Fanti omens.' *Africa*, **13**, 2, 1940: 150–159.
See also no. 342.

Ga

1027 ADJEI, AKO. 'Mortuary usages of the Ga people of the Gold Coast.' *Amer. anthropologist*, **45**, 1, Jan.–March 1943: 84–98.

1028 ALLOTEY–PAPPOE, EBENEZER. 'The Homowo festival: the harvest festival of the Ga people.' *Ghana bull. theology*, **1**, 7, Dec. 1959: 1–3.

1029 ALLOTT, A. N. 'A note on the Ga law of succession.' *Bull. Sch. Orient. Afr. Stud.*, **151**, 1, 1953: 164–169.

1030 AMMAH, E. A. *Infant outdooring in Ga society*. Accra, the author, 1958. 15 pp.

1031 BOHNER, T. *Der Schuhmacher Gottes: ein deutsches Leben in Africa*. Frankfurt, Rütten u. Löning, 1935. 275 pp.

1032 BROWN, E. J. P. 'Lante gyan we Homowo.' *Gold Coast and Ashanti Reader, Book 1. 237–240*

1033 BRUCE–MAYERS, J. M. 'The connubial institutions of the Gas.' *J. Roy. Afr. Soc.*, **30**, 121, Oct. 1931: 399–409.

1034 CLARKE, JOHN HENRIK. 'La célébration d'une viellée funèbre dans la tribu Ga du Ghana.' *Présence afr.*, **23**, déc. 1958–janv. 1959: 107–112.

1035 FIELD, MARGARET JOYCE. 'The *Asamanukpai* of the Gold Coast.' *Man*, **34**, 211. Dec. 1934: 186–189.

1036 —— *Religion and medicine of the Ga people.* O.U.P., 1937. 214 pp. Reprinted with a new preface, O.U.P., Accra, Presbyterian Book Depot, 1961.

1037 —— *The social organization of the Ga people.* Crown Agents, 1940. xiii, 231 pp.

1038 LEVY-ERELL, L. 'Das Homowah-Fest in Accra.' *Atlantis*, **6**, 2, 1930: 345–347.

See also nos. 882, 2159.

Guang (*Gonja, Frafra*)

1039 FRAFRA, AZURE. 'Warrior prince of the Northern Territories.' *W. Afr. Rev.*, **21**, 279, Dec. 1950: 1443–1445.

1040 FORTES, MEYER, ed. *Marriage in tribal societies.* Published for the Department of Archaeology and Anthropology by C.U.P., 1962. 157 pp. (Cambridge papers in social anthropology, no. 3.)

1041 GILL, J. WITHERS. *A short history of Salaga: translated from a Hausa manuscript.* Accra, Govt. Printer, 1924. 16 pp.

1042 GOODY, ESTHER N. 'Conjugal separation and divorce among the Gonja of northern Ghana' (in FORTES, M., ed. *Marriage in tribal societies*, 1962: 14–54).

1043 HILTON, THOMAS ERIC. 'Frafra resettlement and the population problem in Zuarungu.' *Universitas*, **3**, 5, 1959: 144–146.

Gurunsi

1044 BLANLUET, P. 'Enquête sur l'enfant de l'A.O.F.: l' enfant gourounsi.' *Bull. Enseign. A.O.F.*, **21**, 78, janv.–mars. 1932: 8–19.

1045 DE COUTOULY, FRANÇOIS. 'Enquête sur l'habitation gourounsi (cercle de Koudougou).' *Rev. anthrop.*, **41**, 7/9, 1931: 244–254.

1046 DITTMER, KUNZ. 'Afrika-Expedition des Hamburgischen Museums für Völkerkunde.' [Haute-Volta-Gurunsi.] *Z. f. Ethnol.*, **80**, 1, 1955: 138–140.

1047 NICOLAS, FRANÇOIS J. 'La question de l'ethnique "Gourounsi" en Haute-Volta (A.O.F.).' *Africa*, 22, 2, April 1952: 170–172.

1048 PONTON, GEORGES L. 'Les Gourounsi du groupe voltaïque.' *Outre-mer*, **4**, avr.–sept., 1933: 99–117.

1049   ZWERNEMANN, JÜRGEN. 'Shall we use the word "Gurunsi"?' *Africa*, **28**, 2, April 1958: 123–125.

Isala

1050   POLARIS. 'Local history in Tumu.' *West Africa*, 30 April, 7 May, 1955: 398, 411.

Konkomba

1051   BIRMINGHAM, W. B., AND TAIT, DAVID. 'Standards of living in the Gold Coast: a comment.' *Universitas*, **1**, 3, June/Dec. 1954.

1052   CORNEVIN, ROBERT. 'L'enterrement d'un chef konkomba.' *Africa*, **24**, 3, July 1954: 247–250.

1053   FROELICH, JEAN CLAUDE. 'Le kinan des Konkomba du Nord Togo. *Notes afr. IFAN*, **80**, oct. 1958: 103–104.

1054   —— 'Les Konkomba du Nord-Togo.' *Bull. IFAN*, **11**, 3/4, juil.–oct. 1949: 409–437.

1055   —— 'La tribu Konkomba du Nord-Togo.' *Mém, IFAN*, **37**, 1954: 257 pp.

1056   TAIT, DAVID. 'The family, household, and minor lineage of the Konkomba.' *Africa*, **26**, 3, July 1956: 219–249; Oct. 1956: 332–341.

1057   —— 'History and social organisation.' [Konkomba and Dagomba.] *Trans. Gold Coast & Togoland Hist. Soc.*, **1**, 1955: 193–210.

1058   —— 'Konkomba.' [Article in] *Encyclopaedia Britannica*. 1960 ed.

1059   —— 'Konkomba friendship relations.' *Afr. Studies*, **13**, 2, 1954: 77–84.

1060   —— *The Konkomba of northern Ghana*. International African Institute; O.U.P., 1961. 255 pp.

1061   ——'Konkomba *osuo* [sorcerer].' *Man*, **55**, 162, Oct. 1955: 152–153.

1062   —— 'Konkomba sorcery.' *J. Roy. Anthrop. Inst.*, **84**, 1/2, 1954: 66–74.

1063   —— 'The place of libation in Konkomba ritual.' *Bull. IFAN*, **17** (B), 1/2, janv.–avr. 1955: 168–172.

1064   —— 'The political system of Konkomba.' *Africa*, **23**, 3, July 1953: 213–223.

1065 TAIT, DAVID. 'The role of the diviner in Konkomba society.' *Man*, **52**, 249, Nov. 1952: 167–168.

1066 —— 'Spirits of the bush: a note on personal religion among the Konkomba.' *Universitas*, **1**, 1, Dec. 1953: 17–18.

1067 —— 'Structural change in the Northern Territories of the Gold Coast.' *W. Afr. Inst. Social & Econ. Research, Annual Conference, March* 1955: 43–51.

See also no. 37 for a bibliography of the writings of David Tait.

Kwahu

1068 RAPP, EUGEN LUDWIG. 'The African explains witchcraft: Akan (Kwahu).' *Africa*, **8**, 4, 1935: 553–554.

1069 WALLIS, J. R. 'The Kwahus—their connection with the Afram Plain.' *Trans. Gold Coast. & Togoland Hist. Soc.*, **1**, 1953: 72–88.

Lefana

1070 HUBER, HUGO. 'Twins among the Lefana in British Togoland. *Anthropos*, **50**, 1/3, 1955: 438–439.

1071 RAPP, EUGEN LUDWIG. 'The African explains witchcraft: Lelemi (Lefana).' *Africa*, **8**, 4, Oct. 1935: 555–556.

Lobi

1072 HINDS, J. H. 'A currency problem in the Lawra district: picturesque money customs of the Lobi and Dagarti people of the Gold Coast.' *W. Afr. Rev.*, **18**, 243, Dec. 1947: 1428–1432.

1073 HOLAS, BOHUMIL. 'Et les flèches entrent en jeu (schéma d'un combat coutoumier en pays lobi).' *Notes afr. IFAN*, **58**, janv. 1953: 16–20.

1074 LABOURET, HENRI. *Les tribus du remeau lobi (Volta Noire moyenne)*. Paris, Institut d'Ethnologie, 1931. vii, 510 pp.

1075 TRAORE, DOMINIQUE. 'Cérémonies de purification chez les lobi.' *Notes afr. IFAN*, **43**, juil. 1949: 82.

Mossi (Moshi)

1076 BORDARIER, P. 'Avec les Mossis de la Haute-Volta.' *Tropiques*, n.s. **47**, 306, janv. 1949: 13–21.

1077 DELOBSOM, A. A. DIM. 'Les danses mossies et leur signification.' *Rev. anthrop.*, **42**, 1932: 169–173.

1078   DELOBSOM, A. A. DIM. *L'empire du Mogho-Naba: coutumes des Mossi de la Haute-Volta*. Paris, Ed. Domat Monchrestien, 1933. vii, 303 pp.

1079   GASCHEN, H. 'Répartition des groupes sanguins chez les Mossi. *Acta tropica*, **4**, 4, 1947: 338–340.

1080   GILL, J. WITHERS. *The Moshi tribe: a short history*. Accra, Govt. Printer, 1924. 24 pp.

1081   HILTON, THOMAS ERIC. 'Mossi country.' *Universitas*, **4**, 1, 1959: 7–8.

1082   HOLAS, BOHUMIL. 'Teinturiers mossi à Dimbokro.' *Notes afr. IFAN*, **38**, avr. 1948: 18–21.

1083   KABORE, D. Y. 'Les mangeuses d'âmes chez les Mossis. *Notes afr. IFAN*, **24**, Oct. 1944: 17–18.

1084   LE MOAL, G. 'L'histoire et la légende mossi.' *Albums de l'A.O.F.* [Dakar] **3**, déc. 1951: 95–105.

1085   NICOLAS, FRANÇOIS. 'Deux contes des Mosé de la Haute-Volta.' *Notes afr. IFAN*, **61**, janv. 1954: 15–16.

1086   OUEDRAOGO, JOSEPH. 'Les funérailles en pays mossi.' *Bull. IFAN*, **12**, 2, avr. 1950: 441–455.

1087   —— 'La polygamie en pays mossi.' *Notes afr. IFAN*, **50**, avr. 1951: 46–52.

1088   OUEDRAOGO, JOSEPH, AND PROST, ANDRÉ. 'La propriété foncière chez les Mossi.' *Notes afr. IFAN*, **38**, avr. 1948: 16–18.

1089   PROST, ANDRÉ. 'Les aliments crus chez l'indigène Mossi-Bousancé.' *Notes afr. IFAN*, **12**, 1941: 55–56.

1090   —— 'Notes sur l'origine des Mossi.' *Bull. IFAN*, **15**, 3, juil. 1953: 1333–1338.

1091   SKINNER, ELLIOTT P. 'Labour migration and its relationship to socio-cultural change in Mossi society.' *Africa*, **30**, 4, Oct. 1960: 375–399.

1092   TAUXIER, LOUIS. *Nouvelles notes sur le Mossi et le Gourounsi*. Paris, Larose, 1924.

1093   ZAHAN, D. 'L'habitation mossi.' *Bull. IFAN*, **12**, 1, janv. 1950: 223–229.

1094   —— 'Notes sur les marchés mossi du Yatenga.' *Africa*, **24**, 4, Oct. 1954: 370–377.

Nzima

1095 ADJAYE, NANA ANNOR. *Nzima land*. Headley Bros., [1931]. 294 pp.

1096 GROTTANELLI, VINIGI L. 'Asonu worship among the Nzema: a study in Akan art and religion.' *Africa*, **31**, 1, Jan. 1961: 46–59.

1097 —— 'Pre-existence and survival in Nzema beliefs.' *Man*, **60**, 1, 1960.

Tallensi

1098 FORTES, MEYER. 'Children's drawings among the Tallensi.' *Africa*, **13**, 5, July 1940: 293–295.

1099 —— 'Divination among the Tallensi of the Gold Coast.' *Man*, **40**, 9, 1940.

1100 —— *The dynamics of clanship among the Tallensi: being the first part of an analysis of the social structure of a Trans-Volta tribe*. O.U.P. for the International African Institute, 1945. 270 pp.

1101 —— 'Kinship, incest and exogamy among the Tallensi of the Northern Territories of the Gold Coast.' (in BUXTON, L. H. D. *Custom is king*, 1935).

1102 —— *Marriage law among the Tallensi*. Accra, Govt. Printer, 1937. 23 pp.

1103 —— 'Names among the Tallensi of the Gold Coast.' *Afrikanistische Studien*, ed. J. Lukas, 1955: 337–349.

1104 —— 'A note on fertility among the Tallensi of the Gold Coast.' *Sociological Rev.*, **35**, 3/4, July-Oct. 1943: 99–113.

1105 —— *Oedipus and Job in West African religion*. C.U.P., 1959. 81 pp.
Tallensi beliefs in fate and justice.

1106 —— 'Ritual festivals and social cohesion in the hinterland of the Gold Coast.' *Amer. anthropologist*, **38**, 4, 1937: 590–604.

1107 FORTES, MEYER. 'The significance of descent in Tale social structure.' *Africa*, **14**, 7, July 1944: 362–385.

1108 —— *Social and psychological aspects of education in Taleland*. O.U.P. for the International African Institute, 1938. 64 pp. (Supplement to *Africa*, **11**, 4, 1938.)

1109 —— *The web of kinship among the Tallensi*. O.U.P., 1949. 358 pp.
A continuation of *Dynamics of clanship among the Tallensi*, dealing with the problems of social organisation in patriarchal societies.

1110   FORTES, MEYER, AND FORTES, S. L. 'Food in the domestic economy of the Tallensi.' *Africa*, **9**, 2, 1936: 237: 276.

1111   GLUCKMAN, MAX. 'An advance in African sociology.' *Afrikanistische Studien*, **6**, 2, June 1947: 57–76.
Review of *The dynamics of clanship among the Tallensi*, by M. Fortes. (No. 1100).

1112   SOMERFELT, AXEL. *Political cohesion in a stateless society: the Tallensi of the Northern Territories of the Gold Coast*. Oslo, Broggers, 1958. 215 pp.
In Norwegian, with English summary.

1113   WORSLEY, P. M. 'The kinship system of the Tallensi: a revaluation.' *J. Roy. Anthrop. Inst.*, **86**, 1, 1956: 37–75.

Wassaw

1114   NUNN, G. N. N. 'Reconciliation customs in the Gold Coast.' [Tarkwa district.] *Man*, **36**, 201, Sept. 1936: 207–208.

Linguistics

General

1115 BAETA, CHRISTIAN GONÇALVES KWAMI. *Hints to authors of vernacular books.* Sheldon Press, [195-]. 24 pp.

1116 BARNARD, G. L. *Report on the use of English (as the medium of instruction) in Gold Coast schools.* Accra, Govt. Printer, 1956. 74 pp.

1117 BERRY, JACK. *The place-names of Ghana: (problems of standardization in an African territory).* London; Accra, University Bookshop, 1958. 190 pp.

1118 —— *Spoken art in West Africa: an inaugural lecture delivered on 8 December 1960.* University of London, School of Oriental and African Studies, 1961. 24 pp.

1119 BROWN, P. P., AND SCRAGG, J. *Common errors in Gold Coast English: their cause and correction.* Macmillan, 1950. 134 pp.

1120 DICKENS, K. J. 'Orthography in the Gold Coast.' *Africa,* 6, 3, 1933: 317–322.

1121 DUNCAN, JOHN. 'Vernacular broadcasting in the Gold Coast.' *Imperial Rev.,* 11, 6, June 1944: 320.

1122 FAGE, JOHN DONNELLY. 'Some notes on a scheme for the investigation of oral tradition in the Northern Territories of the Gold Coast. *J. Hist. Soc. Nigeria,* 1, 1, 1956: 15–19.

1123 GREENBERG, JOSEPH H. 'Studies in African linguistic classification, 1: The Niger-Congo family.' *S.–W.J. Anthrop.,* 5, 2, summer 1949: 79–100.

1124 —— *Studies in African linguistic classification.* New Haven, Compass Publishing Co., 1955.

1125 GYEBI, T. J. O., AND EDU, JOHN E. *English in the Gold Coast.* Accra, the authors, 1951. 79 pp.

1126 HARMAN, H. A. *The new script and its relation to the languages of the Gold Coast.* Accra, Education Dept., 1930. 43 pp.

1127 HOMBURGER, L. *The Negro-African languages.* Routledge, 1949. 275 pp.

1128 JEFFREYS, M. D. W. 'Some West African language borrowings and lendings.' *Africa,* **5,** 4, Oct. 1932: 503–509.

1129 —— 'Word borrowing' [from West African languages]. *Nigeria,* **21,** 1940: 358–362.

1130 KIRK-GREEN, A. H. M. 'Linguistics at Legon.' *West Africa,* **2289,** April 1961: 395.

1131 KWAANSA, KOBINA (A. H. FILSON). *The language problem of the Gold Coast.* Kumasi, Akan World Press, [1955]. 9 pp.

1132 LERNER, L. D. *The language we speak.* Bureau of Current Affairs, [1950?]. 15 pp. (West African affairs pamphlets, no. 10.)

1133 MOURADIAN, JACQUES. 'Note de sémantique négro-africaine.' *Notes afr. IFAN,* **34,** avr. 1947: 13–14.

1134 OWIREDU, P. A. 'Towards a common language for Ghana.' *Afr. affairs,* **56,** 225, 1957: 295–299.

1135 SIERTSEMA, BERTHA. *A test in phonetics: 500 questions and answers on English pronunciation and how to teach it in West Africa.* The Hague, Nijhoff, 1959. 94 pp.

1136 SPICER, A. 'National and official languages for the Gold Coast.' *W. Afr. Inst. Soc. Econ. Res.,* Annual Conference, March 1955: 4–11.

1137 TRESSAN, LAVERGNE DE. 'Inventaire linguistique de l'Afrique occidentale française et du Togo.' *Mém. IFAN,* **30,** 1953. 240 pp.

1138 WARD, IDA C. 'Verbal tone patterns in West African languages.' *Bull. Sch. Orient. Afr. Studies,* **12,** 3/4, 1948: 831–837.

1139 —— *Report of an investigation of some Gold Coast language problems.* Crown Agents, 1945. 74 pp.

1140 WESTERMANN, DIEDRICH HERMANN. 'African linguistic classification.' *Africa,* **22,** 1952: 250–256.
Review of *Studies in African linguistic classification,* by J. H. Greenberg.

1141 —— *A common script for Twi, Fante, Ga and Ewe. . . with a memorandum on school textbooks in vernaculars, and a note on language conditions north of Ashanti.* Accra, Govt. Printer, 1927. 9 pp.

1142　WESTERMANN, DIEDRICH HERMANN, AND BRYAN, M. A. *Handbook of African languages. Part 2: Languages of West Africa.* O.U.P. for the International African Institute, 1952. 215 pp.

See also nos. 15, 417, 458, 459, 473, 807, 828.

Adangme

1143　BERRY, JACK. 'Some notes on the pronunciation of the Krobo dialect of Adangme.' *Mitt. Inst. f. Orient.*, **5**, 1957: 417–431.

1144　PUPLAMPU, D. A. *Adangme manner of speech: a study of the Adangme language, parts 1 & 2.* Macmillan, 1953. 112 pp.

1145　—— *An Adangme script.* Macmillian, 1953. 20 pp. (Adangme teachers' handbooks, no. 1.)

1146　—— 'The national epic of the Adangme.' *Afr. affairs*, **50**, 1951: 236–241.

1147　RAPP, EUGEN LUDWIG. 'Die Adangme-Ga-Mundart von Agotime in Togo.' *Afrika*, **2**, 1, 1943: 4–58.

1148　—— 'Adangme-Texte.' *Afrika*, **1**, 1, 1942: 55–100.

Akan

1149　COKER, INCREASE H. E. *Grammar of African names: an outline guide to the study and appreciation of African names selected from the Akan (Gold Coast), Yoruba, Ibo, Ijaw, and Efik-Ibibio language groups.* Lagos, Techno-Literary Works, 1954. 36 pp.

1150　MATSON, J. N. 'History in Akan words.' *Trans. Gold Coast & Togoland Hist. Soc.*, **2**, 1956: 63–70.

1151　SAUNDERS, GEORGE F. T. 'Akan vocabulary of diseases.' *Mitt. Inst. f. Orient.*, **4**, 1, 1956: 109–119.

1152　TAYLOR, C. J. 'Some Akan names.' *Nigerian field*, **18**, 1953: 34–37.

Brissa

1153　CHAMBERLAIN, G. D. *A brief account of the Brissa language.* Accra, Govt. Printer, 1930. 53 pp.

Dagomba (Dagbane)

1154　BLAIR, H. A. *Dagomba (Dagbane) dictionary and grammar.* Accra, Govt. Printer, 1941. 151 pp.

1155　SHIRER, W. L. *Dagbane grammar.* Tamale, Assemblies of God Mission, 1939. 89 pp.

1156   TAMAKLOE, E. FORSTER. *Dagomba dictionary and grammar*. Accra, Govt. Printer, 1934.

Ewe

1157   BARRY, JACK. *The pronunciation of Ewe*. Cambridge, Heffer, [1951]. 28 pp.

1158   DREXEL, ALBERT. 'Der Ewe-Typus in seiner systemastischen Eigenart und in seiner sprachgeschichtlichen Stellung.' *Bibliotheca africana*, **4**, 2, 1931: 31–41.

1159   HERMAN, AUGUSTE. *A short Ewe grammar, with English-Ewe-French vocabulary*. 1939. 48 pp.

1160   POTAKEY, F. K. 'Diacritical marks used in Ewe writing.' *Teachers' J.*, **9**, 2, 1937: 128–130.

1161   —— 'Notes on Ewe writing.' *Teachers' J.*, **8**, 3, 1936.

1162   POTAKEY, F. K., AND CHAPMAN, DANIEL A. *Ewe spelling*. Achimota, Achimota Press, 1944. (Ewe studies, no. 2.)

1163   RIEBSTEIN, P. E. *Eléments de grammaire Ewe*. Holland, Mission Catholique Steyl, 1923. 132 pp.

1164   SCHOBER, REINHOLD. 'Die semantische Gestalt des Ewe.' *Anthropos*, **28**, 1933: 621–632.

1165   WESTERMANN, DIEDRICH HERMANN. *Evefiala* (Ewe-English dictionary). Berlin, 1928.

1166   —— *Die Ewe-Sprache in Togo: eine praktische Einführung*. 2nd ed. Berlin, de Gruyter, 1961. x, 95 pp. First published 1939.

1167   —— *Gbesela Yeye, or English-Ewe dictionary*. Berlin, D. Reimer, 1930. 348 pp.

1168   —— *A study of the Ewe language;* translated by A. L. Bickford-Smith. O.U.P., 1930. xiv, 258 pp.

1169   —— *Wörterbuch der Ewe-Sprache;* revised ed. Berlin, Akademie-Verlag, 1954. xxiv, 796 pp. First published 1905.

1170   WIEGRÄBE, PAUL. 'Ewelieder.' *Afrika u. Übersee*, **37**, 3, Aug. 1953: 99–108; Sept. 1954: 155–164. Ewe songs with German text.

Fante

1171   ACQUAAH, G. R. *Mfantse-Akan mbebusem: Fante-Akan proverbs.* Cape Coast, 1940. 124 pp.

1172   APPIAH, A. W. E. *A new script Fante primer.* Cape Coast, 1931. 28 pp.

1173   BARTELS, F. L. *Fante word list with rules of spelling.* Cape Coast, Methodist Book Depot, 1944. 84 pp.

1174   BARTELS, F. L., AND ANNOBIL, J. A. *Mfantse nkasafua dwumadzi: a Fante grammar of function.* 6th ed. Cape Coast, Methodist Book Depot, 1955. 182 pp.

1175   CHRISTENSEN, JAMES BOYD. 'The role of proverbs in Fante culture.' *Africa,* **28**, 3, July 1958: 232–242.

1176   GOLD COAST. MINISTRY OF EDUCATION. *Mfantsa nkasafuka nykerewee nye ho Mbra: a Fanti word list with principles and rules of spelling.* Cape Coast, Methodist Book Depot, 1951. 90 pp.

1177   MASON, C. I., AND BILSON, E. C. *First stage in Fante reading.* Achimota, Achimota Press, 1936. 51 pp.

1178   METHODIST BOOK DEPOT. *Mfantse nkasafua nkyerekyerease: interim Fante-English dictionary.* Cape Coast, Methodist Book Depot, 1955. 68 pp.

1179   WELMERS, W. E. *A descriptive grammar of Fanti.* Baltimore, Linguistic Society of America, 1946. 78 pp.

1180   WOHLGEMUTH, N. 'Ein Fante-Tiermärchen.' *Ethnos,* **5**, 1936: 128–132.

Ga

1181   ARMSTRONG, M. *A new Ga reader.* O.U.P., 1931. 46 pp.

1182   BANNERMAN, C. J. *Ga grammar of function.* [New ed.] Cape Coast, Methodist Book Depot, 1948. 168 pp.

1183   BERRY, JACK. 'A Ga folk tale.' *Bull. Sch. Orient. Afr. Studies,* **12**, 2, 1948: 409–416.

1184   —— *The pronunciation of Ga.* Cambridge, Heffer, [195-]. 24 pp.

1185   FLEISCHER, C. F., AND WILKIE, M. B. 'Specimens of folk-lore of the Ga-people on the Gold Coast.' *Africa,* **3**, 3, 1930: 360–368.

1186   GA SOCIETY. *Ga word list with rules of spelling.* 3rd ed. Cape Coast, 1946. 55 pp.

1187   WILKIE, M. B. *Ga grammar, notes and exercises.* O.U.P., 1930. viii, 239 pp.

Guang (Gonja)

1188   BLAIR, H. A. *Gonja vocabulary and notes*. Accra, Govt. Printer, 1934. iv, 32 pp.

1189   RAPP, EUGEN LUDWIG. *The Gonja language*. Berlin, 1957. 52 pp. (Guang-Studien, 2.)

1190   —— *Sprachproben der wichtigsten Guang-Dialekte*. Berlin, [195–]. 10 pp. (Guang-Studien, 3.)

Konkomba

1191   STEVENS, P. D. 'Konkomba or Dagomba?' *Trans. Gold Coast & Togoland Hist. Soc.*, **I**, 1955: 211–216.

1192   TAIT, DAVID. 'Konkomba nominal classes, with a phonetic commentary by P. D. Stevens.' *Africa*, **24**, 2, April 1954: 130–148.

Mossi

1193   ALEXANDRE, GUSTAVE. 'La langue moré.' *Mém. IFAN*, 1953. 2 vols.

1194   KOENIG, JEAN. 'Pluriel de politesse chez les Mossis.' *Notes afr. IFAN*, **21**, janv. 1944: 12–13.

1195   MATTHEWS, J. H. 'English-Mole vocabulary.' *Gold Coast Rev.*, **5**, 1, Jan.–June 1930: 73–95.

1196   SOCQUET, MGR. '*Manuel-grammaire mossi*.' Dakar, IFAN, 1952. 87 pp. (Initiations afr., 4.)

Nzima

1197   BERRY, JACK. 'Consonant mutation in Nzema.' *Mitt. Inst. f. Orient.*, **3**, 2, 1955: 264–271.

1198   —— 'Some notes on the phonology of the Nzema and Ahanta dialects.' *Bull. Sch. Orient. Afr. Studies*, **17**, 1955: 160–165.

Twi

1199   AKROFI, C. A. *Twi kasa mmara* (*Twi grammar in Twi*). Longmans, 1943. xiii, 110 pp.

1200   —— *Twi Mmebusem: Twi proverbs, with English translations and comments*. Macmillan; Kumasi, Presbyterian Book Depot, 1958. 173 pp.

1201   AKROFI, C. A., AND RAPP, EUGEN LUDWIG. *A Twi spelling book*. Accra, Govt. Printer, 1938. 110 pp.

1202   AKROFI, C. A., AND WATT, J. A. 'Notes on Twi spelling in the new script.' *Teachers' J.*, **5**, 3, 1933: 212–216.

1203 BELLON, I. *Twi lessons for beginners, including a grammatical guide and numerous idioms and phrases.* Revised ed. Kumasi, Basel Mission Book Depot, 1955. xv, 74 pp.

1204 BERRY, JACK. *English, Twi, Asante, Fante dictionary.* Accra, Presbyterian Book Depot; Macmillan, 1960. 146 pp.

1205 —— 'A note on Twi accents.' *Afrikanistische Studien,* ed. J. Lukas, 1955: 295–298.

1206 —— 'Vowel harmony in Twi.' *Bull. Sch. Orient. Afr. Studies,* **19,** 1957: 124–130.

1207 CHRISTALLER, J. G. *Dictionary of the Asante and Fante language called Tshi (Twi).* 2nd ed. revised and enlarged. Basel, Basel Evangelical Missionary Society, 1933. 607 pp.
First published 1881.

1208 HERMAN, AUGUSTE. *A short Twi grammar, with English-Twi-French vocabulary.* 1939. 48 pp.

1209 MEAD, MARGARET. 'A Twi relationship system.' *J. Roy. Anthrop. Inst.,* **67,** July–Dec. 1937: 297–304.

1210 METHODIST BOOK DEPOT. *Twi grammar of function.* Cape Coast, Methodist Book Depot. 1950. 191 pp.

1211 NKETIA, J. H. KWABENA. *The writing of Twi, 1: Asante spelling.* Accra, Scottish Mission Book Depot, [195–]. 26 pp.

1212 OFOSU-APPIAH, L. H., 'On translating the Homeric epithet and simile into Twi.' *Africa,* **30,** 1, Jan. 1960: 41–45.

1213 OTT, A., AND ADAYE, J. J. *English for Twi boys and girls.* Kumasi, Basel Mission Book Depot; Macmillan, 1957. 187 pp.

1214 RAPP, EUGEN LUDWIG, ED. *Five hundred Twi proverbs* [collected by J. J. Adaye]. Akropong, the author, 1934. 12 pp.

1215 —— *An introduction to Twi.* 2nd revised ed. Kumasi, Basel Mission Book Depot; Longmans, 1948. 119 pp.
First published 1936.

1216 —— 'Zur Ausbreitung einer westafrikanischen Stammessprache (das Twi).' *Afrikanistische Studien,* ed. J. Lukas, 1955: 220–230.

1217 WARD, IDA C. *The pronunciation of Twi.* Cambridge, Heffer, 1939.
Illustrated by two double-sided 12-in. gramophone records made by Akufo Addo and W. Ofori Atta, School of Oriental and African Studies.

See also nos. 2141, 2144.

Folklore

Folk tales and proverbs of individual ethnic groups are included with those groups in Ethnology and Linguistics.

1218 BARKER, W. H., AND SINCLAIR, C. *West African folk-tales.* Harrap, 1917. 184 pp.

1219 COURLANDER, HAROLD, AND HERZOG, G. *The cow-tail switch, and other West African stories.* N.Y., Holt, 1947. 143 pp.

1220 COURLANDER, HAROLD, AND PREMPEH, ALBERT KOFI. *The hatshaking dance, and other tales from the Gold Coast.* N.Y., Harcourt, Brace, 1957. 115 pp.

1221 DOUGLAS, A. B. 'The Anansesem in Gold Coast schools.' *Gold Coast Rev.*, 5, 1, 1934: 125–143.

1222 HERSKOVITS, M. J., AND HERSKOVITS, F. S. *Dahomean narrative: a cross-cultural analysis.* Northwestern U.P.; Routledge, 1958. xvi, 490 pp. (African studies, no. 1.)

1223 ITAYEMI, P., AND GURREY, P. *Folk tales & fables.* Penguin Books, 1954. 122 pp. (Penguin West African series, no. 3.)

1224 JABLOW, ALTA. *Yes and no: the intimate folklore of Africa.* N.Y., Horizon Press, 1961. 223 pp.
Mainly West African.

1225 RATTRAY, ROBERT SUTHERLAND. 'The African child in proverb, folklore and fact.' *Africa*, 6, 4, 1933: 456–471.

1226 ST. JOHN-PARSONS, D. *Legends of northern Ghana.* Longmans, 1958. 70 pp.

1227 —— *More legends of northern Ghana.* Longmans, 1960. 69 pp.

1228 SHERLOCK, PHILIP M. *Anansi the Spider Man: Jamaican folk tales, retold by Philip M. Sherlock.* Macmillan, 1956. 86 pp.
Anansi tales originated from West Africa.

Archæology

1229 ALIMEN, H. *The prehistory of Africa;* translated by Alan Houghton Brodrick. Hutchinson, 1957. 438 pp.

1230 ARKELL, A. J. 'Gold Coast copies of 5th–7th century bronze lamps.' *Antiquity,* **24,** 93, March 1950: 38–40.

1231 BEQUAERT, MAURICE. 'Pierres trouvées de la Côte d'Or et essai de l'interprétation.' *Bull. roy. Belge. Anthrop. et Préhist.,* **40/41,** 1949–50: 273–274.

1232 BRAUNHOLTZ, H. J. 'Note on two pottery heads from near Fomena, Ashanti.' *Man,* **34,** 2, 1934.

1233 DAVIDSON, BASIL. *The lost cities of Africa.* Boston, Little, Brown, 1959. 357 pp.

1234 —— *Old Africa rediscovered.* Gollancz, 1959. 287 pp.

1235 DAVIES, OLIVER. 'An archaeological link with ancient Ghana.' *Universitas,* **3,** 6, 1959: 175–176.

1236 —— *Archaeology in Ghana.* Nelson, published on behalf of the University College of Ghana, 1961. 45 pp.

1237 —— 'Earliest man, and how he reached Ghana.' *Universitas,* **3,** 2, 1958: 35–37.

1238 —— 'Galets perforés du Ghana et des pays voisins.' *Notes afr. IFAN,* **86,** avr. 1960: 37–39.

1239 —— 'The invaders of northern Ghana: what archaeologists are teaching the historians.' *Universitas,* **4,** 5, March 1961: 134–136.

1240 —— 'The neolithic revolution in tropical Africa.' *Trans. Hist. Soc. Ghana,* **4,** 2, 1960: 14–20.

1241 —— 'The Old Stone-Age between the Volta and the Niger.' *Bull. IFAN,* **19,** (B), 1957: 592–616.

1242 DURVILLE, GASTON. 'Symboles divins monothéistes sur les plus anciens poids de bronze à peser l'or en Côte d'Ivoire et en Gold Coast.' *Bull. Soc. préhist. franç.,* **47,** 3/4, 1950.

1243   JEFFREYS, M. D. W. 'Who were the aborigines of West Africa?' *W. Afr. Rev.*, **22**, 284, May 1951: 466–467.

1244   Lawrence, A. W. 'The National Museum of the Gold Coast.' *Universitas*, **1**, 2, March 1954: 10–12.

1245   LEAKEY, L. S. B. *Stone Age Africa*. O.U.P., 1936.

1246   LONDON. UNIVERSITY. SCHOOL OF ORIENTAL AND AFRICAN STUDIES. *History and archaeology in Africa: report of a conference held in July 1953 at the School of Oriental & African Studies;* edited by R. A. Hamilton. 1955. 99 pp.

1247   MAUNY, RAYMOND. 'Tableau géographique de l'Ouest Africain au moyen âge, d'après les sources écrites, la tradition et l'archéologie.' *Mém. IFAN*, **61**, 1961. 487 pp.

1248   NUNOO, R. B. 'Excavations at Asebu in the Gold Coast.' *J. W. Afr. Science Association*, Feb. 1957: 12–44.
The site is 10 miles N.E. of Cape Coast.

1249   —— 'A report on excavations at Nsuta Hill, Gold Coast.' *Man*, **48**, 90, July 1948: 73–76.

1250   PEDRALS, DENNIE PIERRE DE. *Archéologie de l'Afrique noire*. Paris, Payot, 1950.

1251   SHAW C. THURSTAN. *Archaeology and the Gold Coast*. Accra, Gold Coast Dept. of Information, 1945. 16 pp.

1252   —— *Excavation at Dawu: report on an excavation in a mound at Dawu, Akuapim, Ghana.* Published by Nelson on behalf of the University College of Ghana, 1961. 90 pp. 55 plates.

1253   WELLS, L. H., ED. 'Symposium on human skeletal remains from the Cape Coast.' *South African J. Science*, **32**, 1935: 603–615.

1254   WILD, ROBERT P. 'An ancient pot from Tarkwa, Gold Coast.' *Man*, **35**, Sept. 1935.

1255   —— 'Baked clay beads from graves near Fomena, Ashanti.' *Man*, **34**, 1, 1934.

1256   —— 'Cuttlefish bone mould casting as practised in the Gold Coast.' *Gold Coast Rev.*, **5**, 1, 1934: 144–150.

1257   —— 'Funerary equipment from Agona-Swedru, Winnebah district, Gold Coast.' *J. Roy. Anthrop. Inst.*, **47**, 1937: 67–76.

1258   —— 'Inhabitants of Gold Coast and Ashanti before the Akan invasion.' *Teachers' J.*, **6**, 3, 1935: 195–201.

1259 WILD, ROBERT P. 'Nyame Akuma, or God axes.' *Gold Coast Rev.*, 5, 1, 1934: 156–165.

1260 —— 'Stone Age pottery from the Gold Coast and Ashanti.' *J. Roy. Anthrop. Inst.*, 64, July–Dec. 1934: 203–216.

1261 —— 'Stone implements of the palaeolithic type from the Gold Coast.' *Gold Coast Rev.*, 5, 1, 1934: 174–180.

1262 —— 'Unusual type of primitive iron smelting furnace at Abompusu, Ashanti.' *Gold Coast Rev.*, 5, 1, 1934: 184–192.

1263 —— 'Vestiges of a pre-Ashanti race at Obuasi (Ashanti).' *Gold Coast Rev.*, 5, 1, Jan.–June 1929: 1–17.

History

General

1264 ADDY, E. A. *Ghana history for primary schools. Book 1: 1450–1800.* Longmans, 1958. 90 pp.

1265 —— *Ghana history for primary schools. Book 2: 1800–1957.* Longmans, 1960. 97 pp.

1266 AGLIONBY, J. O. *A gleam from the golden shore.* Achimota, Achimota Press, 1948. 79 pp.

1267 AGYEMAN, NANA YAW TWUM DUAH. *West Africa on the march: an intimate survey of problems and potentialities.* N.Y., William-Frederick Press, 1952. 73 pp.

1268 AKITA, J. M. 'Documentary material available for historical research in the Gold Coast.' *Trans. Gold Coast & Togoland Hist. Soc.*, **I**, 1952: 21–23.

1269 ATTAFUA, A. B. 'Traditional history.' *Trans. Gold Coast & Togoland Hist. Soc.*, **I**, 1952: 18–20.

1270 AUSTIN, D. *West Africa and the Commonwealth.* Penguin Books, 1957. 124 pp.
Author was tutor at the Institute of Extra-Mural Studies in the University College of the Gold Coast from 1949 to 1955.

1271 BARKER, W. H. *The Gold Coast Colony and Protectorate.* Manchester, Sherratt & Hughes, 1922. 174 pp.

1272 BARTLETT, VERNON. *Struggle for Africa.* Muller, 1953. 251 pp.

1273 BENTWICH, N. *The mandates system.* Longmans, 1930.

1274 BOURRET, F. M. *Ghana: the road to independence, 1919–1957.* Revised ed. O.U.P., 1960. 246 pp.
Previous ed. published as *The Gold Coast, 1919–1951.* First published 1949.

1275 —— *The Gold Coast and British Togoland, 1919–1946.* Stanford U.P., 1949. 231 pp.

1276 BOUSQUET, GEORGES HENRI. *Les Berbères: histoire et institutions.* Paris, Presses Universitaires, 1957. 116 pp.

1277 [BOWEN, CHARLES] *"West African way": the story of the Burma Campaigns, 1943–1945: 5th Bn. Gold Coast Regt., 81 West African Division.* Obuasi, Ashanti Times, [195–]. 84 pp.

1278 BRADLEY, KENNETH. 'Gold Coast impressions.' *Blackwood's Magazine,* **261,** 1947: 1–9.

1279 *A brief history of the Gold Coast Regiment, W.A.F.F.* 11 pp.

1280 BROOKS, H. 'The Gold Coast Historical Society.' *W. Afr. Rev.,* **17,** 227, Aug. 1946: 935.

1281 BROWN, GODFREY N. *An active history of Ghana.* Allen & Unwin, 1961. 2 vols.
Vol 1: From the earliest times to 1844.
Vol 2: Since 1845.

1282 BUSIA, KOFI ABREFA. 'West Africa in the 20th century.' *J. World History,* **4,** 1, 1957: 203–217.

1283 CAMPBELL, JOHN MACLEOD. *African history in the making.* Edinburgh House Press, 1956. 126 pp.
Report on the Cambridge Conference on African Education, 1952.

1284 CARLAND, G. B. 'The Gold Coast: an historical approach.' *Afr. affairs,* **46,** 183, April 1947: 89–97.

1285 CHAZALAS, A. *Territoires africaines sous mandat de la France: Cameroun et Togo.* Paris, Soc. Ed. Geog., Maritimes et Coloniales, 1931.

1286 CLARIDGE, WILLIAM W. *A history of the Gold Coast and Ashanti.* Murray, 1915. 2 vols.
Contains accounts of the early period of British occupation and settlements by other Europeans.

1287 CLARKE, JOHN H. 'Old Ghana.' *Negro Hist. Bull.,* **23,** Feb. 1960: 116–117.

1288 —— 'New Ghana.' *Negro Hist. Bull.,* **23,** Feb. 1960: 117–118.

1289 COHEN, SIR ANDREW. *British policy in changing Africa.* Routledge, 1959. ix, 118 pp.

1290 COMMISSARIAT DE LA RÉPUBLIQUE FRANÇAISE AU TOGO. *Guide de la colonisation au Togo.* Paris, Larose, 1926. 198 pp.

1291 CORNEVIN, ROBERT. *Histoire de l'Afrique des origines à nos jours.* Paris, 1956.

1292 —— *Histoire des peuples de l'Afrique noire.* Paris, 1960.

1293 ELIOT, SIR E. C. *Broken atoms.* Bles, 1938.

1294 EVANS, I. L. *The British in tropical Africa.* C.U.P., 1929.

1295 EYRE-SMITH, ST. J. *A brief review of the history and social organization of the people of the Northern Territories of the Gold Coast.* Accra, Govt. Printer, 1933. 45 pp.

1296 FABIAN COLONIAL BUREAU. *Downing Street and the colonies.* 1942.

1297 —— *International action and the colonies: report of a committee of the Fabian Colonial Bureau.* 1943.

1298 FAGE, JOHN DONNELLY. *An atlas of African history.* E. Arnold, 1958. 64 pp.

1299 —— *Ghana: a historical interpretation.* Wisconsin U.P., 1959. 122 pp.

1300 —— *An introduction to the history of West Africa.* 2nd ed. C.U.P., 1959. xii, 214 pp.

1301 —— 'Some general considerations relevant to historical research in the Gold Coast.' *Trans. Gold Coast & Togoland Hist Soc.*, **I**, 1952: 24–29.

1302 FULL, A. *Fünfzig Jahre Togo.* Berlin, 1935.

1303 GOLD COAST ABORIGINES' RIGHTS PROTECTION SOCIETY. *Memorandum of the case of the Gold Coast for a memorial to be presented to His Majesty the King Emperor in Council. . . for the amendment of the Gold Coast Colony (Legislative Council) Order in Council, 1925.*

1304 —— *Petition to the House of Commons.* 1935.

1305 'A Gold Coast chronology.' *W. Afr. Rev.*, July 1951: 748–749.

1306 GOODY, JACK. 'A note on the penetration of Islam into the west of the Northern Territories of the Gold Coast.' *Trans. Gold Coast & Togoland Hist. Soc.*, **I**, 1953: 45–46.

1307 GREAT BRITAIN. WAR OFFICE. *Military report on the Gold Coast, Ashanti, the Northern Territories and Mandated Togoland. Vol 1: General.* H.M.S.O., 1931.

1308 GUGGISBERG, SIR FREDERICK GORDON. *The Gold Coast: a review of events of 1920–1926 and the prospects of 1927–1928.* Accra, Govt. Printer, 1927.

1309 —— *Post-war Gold Coast: a review of the events of 1923, with a statement showing the policy adopted by the government for the progress of the people.* 1924. 180 pp.

1310 HAILEY, M. *An African survey.* Revised ed. O.U.P., 1956. 1676 pp. Limited to Africa south of the Sahara. A well documented survey brought up-to-date to the end of 1955.

1311 HAINES, C. GROVE, ED. *Africa today.* Baltimore, Johns Hopkins Press, 1955. xvi, 510 pp.

1312 HAIR, PAUL EDWARD HEDLEY. *A history of West Africa: for schools and colleges.* E. Arnold, 1959. Pupils' book, 113 pp. Teachers' book, 111 pp.

1313 HANCOCK, W. K. *A survey of British Commonwealth affairs.* O.U.P., 1937–42. 2 vols.

1314 HANNA, A. J. *European rule in Africa.* Published for the Historical Association by Routledge, 1961. 36 pp.

1315 HARDY, GEORGES. *Vue genérale de l'histoire d'Afrique.* Paris, 1952.

1316 HEMINGFORD, DENNIS GEORGE RUDDOCK HERBERT, 2ND BARON. *The Gold Coast: an address to the Annual Meeting of the Anti-Slavery Society on 3rd Sept. 1953.* Anti-Slavery Society, 1953. 6 pp.

1317 HOWARD, C., ED. *West African explorers.* O.U.P., 1951. ix, 598 pp. (World's classics, no. 523.)

1318 KANE, ROBERT S. *Africa A to Z.* N.Y., Doubleday, 1961. 408 pp.

1319 KESSIE, KOHANENANA KOBINA. *Colonies: what Africa thinks.* African Economic Union, 1939. 28 pp.

1320 LABOUR PARTY (GREAT BRITAIN). *The colonies: the Labour Party's post-war policy for the African and Pacific colonies.* 1943.

1321 —— *The Empire in Africa: Labour's policy.* 1920.

1322 LUCAS, C. P. *Historical geography of the British colonies. Vol 3: West Africa.* Washington, D.C., National Education Association, 1950.

1323 MACMILLAN, W. M. *Africa emergent.* Penguin Books, 1949.

1324 MAROIX, GÉNÉRAL. *Le Togo, pays d'influence française.* Paris, Larose, 1937.

1325 MARTONNE, DE. *Les résultats scientifiques de la mission de délimination du Togo.* 1930.

1326 MATE, C. M. O. *A visual history of Ghana.* Evans, 1959. 64 pp.

1327 MEEK, C. K. *Europe and West Africa: some problems and adjustments.* O.U.P., 1940. 143 pp. (University of London. Heath Clark Lectures.)

1328   MOBERLY, F. J. *History of the Great War. Military operations in Togo and the Camerouns, 1914–18.* H.M.S.O., 1931.

1329   MONTMARD, ANDRÉ. *La Gold Coast: études, enquêtes, conférences.* Dakar, Guv. Gén. de l'A.O.F., Serv. de l'Inform., 1949. 76 pp.

1330   MURDOCK, GEORGE PETER. *Africa, its peoples and their cultural history.* N.Y., McGraw-Hill, 1959.

1331   NAINE, D. T., AND SURET-CANALE, J. *Histoire de l'Afrique occidentale.* Conakry, 1960.

1332   OWUSU, SETH AMOAKO. *Political institutions of the coastal areas of the Gold Coast as influenced by European contact.* [1934].

1333   REICHHOLD, WALTER. *Westafrika.* Bonn, Deutsche Afrika-Gesellschaft, 1958. (Länder Afrikas, no. 7.)

1334   REINDORF, CARL CHRISTIAN. *The history of the Gold Coast and Asante.* 2nd ed. Basel, Mission Book Depot, 1951. 351 pp.
        The historical tradition of the Ga people, 1500–1860. First published 1895.

1335   ROBERTS, T., ED. *The new nations of West Africa.* N.Y., Wilson, 1960. 179 pp.

1336   ROGERS, R. S. *A history of the Ghana Army. Vol 1.* Accra, Govt. Printer, 1959. 87 pp.

1337   ROOLVINK, ROELOF, AND OTHERS. *Historical atlas of the Muslim peoples.* Allen & Unwin, 1958. xi pp. 40 maps.

1338   ROYAL INSTITUTE OF INTERNATIONAL AFFAIRS. *The colonial problem: a report by a study group of members of the Royal Institute of International Affairs.* 1937.

1339   RUMPF, HELMUT. *Westafrika: Geschichte einer Küste.* Berlin, Junker & Dünnhaupt, 1943. 121 pp.

1340   SAMUEL, H. L. *The British colonial system and its future: an address to the Anti-Slavery and Aborigines' Protection Society.* [1943].

1341   SAVAGE, KATHERINE. *The story of Africa south of the Sahara.* Bodley Head, 1961. 192 pp.

1342   TOGOLAND BOUNDARY COMMISSION, 1927–1929 *Final report of the two commissioners.* Lomé, Mission Catholique, 1929. 84 pp.

1343   UDOMA, E. UDO. *The lion and the oil-palm, and The clash of cultures.* Dublin, University Press, 1943. 36 pp.
        British rule in West Africa.

1344 UNITED NATIONS. *Report on Togoland under United Kingdom administration, together with related documents.* 1952. 46 pp.

1345 WARD, WILLIAM ERNEST FRANK. *A history of Ghana.* 2nd ed. Allen & Unwin, 1958. 434 pp.
The standard history, from the earliest times. Well documented. First published 1948.

1346 —— *A short history of Ghana.* 7th ed. Longmans, 1957. 275 pp.
First published as *A short history of the Gold Coast,* 1935.

1347 WESTERMANN, DIEDRICH HERMANN. *Geschichte Afrikas: Staatenbildungen Südlich der Sahara.* Cologne, Graven Verlag, 1952. 492 pp.

1348 WILKS, IVOR. *The northern factor in Ashanti history.* Accra, University College of Ghana, Institute of African Studies, 1961. 46 pp.

1349 —— 'A note on the traditional history of Mampong.' *Trans. Hist. Soc. Ghana,* **4**, 2, 1960: 26–29.

1350 —— 'A note on Twifo and Akwamu.' *Trans. Hist. Soc. Ghana,* **3**, 1957: 215–217.

1351 WODDIS, JACK. *Africa: the lion awakes.* Lawrence & Wishart, 1961.

1352 —— *Africa: the roots of revolt.* Lawrence & Wishart, 1960. xiii, 285 pp.

1353 WOLFSON, FREDA. *Pageant of Ghana.* O.U.P., 1958. 266 pp. (West African history series.)
Extracts from works of writers on the Gold Coast from its discovery by the Portuguese in 1471 to 1957.

1354 YOUELL, GEORGE. *Africa marches.* S.P.C.K., 1949. 144 pp.
West African soldiers in the Second World War.

See also nos. 27, 29, 34.

Ancient Ghana

1355 AL ADAWI, I. A. 'Description of the Sudan by Muslim geographers and travellers.' *Sudan Notes and Records,* **35**, 2, 1954: 5–16.

1356 BATTUTA, IBN. *The travels of Ibn Battuta, A.D. 1325–1354;* translated with revisions and notes from the Arabic text edited by C. Defrémery and B. R. Sanguinetti, by H. A. R. Gibb. C.U.P. for the Hakluyt Society, 1958. Vol. 1. xvii, 269 pp.
Vol. 2. xi, 271–537 pp. 1962.
Travels in Asia and North Africa, including western Sudan.

1357 BOULNOIS, J., AND HAMA, B. *L'empire de Gao.* Paris, Maisonneuve, 1956. 182 pp.

1358 BOVILL, E. W. *Caravans of the old Sahara.* O.U.P., 1933. 300 pp.

1359 —— *The golden trade of the Moors.* O.U.P., 1958. 281 pp.
One of the best accounts of the ancient kingdoms south of the Sahara desert, including Ghana and Mali. A revision of *Caravans of the old Sahara*, 1933.

1360 —— 'The Moorish invasion of the Sudan.' *J. Roy. Afr. Soc.,* **26,** 1926: 245–262, 380–387. *Africa,* **27,** 1927: 47–56.

1361 CAPOT-REY, ROBERT. *Le Sahara français.* Paris, Presses Universitaires de France, 1953.

1362 CONTON, WILLIAM F. *West Africa in history. Vol 1: Before the Europeans.* Allen & Unwin, 1961. 93 pp.

1363 DANQUAH, JOSEPH BOAKYE. 'The Akan claim to origin from Ghana.' *W. Afr. Rev.,* Nov. 1955: 968–970; Dec. 1955: 1107–1111.
A reply to R. Mauny's views on ancient Ghana.

1364 —— *Revelation of culture in Ghana: lectures and essays of discovery in the search for the ancient origins of a progressive people.* [Accra, 1961.] iv, 273 pp. (Typescript.)

1365 DE GRAFT JOHNSON, J. C. 'African empires of the past.' *Présence afr.,* avr.–mai 1957: 58–64.

1366 ——*African glory: the story of vanished Negro civilizations.* Watts, 1954. 209 pp.
The ancient empires of western Africa, Mali, Songhai and Ghana.

1367 —— *Le civilta scompare dell' Africa.* [African glory.] Rome, Feltrinelli, 1957.

1368 —— *Velikost a slava Afriky.* [African glory.] Prague, Melantrich, 1956.

1369 'L'Empire du Mali.' *Notes afr. IFAN,* **82/83,** avr.–juil. 1959.

1370 FAGE, JOHN DONNELLY. 'Ancient Ghana: a review of the evidence.' *Trans. Hist. Soc. Ghana,* **3,** 1957: 77–98.

1371 —— 'Some problems of Gold Coast history.' *Universitas,* **1,** 6, 1955: 5–9.

1372 GAUTIER, EMILE FELIX. *Sahara: the great desert.* N.Y., Columbia U.P., 1935.

1373 'The Ghana question: where the experts disagree.' *W. Afr. Rev.,* March 1957: 267–272.

1374 HODGKIN, T. 'Ancient chroniclers of West Africa's past.' *Courier*, 12, 1959: 15–20.

1375 —— 'The civilisation of Ghana.' *West Africa*, 4 April 1953: 291.

1376 —— 'Koumbi Saleh and the capital of Ghana.' *West Africa*, 28 March 1953: 271–272.

1377 HUTTON, J. S. 'Medieval Ghanata and modern Ghana.' *Bantu*, 6, June 1957: 35–46.

1378 KHALDOUN, IBN. *Histoire des Berbères et des dynasties musulmanes de l'Afrique septentrionale;* trans. by M. G. De Slane. New ed. by P. Casanova. Paris, Geuthner, 1925–56. 4 vols.

1379 —— *The Muqaddimah: an introduction to history;* trans. and edited by F. Rosenthal. Routledge, 1958. 3 vols.

1380 KWAPONG, A. A. 'Africa antiqua.' *Trans. Gold Coast & Togoland Hist. Soc.*, 2, 1956: 1–12.

1381 LEWIS, BERNARD. *The Arabs in history.* Hutchinson, 1950. 196 pp.

1382 LHOTE, HENRI. 'Au sujet d'objets anciens de la région de Tombouctou et des puits de l'Azaouad.' *Notes afr. IFAN*, 55, juil. 1952: 79–82.

1383 —— *Les Touaregs du Hoggar.* 2nd ed. Paris, Payot, 1955.

1384 MACALL, DANIEL F. 'The traditions of the founding of Sijilmassa and Ghana.' *Trans. Hist. Soc. Ghana*, 5, 1, 1961: 3–32.

1385 MALDONADO, EDUARDO. 'Bosquejo historico del imperio Mali. *Africa* [*Madrid*], 241, 1962: 10–13.

1386 MATHEWS, K. D. *Cities in the sand.* Philadelphia, 1957.

1387 MAUNY, RAYMOND. 'La civilisation de Ghana.' *Bull. Inform. A.O.F.*, 123, janv. 1952: 14–17.

1388 —— 'Essai sur l'histoire des métaux en Afrique occidentale.' *Bull. IFAN*, 14, 2, avr. 1952: 545–596.

1389 —— 'État actuel de la question de Ghana.' *Bull. IFAN*, 13, 2, avr. 1951: 463–475.

1390 —— 'État actuel de nos connaissances sur la préhistoire du Dahomey et du Togo.' *Études dahoméennes*, 4, 1950: 5–11.

1391 —— 'Niches murales de la maison fouillée à Koumbi Saleh.' *Notes afr. IFAN*, 46, avr. 1950: 34–35.

1392   MAUNY, RAYMOND. 'Notes on the protohistoric period in West Africa.' *J. W. Afr. Science Association*, **2**, 2, Feb. 1957: 207–208.

1393   —— 'Objets anciens de la région de Tombouctou.' *Notes afr. IFAN*, **53**, janv. 1952: 9–11.

1394   —— 'The question of Ghana.' *Africa*, **24**, 3, July 1954: 200–213. An important statement of evidence, with a plan of the ruins of Koumbi Saleh, the reputed site of the capital of the Ghana Empire.

1395   MEYEROWITZ, EVA L. R. 'The Akan and Ghana.' *Man*, **57**, June 1957: 83–88.

1396   —— 'A note on the origin of Ghana.' *Afr. affairs*, **51**, 205, Oct. 1952: 319–323.

1397   MONTEIL, CHARLES. 'Les empires de Mali.' *Bull. Comité d'Études Hist. et Sci. A.O.F.*, **12**, 1929: 291–447.

1398   —— 'Les "Ghâna" des géographes arabes et des Européens.' *Hesperis*, [*Rabat*], 1951: 441–452.

1399   PALMER, SIR HERBERT RICHMOND. *The Bornu Sahara and Sudan.* Murray, 1936. viii, 296 pp.

1400   —— *The Carthaginian voyage to West Africa in 500 B.C., together with Sultan Mohammed Bello's account of the origin of the Fulbe.* Bathurst, Govt. Printer, 1931. 51 pp.

1401   —— *Sudanese memoirs: being mainly translations of a number of Arabic manuscripts relating to the central and western Sudan.* Lagos, Govt. Printer, 1928. 3 vols.

1402   ROUCH, JEAN. 'Contribution à l'histoire du Songhay.' *Mém. IFAN*, **29**, 1953: 169–170.

1403   THOMASSEY, P. 'Notes sur la géographie et l'habitat de la région de Koumbi Saleh.' *Bull. IFAN*, **13**, 2, avr. 1951: 476–486.

1404   THOMASSEY, P., AND MAUNY, RAYMOND. 'Campagne de fouilles a Koumbi Saleh.' *Bull. IFAN*, **13**, 2, avr. 1951: 438–462.

1405   URVOY, YVES. *Histoire des populations du Soudan Central.* Paris, Larose, 1936.

1406   VUILLET, J. 'Essai d'interpretation des traditions légendaires sur les origines des vieux empires soudanais.' *C. R. Acad. Sci. colon.*, **10**, avr. 1950: 268–287.

1407   WILLIAMS, JOSEPH J. *Hebrewisms of West Africa: from Nile to Niger with the Jew.* Longmans, 1930. 443 pp. A claim that the early peoples from Israel migrated to the Sudan.

1408 WINGFIELD, R. J. *The story of old Ghana, Melle and Songhai.* C.U.P., 1957. 60 pp.

15th–17th Centuries–European contact

1409 APPLETON, LESLIE. 'Elmina: most ancient of all the Gold Coast castles.' *W. Afr. Rev.*, Jan. 1953: 16–17.

1410 —— 'Traders' castle.' [Cape Coast.] *W. Afr. Rev.*, **23**, 293, Feb. 1952: 116–119.

1411 ASTLEY, THOMAS, Comp. *A new general collection of voyages and travels . . . in Europe, Asia, Africa and America. Vol 2: Voyages and travels along the western coast of Africa . . . with the geography and the natural history of the neighbouring countries.* London, printed for Thomas Astley, 1745. 732 pp.

1412 AZURARA, GOMES EANNES DE. *Conquests and discoveries of Henry the Navigator, being the chronicles of Azurara: Portuguese navigators and colonisers of the 15th and 16th centuries;* edited by V. de Castro e Almeida, trans. by Bernard Miall. Allen & Unwin, 1936. 253 pp.

1413 BANTON, MICHAEL. 'The Swedes at Cape Coast.' *West Africa*, 2023, 1956: 5.
Swedish Africa Company.

1414 BARTELS, F. L. 'Jacobus Eliza Johannes Capitein, 1717–47.' *Trans. Hist. Soc. Ghana*, **4**, 1959: 3–13.

1415 BLAKE, J. W. *European beginnings in West Africa, 1454–1578: a survey of the first century of white enterprise in West Africa*, Longmans, 1937. 212 pp. (Royal Empire Society. Imperial studies, no. 14.)

1416 —— *Europeans in West Africa, 1450–1560: documents to illustrate the nature and scope of Portuguese enterprise in West Africa, the abortive attempt of Castilians to create an empire there, and the early English voyages to Barbary and Guinea.* Hakluyt Society, 1942. 2 vols.

1417 BOAHEN, A. ADU. 'The African Association, 1788–1805.' *Trans. Hist. Soc. Ghana*, **5**, 1, 1961: 43–64.

1418 BOATENG, E. A. 'Some notes on the classification of Gold Coast settlements.' *Universitas*, **I**, 3, 1954: 16–18; 1955: 19–21.

1419 BRAUN, SAMUEL. *Schiffahrten.* [Voyages to West Africa.] Basel, Reinhardt, [194–]. 160 pp.
Facsimile reprint of the edition of 1624.

1420 BRØNDSTED, JOHANNES. *Vore gamle tropakolonier.* [Our former tropical colonies] Copenhagen, Westermann, 1952. 2 vols.
Vol 1: Danish East Indies and Gold Coast. Vol 2: West Indies.

1421 BUXTON, T. F. *The African slave trade and its remedy. Part 1: The slave trade. Part 2: The remedy.* Murray, 1840.

1422 CADAMOSTO, ALOISE DE. *The voyages of Cadamosto and other documents on western Africa in the second half of the fifteenth century;* trans. and ed. by G. R. Crone. Hakluyt Society, 1937. 159 pp.

1423 CANOT, T. *Adventures of an African slaver, being a true account of the life of Captain Theodore Canot, trader in gold, ivory and slaves on the coast of Guinea. . . as told in 1854 to Brantz Mayer.* N.Y., Boni, 1928. 376 pp.

1424 CAVE, R. M. *Gold Coast forts.* Nelson, 1957. 60 pp. (Background to modern Africa series.]

1425 COOMBS, DOUGLAS. 'The place of the 'Certificate of apologie' in Ghanaian history.' *Trans. Hist. Soc. Ghana,* **3,** 1957: 180–193.

1426 COUPLAND, SIR REGINALD. *The British Anti-Slavery Movement.* Hutchinson, 1933.

1427 DAVIES, K. G. *The Royal African Company.* Longmans, 1957. 396 pp.

1428 DONNAN, ELIZABETH, ED. *Documents illustrative of the history of the slave trade to America.* Washington, D.C., Carnegie Institution of Washington, 1930–35. 4 vols.

1429 DU BOIS, W. E. BURGHARDT. *The suppression of the African slave-trade to the United States of America, 1638–1870.* Cambridge, Mass., [1916]. xi, 335 pp.

1430 FAGE, JOHN DONNELLY. 'A new check list of the forts and castles of Ghana.' *Trans. Hist. Soc. Ghana,* **4,** 1959: 57–67.

1431 FRASER, JAN J. 'What happened to the Dutch?' [Departure of the Dutch from the Gold Coast.] *W. Afr. Rev.,* Feb. 1960: 65–68.

1432 FURLEY, JOHN T. 'Provisional list of some Portuguese Governors of the Captaincy Da Mina.' *Trans. Gold Coast & Togoland Hist. Soc.,* **2,** 1956: 53–62.

1433 —— 'Notes on some Portuguese Governors of the Captaincy Da Mina.' *Trans. Hist. Soc. Ghana,* **3,** 1957: 194–214.

1434 GALLAGHER, J. 'Fowell Buxton and the new African policy, 1838–42.' *Cambridge hist. J.,* **11,** 1950: 36–58.

1435 GIROUARD, MARK. 'Elmina's other fort.' [St. Iago.] *W. Afr. Rev.,* Jan. 1962: 21–23.

1436 HAZEWINKEL, H. C. 'Twee attestaties over de Nederlandsche kolonisatie aan de Goudkust.' *Bijd. Hist. Gen.* [*Utrecht*], **53**, 1932:246.

1437 *Historic Christiansborg: a brief account of the history and construction of the Castle of Christiansborg*, Accra, Ghana. Accra, Govt. Printer, 1961. 8 pp.

1438 *Historic Elmina: a brief account of the history and structure of Elmina Castle*. Accra, Govt. Printer, [1961]. 8 pp.

1439 KLEIST, ALICE M. 'The English African trade under the Tudors.' *Trans. Hist. Soc. Ghana*, **3**, 1957: 137–150.

1440 LAWRENCE, A. W. 'Some source books for West African history.' *J. Afr. Hist.*, **2**, 2, 1961: 227–234.

1441 LLOYD, CHRISTOPHER. *The navy and the slave trade: the suppression of the African slave trade in the nineteenth century.* Longmans, 1949. xiii, 314 pp.

1442 MACGREGOR, I. A. 'Europe and the East' (in *New Cambridge Modern History*, 2: *The Reformation*, 591–614).
The Portuguese in Africa.

1443 MACINNES, C. M. *England and Slavery.* Arrowsmith, 1934.

1444 MARTIN, E. C. *The British West African settlements, 1750–1821: a study in local administration.* Longmans, for the Royal Colonial Institute, 1927. 186 pp.

1445 MATSON, J. N. 'The French at Amoku.' *Trans. Gold Coast & Togoland Hist. Soc.*, **1**, 1953: 47–62.

1446 MEYEROWITZ, EVA L. R. 'The tradition of Tafo from about 1600 to 1740 from material given to me by the Tafohene Nana Yao Dabanka and his Elders in 1946.' *Trans. Hist. Soc. Ghana*, **4**, 2, 1960: 30–32.

1447 MILLS, JOHN TAYLER. 'The ghost of James Fort.' *W. Afr. Rev.*, July 1950: 821–822.

1448 MONOD, T. *De la première découverte de Guinée, par Diogo Gomes.* Bissao, 1958.

1449 NABER, S. P. L'HONORÉ. *De Nederlands in Guinee en Brazilië.* The Hague, 1931.

1450 NEWBURY, C. W. *The western Slave Coast and its rulers: European trade and administration among the Yoruba and Adja-speaking peoples of south-western Nigeria, southern Dahomey and Togo.* Oxford, Clarendon Press, 1961. 234 pp.

1451   O'NEIL, B. H. ST. J. *Report to the Monuments and Relics Commission of the Gold Coast upon the historical growth, archaeological importance, the general condition and the present use of the castles and forts of the Gold Coast with a view to their better preservation as ancient monuments.* 1951. [34] pp. (Typescript.)
An important survey by the Chief Inspector of Ancient Monuments, Great Britain.

1452   OWEN, NICHOLAS. *Journal of a slave dealer from the year 1746 to the year 1757;* edited by Eveline Martin. Routledge, 1930. viii, 120 pp.

1453   PARRY, J. H. *Europe and a wider world, 1415–1715.* Hutchinson, 1949.

1454   PEREIRA, DUARTE PACHECO. *Esmeraldo de situ orbis;* trans. and ed. by G. H. T. Kimble. Hakluyt Society, 1937. xxxv, 193 pp.
A guide to navigation of the African continent, written 1505–1508. Pacheco was Governor of S. Jorze da Mina from 1520 to 1522.

1455   —— *Esmeraldo de situ orbis;* ed. by R. Mauny. Bissau, Centro de Estudos da Guine Portuguesa, 1956.

1456   PERHAM, MARGERY, AND SIMMONS, J. *African discovery: an anthology of exploration.* Faber, 1942.

1457   PRESTAGE, EDGAR. *The Portuguese pioneers.* Black, 1933.

1458   PRIESTLEY, MARGARET. 'A note on Fort William, Anomabu.' *Trans. Gold Coast & Togoland Hist. Soc.,* **2**, 1956: 46–48.

1459   RATELBAND, K. *Vijf dagregisters van het Kesteel Sao Jorge Da Mina (Elmina) aan de Goudkust (1645–1647).* The Hague, Nijhoff, 1953. cx, 439 pp.

1460   ROUSSIER, P. *L'établissement d'Issigny, 1687–1702.* Paris, 1935.

1461   RYDER, A. F. C. 'The re-establishment of Portuguese factories on the Costa da Mina to the mid eighteenth century.' *J. Hist. Soc. Nigeria,* **I**, 3, 1958: 157–183.

1462   SHARP, N. A. DYCE. 'Cape Coast: an historical sketch, from 1610 to 1725.' *Trans. Cape Coast Hist. Soc.,* **I**, 1, 1936: 7–15.

1463   SWEDISH–AFRICAN COMPANY. *Translations of documents, etc., exchanged between Sweden and the Gold Coast in the 17th century. . . presented by the King of Sweden to the Prime Minister on 6th March, 1957.*

1464   TREND, JOHN BRANDE. *Portugal.* Benn, 1957. xii, 13–218 pp.

1465 VARLEY, W. J. 'The castles and forts of the Gold Coast.' *Trans. Gold Coast & Togoland Hist. Soc.*, **I**, 1952: 1–17.

1466 WARTEMBERG, J. SYLVANUS. *Sao Jorge d'El Mina, premier West African settlement: its tradition and customs.* Ilfracombe, Stockwell, 1951. 166 pp.

1467 WILKS, IVOR. 'The rise of the Akwamu Empire, 1650–1710.' *Trans. Hist. Soc. Ghana*, **3**, 1957: 99–136.

1468 WILLIAMS, ERIC. *Capitalism and slavery.* N. Carolina U.P., 1944.

1469 WOLFSON, FREDA. 'Early English traders in Ghana.' *West Africa*, **2079**, 1957: 155–156.

1470 WYNDHAM, H. A. *The Atlantic and emancipation.* O.U.P., 1937. xvi, 300 pp. (Problems of imperial trusteeship.)

1471 —— *The Atlantic and slavery.* O.U.P., 1935.

See also nos. 224, 377.

18th–19th Centuries

1472 AHUMA, S.R.B.A. *Memoirs of West African celebrities, Europe, etc. (1700–1850), with special reference to the Gold Coast.* Marples, 1905. 260 pp.

1473 AKITA, J. M. 'The transfer of the seat of government from Cape Coast to Accra [in 1877].' *Gold Coast Teachers' J.*, **I**, 1956: 42–47.

1474 ANSTEY, R. T. 'British trade and policy in west central Africa between 1816 and the early 1880s.' *Trans. Hist. Soc. Ghana*, **3**, 1957: 47–71.

1475 BERBAIN, SIMONE. 'Étude sur la traite des noirs au golfe de Guinée: le comptoir français de Juda (Ouidah) au XVIIIe siècle.' *Mém. IFAN*, 1942. 125 pp.

1476 BOAHEN, A. ADU. *British penetration of the Sahara and western Sudan, 1788–1861.* (Unpublished thesis, University of London, 1959.)

1477 CLARKE, F.A.S. 'The drama of Kumasi.' [1900.] *W. Afr. Rev.*, March 1950: 265–271.

1478 —— 'Wolseley's march to Kumasi.' *W. Afr. Rev.*, Dec. 1949.

1479 CONHAIM, R. I. *British policy on the Gold Coast, 1874–1901.* (Unpublished thesis, University of California, 1959.)

1480   CROWE, S. E. *The Berlin West African Conference, 1884–1885.*
Longmans, 1942. 249 pp. (Imperial studies, no. 19.)

1481   DALTON, HEATHER. *The development of the Gold Coast under British
administration, 1874–1901.* (Unpublished thesis, University of
Ghana, 1957. 322 pp.)

1482   DANQUAH, JOSEPH BOAKYE. 'The historical significance of the Bond
of 1844.' *Trans. Hist. Soc. Ghana,* **3,** 1957: 3–29.

1483   ENFIELD, D. E. *L. E. L.: a mystery of the thirties.* Hogarth Press,
1928. 201 pp.
Letitia Elizabeth Landon, wife of Capt. George Maclean.

1484   FAGE, JOHN DONNELLY. 'The administration of George Maclean on
the Gold Coast, 1830–44.' *Trans. Gold Coast & Togoland Hist.
Soc.,* **I,** 1954: 104–120.

1485   GRIFFITH, SIR WILLIAM BRANDFORD. 'West Africa in the 1880's.'
West Africa Annual, 1954: 17–25.

1486   JACKSON, R. M. *Journal of a voyage to the west coast of Africa in 1826.*
Letchworth, 1934. 159 pp.

1487   JONES-QUARTEY, K. A. B. 'Sierra Leone's role in the development of
Ghana, 1820–1930.' *Sierra Leone Studies,* **10,** 1958: 73–84.

1488   MASTERS, W. E. *Kumasi—then and now, 1875–1925.* London, The
School Press, [1926]. 15 pp. (Reprinted from the *London Hospital
Gazette,* Nov. 1926.)

1489   MELLOR, G. R. *British imperial trusteeship, 1783–1850.* Faber, 1951.
499 pp.

1490   METCALFE, G. E. 'After Maclean: some aspects of British Gold Coast
policy in the mid-nineteenth century.' *Trans. Gold Coast &
Togoland Hist. Soc.,* **I,** 1955: 178–192.
Capt. George Maclean (1801–1847) was British Administrator in
the Gold Coast from 1830 to 1844.

1491   MOSELEY, MABOTH. 'Soldiers of the Queen in Ashanti' [1873]. *W.
Afr. Rev.,* Dec. 1952: 1236–1239.

1492   NEWTON, A. P. 'British enterprise in tropical Africa, 1783–1870'
(in *Cambridge History of the British Empire,* **2;** 635–675).

1493   NØRREGAARD, GEORG. *Englands køb af de Danske besiddelser i Ostindien
og Afrika, 1845 og 1850.* København, Bianco Lunos, 1936. 78 pp.

1494   PRIESTLEY, MARGARET. 'The Ashanti question and the British
eighteenth-century origins.' *J. Afr. Hist.,* **2,** 1, 1961: 35–59.

1495 PRIESTLEY, MARGARET, AND WILKS, IVOR. 'The Ashanti kings in the eighteenth century: a revised chronology.' *J. Afr. Hist.*, **1**, 1, 1960: 83–96.

1496 SWANZY, HENRY. 'A trading family in the nineteenth century Gold Coast (the Swanzys).' *Trans. Gold Coast & Togoland Hist. Soc.*, **2**, 1956: 87–120.

1497 TORDOFF, W. 'The exile and repatriation of Nana Prempeh I of Ashanti (1896–1924).' *Trans. Hist. Soc. Ghana*, **4**, 2, 1960: 33–58.

1498 WASSERMAN, B. 'The Ashanti War of 1900: a study in cultural conflict.' *Africa*, **31**, 2, April 1961: 167–178.

1499 WOLFSON, FREDA. 'British relations with the Gold Coast, 1843–1880.' *Bull. Inst. Hist. Res.*, **24**, 70, Nov. 1951: 182–186.

See also nos. 31, 270.

Government and Politics, 20th Century

The Gold Coast

1500 ACHIMOTA AND KUMASI DISCUSSION GROUPS. *Towards national development: post-war Gold Coast;* edited by M. Ribeiro. Achimota, 1945. 120 pp.

1501 ACHIMOTA DISCUSSION GROUP. *Pointers to progress: the Gold Coast in the next five years;* edited by C. T. Shaw. Achimota, 1942. 87 pp.

1502 —— *Quo vadimus, or Gold Coast future;* edited by C. S. Deakin. Achimota, 1940.
Report of a conference called by members of the Achimota School staff, January 1939.

1503 AKPAN, N. V. *Epitaph to indirect rule.* Cassell, 1956. 202 pp.

1504 AMPAH, E. B. K. *The tears of Dr. Kwame Nkrumah: the rise of the Convention People's Party.* Cape Coast, Prospect Printing Press, [1951]. 29 pp.

1505 APTER, D. E. *The Gold Coast in transition.* Princeton U.P., O.U.P., 1955. 355 pp.
Political change in the Gold Coast prior to independence.

1506 —— 'Some economic factors in the political development of the Gold Coast.' *J. Econ. Hist.,* **14,** 4, Oct. 1954: 409–427.

1507 ARDEN-CLARKE, SIR CHARLES N. 'Eight years of transition in Ghana.' *Afr. affairs,* **57,** 226, 1958: 29–37.

1508 —— 'Gold Coast into Ghana: some problems of transition.' *Int. affairs,* **34,** 1, 1958: 49–56.

1509 ASEKRE, B. A. *An analysis of the Gold Coast evolution.* N.Y., Rosenberg, 1937. 8 pp.

1510 AUSTIN, DENNIS. 'The working committee of the United Gold Coast Convention.' *J. Afr. hist.,* **2,** 2, 1961: 273–297.
The political scene from 1947–51, the U.G.C.C. and C.P.P.

1511 BENNETT, GEORGE. 'The Gold Coast general election of 1954.' *Parl. affairs*, **7**, 4, Autumn 1954: 430–439.

1512 BOATENG, E. A. 'The evolution of the political map of the Gold Coast.' *Bull. Gold Coast Geog. Association*, **1**, 2, 1956: 16–19.

1513 BOSOMPEM, J. E. Y. *The Legislative Assembly of the Gold Coast.* Accra, the author, 1955. 70 pp.

1514 BRIGGS, A. 'Nationalism in the Gold Coast.' *Fortnightly*, 1023–4, March–April 1952: 152–157, 231–236.

1515 —— 'People and constitution in the Gold Coast.' *West Africa*, **1827–1838**, March–May 1952: 173 +

1516 BURNS, SIR ALAN. *Colour prejudice, with particular reference to the relationship between whites and negroes.* Allen & Unwin, 1948. 164 pp.

1517 BUSIA, KOFI ABREFA. 'The Gold Coast and Nigeria on the road to self-government' (in HAINES, C. G., *Africa today*, 1955: 289–304).

1518 —— *Judge for yourself.* Accra, 1956.

1519 —— 'The present situation and aspirations of élites in the Gold Coast.' *Int. Soc. Sci. Bull.*, **8**, 3, 1956: 424–431.

1520 —— 'The prospects for parliamentary democracy in the Gold Coast.' *Parl. affairs*, **5**, 4, 1952.

1521 —— *Self government for the Gold Coast.* Bureau of Current Affairs, 1951. 16 pp. (West African affairs pamphlets, no. 9.)

1522 CARBON FERRIÈRE, JACQUES DE. *La Gold Coast: administration, finances, économie.* Paris, 1937. 207 pp.

1523 CARR-GREGG, J. R. E. *Self-rule in Africa: recent advances in the Gold Coast.* N.Y., Carnegie Endowment for International Peace, 1951. (Reprint from International Conciliation, Sept. 1951: 319–382.)

1524 CHAPMAN, DANIEL A. *The Anlo constitution.* Achimota, Achimota Press, 1944. 8 pp. (Ewe studies, no. 1.)

1525 CHRISTENSEN, JAMES B. 'African political systems: indirect rule and democratic processes.' *Phylon*, **15**, 1, 1954: 69–83.

1526 COFFEE, MARY. *The self-government movement in the Gold Coast, West Africa.* Washington, D.C., Howard University, 1954. 153 pp. (Unpublished thesis.)

1527 COMMITTEE ON YOUTH ORGANIZATION. *The Ghana Youth Manifesto: towards self-government.* Kumasi, 1948.

1528   CONVENTION PEOPLE'S PARTY. *Forward to freedom with the common people: manifesto for the general election, 1954.* Accra, C.P.P., 1954. 20 pp.

1529   CUDJOE, SETH D. *Aids to African autonomy: a review of education and politics in the Gold Coast.* College Press, 1950. 62 pp.

1530   DAILY GRAPHIC. ACCRA. *The Gold Coast and the constitution.* 1952. 31 pp.

1531   —— *Proposals on constitutional reform.* 1952. 28 pp.

1532   DANQUAH, JOSEPH BOAKYE. *The country's demand.* Saltpond, United Gold Coast Convention, 1950.

1533   —— *The doyen speaks:* a collection of speeches and letters by Dr. J. B. Danquah, collected by H. K. Akyeampong and edited by Moses Danquah. Accra, 1956. 58 pp.

1534   —— *First steps towards a national fund.* Accra, Gold Coast Youth Conference, 1938.

1535   —— *Friendship and Empire:* Gold Coast edition with speeches by A. Creech Jones and Herbert Morrison. Fabian Colonial Bureau, 1949. 35 pp.

1536   —— *Liberty of the subject: a monograph on the Gold Coast cocoa hold-up and boycott of foreign goods (1937–38), with prolegomena on the historical motives behind the Farmers' Movement.* Kibi, Boakie Publishing Co., [1938]. 63 pp.

1537   —— *Self-help and expansion: a review of the work and aims of the Youth Conference, with a statement of its policy for 1943, and the action consequent upon that policy.* Accra, Gold Coast Youth Conference, [1943]. 29 pp.

1538   —— *Ten-point programme and reaffirmation of policy.* Cape Coast, United Gold Coast Convention, 1950.

1539   DANQUAH, MOSES. *Political agitation in the Gold Coast.* Accra, United Gold Coast Convention, 1950.

1540   DAVIDSON, B., AND ADEMOLA, A., EDS. *The new West Africa: problems of independence.* Allen & Unwin, 1953. 184 pp.
       Political and social changes in the Gold Coast and Nigeria.

1541   DOVE, G. F. K. *The political philosophy of Kwame Nkrumah.* Washington, D.C., Howard University, 1955. 87 pp. (Unpublished thesis.)

1542 DRAKE, ST. C. 'Prospects for democracy in the Gold Coast.' *Ann. Amer. Acad. Pol. Soc. Sci.*, **306,** July 1956: 78–87.

1543 EDU, JOHN E. *The amazing story of the C.P.P.* Accra, New Gold Coast Publishing Co., 1954. 47 pp.

1544 —— *Gold Coast self-government (a brief review).* Cape Coast, the author, 1950. 53pp.

1545 —— *How Dr. Nkrumah conquered colonialism.* Accra, Heal Press, 1954. 44 pp.

1546 'Eweland unification: what are the facts? A government memorandum of some importance.' *W. Afr. Rev.*, **19,** 245, Feb. 1948: 141–143; March 1948: 256–257.

1547 FRAFRA, AZURE. 'Gold Coast Northern Territories and the new democracy: some points in its history and its place in the future.' *W. Afr. Rev.*, **21,** 268, Jan. 1950: 33–36.

1548 GOHOHO, M. F. *The Gold Coast adventure.* Accra, the author, [1952?]. 51 pp.

1549 *Gold Coast and the Constitution.* Accra, West African Graphic, 1952. 31 pp.

1550 GOLD COAST YOUTH CONFERENCE, CAPE COAST, 1938. *First steps towards a national fund; Better education and health; Trade and commerce; Marriage and inheritance; Funeral customs; The Syrian.* Accra, 1938.

1551 GOLD COAST YOUTH CONFERENCE, 1940. *Something to hate.* Accra, 1940.
    On 'The problem of our social and economic reconstruction in war and peace'. Akropong, 1940.

1552 GOLD COAST YOUTH CONFERENCE, 1942. *Are we to sit down?* Accra, 1942. 44 pp.
    Foreword by Dr. J. B. Danquah.

1553 GUNTHER, JOHN. *Inside Africa.* H. Hamilton, 1955. 960 pp.
    Includes concise references to the Gold Coast before independence.

1554 HAILEY, LORD. *Native administration in the British African territories. Part 3: West Africa, Nigeria, Gold Coast, Sierra Leone, Gambia.* H.M.S.O., 1950–3. 5 vols.

1555 HATCH, JOHN. 'Policies and politics in the Gold Coast.' *Africa south*, **1,** 1, Oct.–Dec. 1956: 107–115.

1556 HAYFORD, CASELY (i.e. Joseph Ephraim Casely). *Gold Coast native institutions: with thoughts upon a healthy imperial policy for the Gold Coast and Ashanti.* Sweet & Maxwell, 1913. 304 pp.

1557 —— *West African leadership,* by Magnus J. Sampson; [being] public speeches delivered by the Hon. J. E. Casely Hayford. Ilfracombe, Stockwell, [1949]. 160 pp.

1558 HODGKIN, THOMAS. *Freedom for the Gold Coast?* London, Union of Democratic Control, 1951. 14 pp.

1559 —— *Nationalism in colonial Africa.* Muller, 1956. 216 pp.

1560 IMORU, A. *The northerners' future in the balance.* Accra, United Press, [1953?]. 14 pp.

1561 JACKSON, B. WARD (i.e. Barbara E. Ward). 'The Gold Coast: an experiment in partnership.' *Foreign affairs* [N.Y.] **32,** 4, July 1954: 608–616.

1562 JONES–QUARTEY, K. A. B. 'Anglo-African journals and journalists in the nineteenth and early twentieth centuries.' *Tran. Hist. Soc. Ghana,* **4,** 1959: 47–56.

1563 —— *Problems of the press.* Bureau of Current Affairs, [195–]. 15 pp. (*West African affairs pamphlets, no. 5*).

1564 —— 'Thought and expression in the Gold Coast press, 1874–1930.' *Universitas,* **3,** 3, 1958: 72–75; **3,** 4, 113–116.

1565 KIMBLE, DAVID. *The machinery of self-government.* Penguin Books, 1953. 124 pp. (Penguin West African series.)

1566 —— *A political history of the Gold Coast, 1850–1929.* O.U.P., 1962. 516 pp.

1567 —— *Public opinion and government.* Bureau of Current Affairs, [1954?]. (West African affairs pamphlets, no. 2.)

1568 —— *The rise of nationalism in the Gold Coast, 1908–1928.* (Unpublished thesis, University of Ghana, 1960. 2 vols.)

1569 KWABENA BONNE III, NII. *Milestones in the history of the Gold Coast: autobiography of Nii Kwabena Bonne III, Osu Alata Mantse, also Nana Owusu Akenten III, Oyokohene of Techiman Ashanti.* Diplomatist Press, 1954. 92 pp.

1570 KWAW-SWANZY, B. E. *Constitutional development of the Gold Coast, 1901–25.* (Unpublished thesis, Cambridge University, 1955.)

1571   KYEREMATEN, A. A. Y. 'West Africa in transition.' *Africana*, **1, 2,** April 1949: 3–4.

1572   LE GROS CLARK, F., AND OTHERS. *The new West Africa: problems of independence.* Allen & Unwin, 1953. 184 pp.

1573   LEMKIN, J. Ed. *Race and power: studies of leadership in five British dependencies.* Bow Group, 1956.
    High tide along the Gold Coast, by J. Seekings, pp. 37–56.

1574   MCCARTHY, J. C. *The 'Trials of Ghana':* (towards self-government). Accra, 1950.

1575   MACMILLAN, W. M. *African development: political and social reconstruction: the peculiar case of the Gold Coast Colony.* 1940.

1576   MATE KOLE, NENE AZZU. 'The Gold Coast: development in native states.' *Corona*, **2,** 12, Dec. 1950: 446–449.

1577   MUNGER, EDWIN S. *African field reports, 1952–1961.* Cape Town, Struik, 1961. 808 pp.
    American Universities Field Staff reports.

1578   NATIONAL DEMOCRATIC PARTY. *The road to sure, solid self-government; the manifesto of the National Democratic Party.* Accra, 1951.

1579   NATIONAL LIBERATION MOVEMENT. *Statement by the National Liberation Movement and its allies on the Gold Coast Government's constitutional proposals for Gold Coast independence.* Kumasi, Abura Printing Works, 1956. 8 pp.

1580   NICHOLSON, MARJORIE. *West African ferment.* Fabian Publications, 1950. 44 pp.

1581   NKRUMAH, KWAME. *Address by the Prime Minister to the Trans-Volta Togoland Council, Ho, Tuesday 24th August, 1954.* Accra, Govt. Printer, 1954. 4 pp.

1582   —— *Education and nationalism in West Africa.* 1943.

1583   —— *Motion for Gold Coast independence made by the Prime Minister in the Legislative Assembly of 3rd August, 1956.* Accra, Govt. Printer, 1956.

1584   —— 'Movement for colonial freedom.' *Phylon [Atlanta].* **16, 4,** 1955: 397–409.

1585   —— *Padmore the missionary: an address on the opening of the George Padmore Memorial Library, 30th June 1961.* Accra, Govt. Printer, 1961. 5pp.

9

1586   NKRUMAH, KWAME. *Revised constitutional proposals: speech delivered in the Legislative Assembly on November 12th, 1956.* 14 pp. (Supplement to *The Gold Coast today*, I, 24, Dec. 1956.)

1587   —— *Towards colonial freedom.* London, 1947.

1588   ——*What I mean by Positive Action.* Accra, C.P.P., 1949.

1589   PADMORE, GEORGE. *Africa: Britain's third empire.* Dobson, 1949.

1590   —— *Africa and the world peace.* 1937.

1591   —— *The Gold Coast revolution: the struggle of an African people from slavery to freedom.* Dobson, 1953. 272 pp.

1592   —— 'Pan-Africanism and Ghana.' *United Asia*, 9, 1, 1957: 50–54.

1593   —— *Pan-Africanism or communism? The coming struggle for Africa.* Dobson, 1956. 463 pp. Also published Accra, Guinea Press.

1594   POKU, OHENANA JOHN KOFI. *Hints on "Yeate yen ho" (Federation): Asante and English.* Kumasi, Abura Printing Works, [1955]. [46] pp. Author is General Secretary, Asante Farmers' Union.

1595   POLARIS. 'The N.T.'s in Gold Coast politics.' *West Africa*, 8 May—5 June, 1954.

1596   PRICE, J. H. *The Gold Coast election, 1951.* Bureau of Current Affairs, [195-]. 15 pp. (West African affairs pamphlets, no. 11.)

1597   PUBLIUS SERVUS. *The civil service.* Bureau of Current Affairs, [195-]. (West African affairs pamphlets, no. 18.)

1598   REDMAYNE, P. *The Gold Coast yesterday and today.* Chatto & Windus, 1938. 124 pp.

1599   RICHARDSON, K. E. *Self-help: the recipe for national progress (food for reflection).* Cape Coast, the author, [1950]. 64 pp.

1600   ROBINSON, KWASI. 'Background to Gold Coast nationalism.' *West Africa*, 1741–9, 8 July—2 Sept. 1950.

1601   RUSSELL, A. C., AND OTHERS. 'The Gold Coast general election, 1951.' *J. Afr. admin.*, 3, 2, April 1951: 65–77.

1602   SEEKINGS, JOHN. 'High tide along the Gold Coast' (in LEMKIN, J., *Race and power*, 1956: 37–56).

1603   SHAW, C. THURSTAN. 'Further difficulties of indirect rule in the Gold Coast.' *Man*, 45, 20, March-April 1945: 27–30.

1604   TIMOTHY, E. BANKOLE. *Bankole Timothy's notebook.* Accra, 1953. 31 pp.

1605 TIMOTHY, E. BANKOLE. 'The press in West Africa.' *Afr. world*, Oct. 1951: 11–12.

1606 UNITED GOLD COAST CONVENTION (The Peoples' Organisation). *Letter to Nananom in Council touching the controversial issues in the Coussey Report*. Saltpond, 1950. 16 pp. (Chairman, George A. Grant.)

1607 —— *The 'P' plan: U.G.C.C.'s seven-point scheme for Gold Coast liberation*. Saltpond, U.G.C.C., 1952. 14 pp. (Forward by George A. Grant.)

1608 UNITED NATIONS. TRUSTEESHIP COUNCIL. *The Ewe problem*. N.Y. United Nations, 1951. (T.L. 131.)

1609 —— *Special report on the Ewe and Togoland unification problem, together with related documents*. N.Y., United Nations, 1954. 57 pp. (U.N. visiting mission, 1952. T/1105.) (Chairman, Roy A. Peachey.)

1610 WALLACE-JOHNSON, ISAAC T. 'A full and illustrated report of the proceedings of the restoration of the Ashanti Confederacy, January 31–February 4, 1935.' [Kumasi]. *West African Sentinel*, [1935]. 40 pp.

1611 *Why C.M.B.—C.P.C. probe! Petitions submitted by Asanteman Council, farmers, N.L.M. & allies, and the Opposition in the Legislative Assembly*. Kumasi, Abura Printing Works, [1955?]. 57 pp.

1612 WISEMAN, H. V. 'The Gold Coast, from executive council to responsible cabinet.' *Parl. affairs*, **10**, 1, Winter 1956–57: 27–35.

1613 YEN, KWESI. *The achievements of Dr. Kwame Nkrumah*. Accra, Heal Press, [1954]. 19 pp.

1614 —— *The street boys on the march to freedom*. Accra, Quality Press, 1954. 23 pp.

Ghana

1615 ADAM, THOMAS R. *Government and politics in Africa south of the Sahara*. N.Y., Random House, 1959.

1616 AFRIKA INSTITUUT, LEIDEN. *Ghana, 6 Maart 1957*. Rotterdam, Afrika Instituut, 1957. 43 pp.

1617 'After the Queen's tour—what?' *Africa report*, Dec. 1961: 11.

1618 AGARWALA, C. B. 'The government of Ghana.' *Foreign Affairs Reports*, **9**, 8, août 1960: 87–95.

1619   ALL-AFRICAN PEOPLE'S CONFERENCE. ACCRA, 1958. *Conference resolution on imperialism and colonialism.* Accra, Govt. Printer, 1959. 12 pp.

1620   AMAMOO, JOSEPH G. 'Ghana and the western democracies.' *Afr. affairs,* **58,** 230, Jan. 1959: 54–60.

1621   —— *The new Ghana: the birth of a nation.* Pan Books, 1958. 145 pp.

1622   AMPAH, E. B. K. *Osagyefo in the Central Region.* Accra, Guinea Press, [1960]. 67 pp.

1623   ARDEN-CLARKE, SIR CHARLES N. 'The west and Africa's challenge.' *Afr. affairs,* **60,** 241, Oct. 1961: 501–507.

1624   ARTHUR, JOHN. *Freedom for Africa.* Accra, the author, 1961. 199 pp. [Printed in Leipzig.]

1625   —— *"Mile 51": in honour of Osagyefo's 51st birthday.* Accra, Guinea Press, 1960. 84 pp.

1626   —— *One Africa: published in honour of Osagyefo's 52nd birthday.* [Accra, the author, 1961.] 76 pp. [Printed in the German Democratic Republic.]

1627   ASANTE, K. B. 'Towards the future in Ghana.' *Afr. affairs,* **57,** 226, Jan. 1956: 52–57.

1628   AUSTIN, DENNIS. 'The Ghana Parliament's first year.' *Parl. affairs,* **II,** 3, summer 1958: 350–360.

1629   —— 'The Ghana government.' *Africa south,* **3,** 3, April–June 1959: 90–96.

1630   —— 'Ghana since independence.' *World today,* Oct. 1961: 424–435.

1631   —— 'Ghana's north to-day.' *W. Afr. Rev.,* Aug. 1960: 18–22.

1632   BELGRADE CONFERENCE, 1961. *The conference of Heads of State or Government of non-aligned countries, Belgrade, September 1–6, 1961.* Accra, Ministry of Information, 1961. 339 pp.

1633   BOYON, J. *Naissance d'un état africain: le Ghana.* Paris, Colin, 1958. 273 pp.

1634   BRETTON, HENRY L. 'Current political thought and practice in Ghana.' *Amer. Pol. Sci. Rev.,* **52,** 1, March 1958: 46–63.

1635   BRITISH SOCIETY FOR INTERNATIONAL UNDERSTANDING. *Ghana.* 1957. 20 pp.

1636   —— *Ghana since independence.* 1959. 24 pp.

1637 BRUWER, J. F. 'Die geboorte van 'n onafhanklike staat in Afrika—Ghana.' [Birth of an independent state—Ghana.] *J. Racial affairs*, **8**, 2, Jan. 1957: 52–67.

1638 BUDU-ACQUAH, K. *Ghana: the morning after*... Goodwin Press, 1961. 127 pp.

1639 CAMERON, J. *The African revolution*. Thames & Hudson, 1961. 199 pp.

1640 CARTER, GWENDOLEN MARGARET. *Independence for Africa*. Thames & Hudson, 1961. xix, 172 pp.

1641 CASABLANCA CONFERENCE, 1961. [*Report of*] *Conference of Heads of African States at Casablanca, 3rd–7th January, 1961*. Accra, Govt. Printer, 1961. 12 pp.

1642 CHAPMAN, DANIEL A. *Radio, television & press interviews, December 3, 1957–May 23, 1958, given by His Excellency Daniel A. Chapman, Ambassador of Ghana to the United States*. Washington, D.C., Embassy of Ghana, 1958. 38 pp. (Typescript.)

1643 —— *Speeches delivered November 14, 1957–July 9, 1958, by His Excellency Daniel A. Chapman, Ambassador of Ghana to the United States*. Washington, D.C., Embassy of Ghana, 1958. 33 pp. (Typescript.)

1644 CONFERENCE OF INDEPENDENT AFRICAN STATES, ACCRA, 1958. *General report*. Accra, Govt. Printer, [1959]. 44 pp. Text in English and French.

1645 —— *Final communiqué*. Accra, Govt. Printer, 1958.

1646 CROCKER, W. R. *Self-government for the colonies*. Allen & Unwin, 1959. vi, 177 pp.

1647 CROWDER, M. *Pagans and politicians*. Hutchinson, 1959. 224 pp.

1648 DE SMITH, S. A. 'The independence of Ghana.' *Modern Law Rev.*, **20**, 1957: 347–363.

1649 *Deutsche Aussenpolitik: Afrikanische Gegenwartsfragen*. Berlin, Rütten & Loening, 1960. 219 pp.

1650 DONKOR, ALBERT. *A soliloquy of Africa: a special dedication to the late George Padmore*. Accra, Guinea Press, [1960]. 16 pp.

1651 DUBROWIN, L. *Goldküste errang Unabhängigkeit*. Presse der Sowjetunion [Berlin]. 1957.

1652 DUCHEIN, R. N. *The Pan-African manifesto*. Accra, Guinea Press, [1959].

1653 EDU, JOHN E. *Would you be a Ghana hero?* Accra, the author, 1959.

1654 *Ghana.* Africa Bureau, 1957. 4 pp. (Background facts, no. 1.)

1655 'Ghana's first five years.' *W. Afr. Rev.*, Jan. 1962: 16–17.

1656 'Ghana's role in world affairs.' *Afr. World Annual*, 1961: 36–37.

1657 HANSARD SOCIETY FOR PARLIAMENTARY GOVERNMENT. *The Parliament of Ghana* [by Peter Regent]. Hansard Society, 1959. 23 pp.

1658 —— *What are the problems of parliamentary government in West Africa?* The report of a conference held by the Hansard Society for Parliamentary Government at St. Edmund Hall, Oxford, September 1957, under the chairmanship of Geoffrey de Freitas, M. P. Hansard Society, [1958]. 180 pp.

1659 HILTON, THOMAS ERIC. 'Land planning and resettlement in northern Ghana.' *Geography* [*Sheffield*], **44**, Nov. 1959: 227–240.

1660 HINTZE, U. *Wie Ghana seine Unabhängigkeit erkämpfte.* Deutsche Außenpolitik, 1957.

1661 HUTCHINSON, A. *Road to Ghana.* Gollancz, 1960. 190 pp.
An account by one of the accused in the South African treason trial.

1662 JAHODA, GUSTAV. *White man: a study of the attitudes of Africans to Europeans in Ghana before independence.* O.U.P., 1961. 144 pp.

1663 JANTZEN, GUNTHER. *Ghana: Betrachtungen zum Unabhängigkeitstag am 6. März, 1957.* Bonn, Deutsche Afrika-Gesellschaft, 1957. (Schriftenreihe, 2.) 24 pp.

1664 JONES-QUARTEY, K. A. B. 'Press and nationalism in Ghana.' *United Asia*, **9**, 1, 1957: 55–60.

1665 KIMBLE, GEORGE H. T. 'Ghana.' *Focus*, **9**, 8, April 1959: 6.

1666 LARMIE, E. B. *A republic for Ghana?* Accra, the author, 1959. 8 pp.

1667 LEGUM, COLIN. *Bandung, Cairo & Accra: a report on the first Conference of Independent African States.* Africa Bureau, 1958. 32 pp.

1668 LINZE, DIETRICH W. 'Ghana: Gliedstaat des Britischen Commonwealth of Nations.' Mitt. Inst. Auslandsbeziehungen, **9**, 4, Oct.–Dec. 1959: 234–247.

1669 MELADY, THOMAS P. *An evaluation of the United States' position in Guinea, Liberia and Ghana.* Pittsburgh, Duquesne University, Institute of African Affairs, 1960. 18 pp.

1670 MENDIAUX, EDOUARD. *Moscou, Accra et le Congo*. Brussels, Dessart, 1960. 198 pp.

1671 MILSOME, J. R. 'West Africa and U.N.O.' *W. Afr. Rev.*, **30**, 385, 1959: 901–903.

1672 MOELLER DE LADDERSOUS, A. J. 'L'état de Ghana.' *Acad. roy. Sci. colon.*, **3**, 4, 1957: 717–747.

1673 MUNGER, EDWIN S. 'All-African People's Conference: a report' (in MUNGER, E. S. *African field reports, 1952–1961*).

1674 —— 'Ghana: striking a balance between plus and minus' (in MUNGER, E. S. *African field reports, 1952–1961*).

1675 NEW YORK TIMES. *Republic of Ghana: new frontier of democracy. . . new land of opportunity*. 1960. 16 pp.

1676 NKRUMAH, KWAME. *Address at the closing session of the Casablanca Conference on Saturday, 7th January 1961*. Accra, Govt. Printer, 1961. 4 pp.

1677 —— *Address to the resumed session of the 15th General Assembly of the United Nations*. Accra, Ministry of Information, 1961. 48 pp.

1678 —— *An address by Osagyefo Dr. Kwame Nkrumah to the 15th Session of the General Assembly of the United Nations on Friday 23rd September, 1960*. Accra, Govt. Printer, 1960.

1679 —— *Address to the 15th Session of the General Assembly of the United Nations*. N.Y., United Nations, 1960. 17 pp.

1680 —— *An address to the National Assembly on African affairs, August 8, 1960*. Accra, Govt. Printer, 1960. 20 pp.

1681 —— *Africa must be free: a message delivered on the third anniversary of Africa Freedom Day, April 15, 1961*. Accra, Govt. Printer, 1961. 4 pp.

1682 —— *African unity: a speech on opening Africa Unity House in London, 18th March 1961*. Accra, Govt. Printer, 1961. 4 pp.

1683 —— *Appeal for world peace: text of an address to the Conference of Non-Aligned Countries in Belgrade on September 2nd, 1961*. Accra, Govt. Printer, 1962. 19 pp.

1684 —— *Allocution prononcée devant l'Assemblée Nationale sur les affaires africaines*. Accra, Govt. Printer, 1960. 21 pp.

1685 —— *Christmas Eve broadcast, 24th December, 1957*. Accra, Govt. Printer, 1957. 4 pp.

1686 NKRUMAH, KWAME. *The city of Accra: speech declaring Accra a city, on Wednesday 29th March, 1961.* Accra, Govt. Printer, 1961. 4 pp.

1687 —— *The C.P.P. 12th anniversary: a message by Osagyefo.* Accra, Govt. Printer, 1961. 3 pp.

1688 —— *Dawn broadcast on Saturday morning, April 8, 1961.* Accra, Govt. Printer, 1961. 9 pp.

1689 —— *The fight on two fronts: a speech on assuming office as General Secretary of the C.P.P. on May 1, 1961.* Accra, Govt. Printer, 1961. 11 pp.

1690 —— *Ghana's policy at home and abroad: speech given in the Ghana Parliament, August 29, 1957.* Washington, D.C., Ghana Embassy Information Service, 1957. 14 pp.

1691 —— *Guide to party action: address at the first seminar at the Winneba Ideological School, on 3rd February, 1962.* Accra, C.P.P., 1962. 16 pp.

1692 ——*Hands off Africa: some famous speeches, with a tribute to George Padmore.* Accra, Ministry of Local Govt., 1960. 62 pp.

1693 —— *I speak of freedom: a statement of African ideology.* Heinemann, 1961. 291 pp.
      Also published N.Y., Praeger, 1961.

1694 —— *Laying of the foundation stone of the Kwame Nkrumah Institute: an address.* Accra, Govt. Printer, 1961. 9 pp.

1695 —— *New horizons: sessional report on the first session of the first Parliament of Ghana.* Accra, Govt. Printer, 1961. 7 pp.

1696 —— *New Year message on 1st January, 1961.* Accra, Govt. Printer, 1961. 8 pp.

1697 —— *Osagyefo at the United Nations: an address.* Accra, Govt. Printer, 1960. 22 pp.

1698 —— *Osagyefo speaks: two addresses given during the first anniversary of the inauguration of the Republic of Ghana.* Accra, Govt. Printer, 1961. 8 pp.

1699 —— *The road ahead: Osagyefo speaks to the National Assembly on current affairs.* Accra, Govt. Printer, 1961. 9 pp.

1700 —— *Season of goodwill: Osagyefo's New Year broadcast to the nation.* Accra, Govt. Printer, 1962. 15 pp.

1701 —— *South Africa and the Commonwealth: two statements bearing upon South Africa's apartheid system and her decision to withdraw from the Commonwealth, March 1961.* Accra, Govt. Printer, 1961. 4 pp.

1702 NKRUMAH, KWAME. *Speech on foreign policy in the National Assembly on 15th July, 1958.* Accra, Govt. Printer, 1958. 4 pp.

1703 —— *Speech on foreign policy, 16th December, 1959.* Accra, Govt. Printer, 1959. 11 pp.

1704 —— *State opening of Parliament, 4th July, 1961.* Accra, Govt. Printer, 1961. 22 pp.

1705 —— *Statement on certain aspects of African unity.* Accra, Govt. Printer, 1962. 5 pp.

1706 —— *Tragedy in Angola: an address to the National Assembly of Ghana.* Accra, Govt. Printer, 1961. 13 pp.

1707 —— *Visit to Nigeria by the Prime Minister of Ghana, Dr. Kwame Nkrumah: speeches made by Dr. Nkrumah during his tour of the Federation from January 26th to February 6th, 1959.* Accra, Govt. Printer, 1959. 35 pp.

1708 —— *The voice of Africa: speech on the opening of the Ghana External Broadcasting Service.* Accra, Govt. Printer, 1961. 3 pp.

1709 —— *Work for Ghana and the future: broadcast to the nation on 20th September, 1961.* Accra, Govt. Printer, 1961. 6 pp.

1710 OFORI ATTA, W. *The challenge of our time.* Accra, the author, [1960]. 5 pp.
Supports Opposition Presidential candidate, Dr. J. B. Danquah.

1711 —— *The true pioneer (Dr. J. B. Danquah).* Accra, United Party, [1960]. 5 pp.

1712 PFEFFER, KARL HEINZ. *Ghana: menschlich-soziale Grundlagen für die wirtschaftliche Entwicklung eines jungen Staatswesens.* Hamburg, Verlag Weltarchiv, 1961. 81 pp.

1713 —— *Ghana.* Bonn, Schroeder, 1958. 104 pp. (Deutsche Afrika-Gesellschaft der Länder Afrikas, Bd. 5.)

1714 POTEKHIN, I. I. *Ghana segodnya: dnevnik, 1957.* [Ghana today: diary, 1957.] Moscow, Geografizdat, 1959. 158 pp.
A record of Dr. Potekhin's visit to Ghana from 14th October to 23rd December, 1957. He is Director of the Institut Afriki, Akademie Nauk, Moscow.

1715 —— 'Novoe Afrikanskoe Gosudarstvo—Ghana.' [A new African state—Ghana.] *Soviet. Etnogr.,* **2,** 1957: 106–116.

1716 PRÉSENCE AFRICAINE. 'Hier Gold Coast, aujourd'hui Ghana.' *Présence Afr.,* **12,** fev.–mars 1957.

1717 PRICE, J. H. 'How democracy works in Ghana.' *Universitas*, **4,** 4, 1960: 105–106.

1718 RAYMOND, R. *Black star in the wind.* MacGibbon & Kee, 1960. 288 pp.

1719 REDMAYNE, P. *Gold Coast to Ghana.* Murray, 1957. 48 pp.

1720 'The Republic of Ghana.' *Commonwealth survey*, **6,** 15, July 1960: 667.

1721 ROYAL INSTITUTE OF INTERNATIONAL AFFAIRS.*Ghana: a brief political and economic survey.* 1957. 65 pp.

1722 —— *Ghana: a survey of the Gold Coast on the eve of independence.* 1957. 62 pp.

1723 SCHMIDT, U. 'Ein neuer afrikanischer Staat—die Republik Ghana.' *Einheit*, **12**, 1957.

1724 THEOBALD, ROBERT, Ed. *The new nations of West Africa.* N.Y., Wilson, 1960. 179 pp. (The reference shelf, no. 2.)

1725 THE TIMES. *Supplement on Ghana.* 9th Nov. 1959. xii pp.

1726 TOURÉ, SEKOU. *Speech delivered by President Sekou Touré on the occasion of the proclamation of the Republic of Ghana.* Accra, Govt. Printer, 1960. 19 pp.

1727 UNION OF AFRICAN STATES. *Charter for the Union of African States.* Accra, Govt. Printer, 1961. 8 pp.

1728 UNITED PARTY. *Ghana at the cross-roads: a statement by the National Executive of the United Party on the Government's decision to change Ghana into a Republic.* Accra, U.P., 1960. 11 pp.

1729 —— *In defence of Ghana: a statement by the National Executive of the United Party on the Granville Sharp Commission's reports and the Government's White Paper on the reports.* Accra, U.P., 1959. 35 pp.

1730 —— *Unwarranted detention: a plea to the legal conscience.* Accra, U.P., 1959. 15 pp.

1731 UWANAKA, CHARLES U. *The story of Ghana independence.* Lagos, Pacific Printing and Publishing Works, [1957]. 56 pp.

1732 WALTER, GERARD. *Goldküste wird Ghana.* Berlin, Rütten & Loening, 1961. 145 pp. (Taschenbuch Geschichte.)

1733 'The West sets the pace.' *W. Afr. Rev.*, Oct. 1959: 701–703.

1734   'What sort of socialism for Ghana?' *New Commonwealth*, June 1961: 391–392.

1735   WILLIAMS, CHANCELLOR. *The rebirth of African civilization.* Washington D.C., Public Affairs Press, 1961. 328 pp.
Political Ghana, pp. 121–130.

1736   *With friends in Africa.* Belgrade, "Jugoslavia", 1961. [70] pp. Record of the visit of Marshal Tito.

Biography

Collective

1737 DYKE, F. A. *Lebanese and Syrians in the Gold Coast.* Accra, the author, 1953. 50 pp.

1738 FAX, ELTON C. *West Africa vignettes.* N.Y., American Society of African Culture, 1960. 62 pp.
   Includes portraits of Philip Gbeho, Evelyn Amarteifio and Seth D. Cudjoe.

1739 HUTCHINSON, CHARLES FRANCIS. *The pen-pictures of modern Africans and African celebrities.* Vol 1. African Library Press, [1931 ?]. 207 pp.

1740 MELADY, THOMAS P. *Profiles of African leaders.* Macmillan N.Y., 1961. 186 pp.

1741 ROGERS, J. A. *World's great men of color.* N.Y., the author, 1947. 2 vols.
   Includes short biographies of Osei Tutu and King Prempeh (d. 1931).

1742 SAMPSON, MAGNUS J. *Gold Coast men of affairs: past and present.* Ilfracombe, Stockwell, 1937. 224 pp.

1743 SEGAL, RONALD, ED. *Political Africa: a who's who of political personalities and parties.* Stevens, 1961. ix, 475 pp.

Individual

Aggrey, J. E. K. (Vice-Principal of Achimota College)

1744 ADU, AMMISHADDAI. 'The real Aggrey.' *W. Afr. Rev.*, April 1953: 381–384.

1745 CHIRGWIN, A. M. *Yarns on men of Africa.* Edinburgh House Press, 1931. 70 pp.
   Kwegyir Aggrey, p. 55+

1746 GREAT BRITAIN. CENTRAL OFFICE OF INFORMATION. *Aggrey of Africa* (1875–1927). H.M.S.O., 1948. 8 pp. (British Commonwealth leaflets.)

1747 MACARTNEY, W. M. *Dr. Aggrey: ambassador for Africa.* S.C.M. Press, [1949]. 106 pp.

1748 MUSSON, M. *Aggrey of Achimota.* Lutterworth Press, 1944. 56 pp. (Africa's own library, no. 7.)

1749 PARR, JARDINE. *Famous names in Africa.* Evans, 1962. 64 pp. (Records of achievement series.) Dr. Aggrey, pp. 55–60.

1750 SMITH, EDWIN W. *Aggrey of Africa: a study in black and white.* N.Y., Doubleday; S.C.M. Press, 1929. 292 pp.

1751 —— *Aggrey the African,* being Edwin W. Smith's "Aggrey of Africa" edited as a simpler and shorter story by C. Kingsley Williams. Sheldon Press, 1933. 144 pp.

Amo, Anton Wilhelm

1752 LOCHNER, NORBERT. 'Anton Wilhelm Amo: a Ghana scholar in eighteenth century Germany.' *Trans. Hist. Soc. Ghana,* **3,** 1957: 169–179.

Ankrah, R. (Professional boxer)

1753 ANKRAH, R. *My life story.* Accra, Daily Graphic, 1952. 30 pp.

Armattoe, Raphael Ernest Grail

1754 KWAKU, WILLIAM A. 'Raphael Ernest Glikpo Armattoe (1913–1953).' *Afrika und Übersee,* **38,** 3, June 1954: 111–112.

Aron-Kuku

1755 WIEGRÄBE, PAUL. *Aus dem Leben des afrikanischen Evangelisten Aron-Kuku: nach einem Ewe-Originalmanuskript übersetzt.* Bremen, Norddeutsche Missions-Gesellschaft, 1930.

Blankson, George K. (First African member of the British Legislative Council in the Gold Coast)

1756 AKITA, J. M. 'Biographical sketch of George Blankson of Anomabu (1809–1898).' *Trans. Gold Coast & Togoland Hist. Soc.,* **I,** 1955: 217–222.

Boyle, D. (District Commissioner in Ashanti and Accra, 1914–1917)

1757 BOYLE, D. *With ardours manifold.* Hutchinson, 1959. 339 pp.

Brew, Richard

1758 PRIESTLEY, MARGARET. 'Richard Brew: an eighteenth-century trader at Anomabu.' *Trans. Hist. Soc. Ghana,* 4, 1959: 29–46.

Burns, Sir Alan (Governor of the Gold Coast 1941–1947)

1759 BURNS, SIR ALAN. *Colonial civil servant.* Allen & Unwin, 1950. 324 pp.

Danquah, Joseph Boakye (Ghanaian writer, lawyer and politician)

1760 DANQUAH, JOSEPH BOAKYE. *Liberty: a page from the life of J.B.* Accra, H. K. Akyeampong, [1960]. 34 pp.

Duff, Sir Hector

1761 DUFF, SIR HECTOR. *African small chop.* Hodder & Stoughton, 1932.

Ferguson, George Ekem (Surveyor and British agent in the Northern Territories, born at Anomabu in 1864, died 1897)

1762 SAMPSON, MAGNUS J. 'George Ekem Ferguson of Anomabu.' *Trans. Gold Coast & Togoland Hist. Soc.,* 2, 1956: 30–45.

Fraser, Alexander Garden (First Principal of Achimota College)

1763 WARD, WILLIAM ERNEST FRANK. *A.G.F.: 1873–1962.* Accra, Govt. Printer, [1962]. 57 pp.

Freeman, Thomas Birch (Wesleyan Methodist missionary pioneer in West Africa)

1764 BIRTWISTLE, ALLEN. 'Missionary administrator: the story of Thomas Birch Freeman.' *W. Afr. Rev.,* Dec. 1951: 1392–1395.

1765 —— *Thomas Birch Freeman: West African pioneer.* Cargate Press, 1950. 112 pp.

1766 WALKER, F. DEAVILLE. *Thomas Birch Freeman: the son of an American.* S.C.M. Press [1929?]. 221 pp.

Gbedema, Komla Agbeli

1767 MUNGER, EDWIN S. 'Ghana's Finance Minister: Komla Abeli Gbedemah' (in MUNGER, E. S. *African field reports, 1952–1961*).

Griffith, Sir William Brandford

1768 GRIFFITH, SIR WILLIAM BRANDFORD. *The far horizon: portrait of a colonial judge.* Ilfracombe, Stockwell, 1951. 319 pp.

Holt, John (Founder of the merchant shipping line in West Africa)

1769 HOLT, C. R., ED. *The diary of John Holt, 1862–1872.* Liverpool, Young, 1948. 278 pp.

Howard-Bennett, Rosemary (Anglican sister at Mampong)

1770 HOWARD-BENNETT, ROSEMARY. *I choose the cloister.* Hodder & Stoughton, 1956. 125 pp.

Maclean, George (British Administrator in the Gold Coast, 1830–1844)

1771 METCALFE, G. E. *Maclean of the Gold Coast: the life and times of George Maclean, 1801–1847.* O.U.P., 1962. Forthcoming.

1772 MOSELEY, MABOTH. 'Maclean of the Gold Coast.' *W. Afr. Rev.*, March–August 1952: 234+

Nkrumah, Kwame (President of Ghana)

1773 ADAMAFIO, T. *A portrait of the Osagyefo, Dr. Kwame Nkrumah.* Accra, Govt. Printer, 1960. 6 pp.

1774 AMES, SOPHIA RIPLEY. *Nkrumah of Ghana.* Chicago, Rand McNally, 1961. 184 pp.

1775 NKRUMAH, KWAME. *The autobiography of Kwame Nkrumah.* Nelson, 1957. 310 pp. Paperback edition, 1959.
American edition has title: *Ghana, the autobiography of Kwame Nkrumah.*

1776 ——— *Schwarze Fanfare.* Berlin, Paul List Verlag, 1958.
German translation of his autobiography.

1777 PHILLIPS, JOHN. *Kwame Nkrumah and the future of Africa.* Faber, 1960. 272 pp.

1778 POWELL, ERICA. *Kwame Nkrumah of the new Africa;* adapted from *Ghana,* the autobiography of Kwame Nkrumah. Nelson, 1961. iv, 68 pp.

1779 TIMOTHY, E. BANKOLE. *Kwame Nkrumah: his rise to power.* Allen & Unwin, 1955. 201 pp.

Quaque, *Philip* (First African chaplain at Cape Coast)

1780   BARTELS, F. L. 'Philip Quaque, 1741–1816.' *Trans. Gold Coast & Togoland Hist. Soc.*, **I**, 1955: 153–177.

Reindorf, *Carl Christian* (Pastor of the Basel Mission and author of *The history of the Gold Coast and Asante*, 1895)

1781   REINDORF, C. E. *Memoir of late Rev. Carl Christian Reindorf.* Accra, Arrow Printing Press, [192–]. 16 pp.

Law

1782 ADJETEY, PETER A. 'Some legal consequences of polygamous marriage in Ghana.' *Universitas*, 4, 6, 1961: 168–171.

1783 AFRIKA INSTITUUT, LEIDEN. *Future of customary law in Africa*. Leiden, University Press, 1956. 323 pp.

1784 AKYEMPIM, OWUSU. *The native court and its functions*. Kumasi, Adom Press, [1955]. 30 pp.

1785 ALLOTT, A. N. 'The effect of marriage on property in the Gold Coast.' *Int. & Comp. Law Quarterly*, 5, 4, Oct. 1956: 519–533.

1786 —— *Essays in African law, with special reference to the law of Ghana*. Butterworth, 1960. 323 pp.

1787 —— 'Gold Coast law reform' *West Africa*, 2, 9, Feb. 1957: 105, 127.

1788 —— 'Marriage and internal conflict of laws in Ghana.' *J. Afr. Law*, 2, 3, autumn 1958: 164–184.

1789 —— 'Native tribunals in the Gold Coast, 1844–1927: prolegomena to a study of native courts in Ghana.' *J. Afr. Law*, 1, 3, 1957: 165–171.

1790 ANDERSON, JAMES NORMAN DALRYMPLE. *Islamic law in Africa*. H.M.S.O., 1954. viii, 409 pp.

1791 BENNION, F. A. R. *Constitutional law in Ghana*. Butterworth. Forthcoming.

1792 [BRYDEN, A. L.] *Gold Coast death sentences*. Solicitors' Law Stationery Society, 1947. 59 pp. [Privately printed.]

1793 CHRISTIAN COUNCIL OF THE GOLD COAST. *Memorandum on the customary law of inheritance: addressed to the chiefs and people of the Gold Coast*. Achimota, College Press, 1934. 16 pp.

1794 DAVIES, S. G. 'The growth of law in the Gold Coast.' *Universitas*, 2, 1, Dec. 1955: 4–6.

1795 —— *The West African law reports*. Vol 1. Achimota, West African Law Publishing Co., 1956. 288 pp.

1796 ELIAS, TASLIM OLAWALE. *Ghana and Sierra Leone: the development of their laws and constitutions.* Stevens, 1962. 334 pp. (The British Commonwealth: the development of its laws and constitutions, no. 10.)

1797 —— *The nature of African customary law.* Manchester U.P., 1956. xii, 318 pp.

1798 GILLESPIE, W. H. *The Gold Coast police, 1844–1938.* Accra, Govt. Printer, 1955. 91 pp.

1799 GRIFFITH, SIR WILLIAM BRANDFORD. *A digest of and index to the reports of cases decided in the Supreme Court of the Gold Coast Colony.* Accra, Govt. Printer, 1953.

1800 —— *A note on the history of the British courts in the Gold Coast Colony, with a brief account of the changes in the constitution of the Colony.* Accra, Govt. Printer, 1936.

1801 HAMILTON, JOHN A. *Crime and punishment.* Bureau of Current Affairs, 1951. 19 pp. (West African affairs pamphlets, no. 19.)

1802 HANNIGAN, A. ST. J. J. 'The impact of English law upon the existing Gold Coast custom and the possible development of the resulting systems.' *J. Afr. admin.,* **8,** 3, July 1956: 126–132.

1803 —— 'Introduction of registration of title to land.' *Universitas,* **2,** 2, March 1956: 41–43.

1804 —— 'Native custom: its similarity to English conventional custom and its mode of proof.' *J. Afr. law,* **2,** 2, 1958: 101–115.

1805 HEDGES, R. Y. 'Legal education in West Africa.' *J. Soc. Public Teachers of Law,* **6,** 1961: 75–79.

1806 KORSAH, SIR ARKU. *Law in the Republic of Ghana: being a series of addresses in July and November, 1960.* Accra, Ministry of Information, 1961. 29 pp.

1807 LIECK, A. *The trial of Benjamin Knowles.* Hodge, 1933. 215 pp.
      The murder trial of the D.C. of Bekwai.

1808 LOVERIDGE, A. J. 'Note on the development of land tenures in the Gold Coast.' *J. Roy., Afr. Soc.,* **42,** 166, Jan. 1943: 31–33.

1809 —— 'Wills and the customary law in the Gold Coast.' *J. Afr. admin.,* **2,** 4, 1950.

1810 MAIR, LUCY P. 'Land tenure in the Gold Coast.' *Civilisations,* **2,** 2, 1952: 183–188.

1811 MATSON, J. N. 'The Supreme Court and the customary judicial process in the Gold Coast.' *Int. & Comp. Law Quarterly*, **2**, 1, Jan. 1953: 47–59.

1812 MEEK, C. K. *Land law and custom in the colonies.* O.U.P., 1946.

1813 'Native tribunals in the Gold Coast.' *Crown Colonist*, **13**, 144, Nov. 1943: 770.

1814 NIVEN, C. R., AND EGBUNA, ERNEST. *Notes on parliamentary procedure.* Hansard Society, 1957. 15 pp.
Intended for African legislators.

1815 NKRUMAH, KWAME. *The old and the new: law in Africa. Speech at the Conference on Legal Education at the Ghana Law School, Accra, 1962.* Accra, Govt. Printer, 1962. 8 pp.

1816 OFORI, DAVID. *Kibi "ritual murder": an inside story of a sensational so-called "ritual murder" case.* Accra, Heal Press, 1947. 36 pp.

1817 OLLENNU, N. A. 'The influence of English law on West Africa.' *J. Afr. law*, **5**, 1, Spring 1951: 21–35.

1818 —— *Land law in Ghana.*
Forthcoming.

1819 —— *The law of succession in Ghana.* [Accra, Presbyterian Book Depot], 1960. 53 pp.

1820 POGUCKI, R. J. H. 'Customary law of a society in transition.' *Universitas*, **2**, 4, 1956: 119–121.

1821 —— 'A note on the codification of customary land law on the Gold Coast.' *J. Afr. admin.*, **8**, 4, 1956: 192–196.

1822 QUAMIE-KYIAMAH, A. 'The customary oath in the Gold Coast.' *Afr. affairs*, **50**, 199, April 1951: 139–147.

1823 RAMSAY, J. M. 'Land planning in the Northern Territories.' *Gold Coast teachers' J.*, **2**, April 1957: 20–26.

1824 RUBIN, L., AND MURRAY, P. *The constitution and government of Ghana.* Sweet & Maxwell, 1961. xvi, 210 pp. (Law in Africa, no. 1.)

1825 THOMAS, H. B. 'Native tribunals in the Gold Coast Colony.' *J. Comp. Legislation*, **26**, Nov. 1944: 30–35.

1826 WIGHT, MARTIN. *The Gold Coast Legislative Council.* Faber, 1947. 285 pp. (Studies in colonial legislatures; ed. by Margery Perham, vol. 2.)

1827   WILD, R. P. 'Gold Coast laws and their effect on mining' (in GOLD
COAST. GEOLOGICAL SURVEY DEPT. *Gold in the Gold Coast*, by N. R.
JUNNER, 1935).

See also nos. 9, 10, 25, 868, 871, 878, 891, 927, 934, 1029, 2051,
2355, 2378, 2435, 2454, 2455, 2468, 2501.

Local Government

1828 ACCRA. TOWN COUNCIL. *Your questions answered.* Accra, Regional Information Office, 1948. 71 pp.

1829 AKYEA, L. E. O. *The Buem-Krachi District Council (June 1953–June 1959).* Accra, Guinea Press, [1960]. 52 pp.

1830 ALTON, E. B. S. 'The local government training school in the Gold Coast.' *J. Afr. admin.,* **4,** 3, July 1952: 108–113.

1831 AUSTIN, DENNIS. 'Elections in an African rural area.' [Ghana.] *Africa,* **31,** 1, Jan. 1961: 1–18.

1832 BENNETT, GEORGE. 'Local government in practice.' *West Africa,* 25 Sept.–6 Nov. 1954.

1833 BOATENG, J. A. *Problems of local government in Ghana.* 2nd ed. Obuasi, [Ashanti Times] 1957. iv, 11 pp.

1834 CAMERON, I. D., AND COOPER, B. K. *The West African councillor.* 2nd ed. O.U.P., 1961. 224 pp.

1835 CANHAM, P. H. 'Local government in Ashanti.' *Corona,* **1,** 4, May 1949: 16–18.

1836 —— *Report on the Gold Coast general election, 1954.* Cape Coast, 1954.

1837 COWAN, L. GRAY. *Local government in West Africa.* N.Y., Columbia U.P., 1958. x, 292 pp.

1838 EDU, JOHN E. *Your share in local government.* Accra, the author, 1952. 41 pp.

1839 GREENWOOD, ALAN F. 'Ten years of local government in Ghana.' *J. Local Admin. Overseas,* **1,** 1, Jan. 1962: 23–28.

1840 HANNIGAN, A. ST. J. J. 'Local government in the Gold Coast.' *J. Afr. admin.,* **7,** 3, July 1955: 116–123.

1841 HICKS, URSULA K. *Development from below: local government and finance in developing countries of the Commonwealth.* O.U.P., 1961. 549 pp.

1842   INTERNATIONAL UNION OF LOCAL AUTHORITIES. *The tasks of local authorities in development areas.* The Hague, Nijhoff, 1961. 193 pp. Refers to rural development in Ghana.

1843   MCLAREN, C. A. 'Local government training in the Gold Coast.' *J. Afr. admin.*, **9,** 2, April 1957: 63–71.

1844   MAIR, L. P. 'Traditional authorities in Gold Coast local government.' *West Africa*, **2023,** 1955: 1140–1141.

1845   MATE, C. M. O. 'Local government councils and their functions.' *Gold Coast education*, **1,** May 1955: 58–67.

1846   MURRAY, A. H. AND DRYSDALE, J. G. S. 'Town boards in Agona State: an experiment.' *J. Afr. admin.*, **3,** 3, July 1961: 110–112.

1847   PACKENHAM, E. S. 'Notes on the development of the native authorities in the Northern Territories of the Gold Coast.' *J. Afr. admin.*, **2,** 2, April 1950: 26–30.

1848   PAUL, M. E. 'Local government in Ghana.' *West Africa*, **2110/2114,** Sept.–Oct. 1957.

1849   PETERS, W. 'Tradition and change in the Saltpond Sub-District of the Gold Coast Colony.' *J. Afr. admin.*, **6,** 1, Jan. 1954: 5–11.

1850   SEKONDI-TAKORADI. TOWN COUNCIL. *Know your Council.* Accra, Public Relations Dept., 1950. 15 pp.

1851   SMITH, THOMAS EDWARD. *Elections in developing countries: a study of electoral procedures used in tropical Africa, South-East Asia and the Caribbean.* Macmillan, 1960. xvii, 278 pp.

1852   WRAITH, R. E. *Local government.* Penguin Books, 1953. 126 pp. (Penguin West African series.)

1853   —— 'Training for local government in West Africa.' *J. Afr. admin.*, **3,** 4, Oct. 1951: 158–162.

See also nos. 2418, 2434, 2439, 2440, 2441, 2447, 2449, 2460, 2461, 2510.

Demography

1854 BARBOUR, KENNETH MICHAEL, AND PROTHERO, R. MANSELL, Eds. *Essays on African population*. Routledge & Paul, 1961. x, 336 pp.

1855 BOATING, E. A. 'Recent changes in settlement in south-east Gold Coast.' *Inst. Brit. Geog.*, **21**, 1955: 157–169.

1856 BUSIA, KOFI ABREFA. 'Some aspects of the relation of social conditions to human fertility in the Gold Coast' (in LORIMER, F., AND OTHERS. *Culture and human fertility*, 1954: 341–350).

1857 FORTES, MEYER. 'A demographic field study in Ashanti' (in LORIMER, F., AND OTHERS. *Culture and human fertility*, 1954: 253–339).
Survey carried out at Agogo, capital township of Ashanti-Akim.

1858 GIL, BENJAMIN. *Demographic statistics in Ghana*. Seminar on African Demography, Paris, 1959.

1859 GIL, BENJAMIN, AND DE GRAFT JOHNSON, K. T. 'The post-enumeration survey in Ghana.' *Econ. bull.*, **4**, 4, April 1960: 15–18.

1860 GOLD COAST. CENSUS OFFICE. *The Gold Coast, 1931: a review of conditions in the Gold Coast in 1931 as compared with those of 1921, based on figures and facts collected by the Chief Census Officer of 1931, together with a historical, ethnographical and sociological survey of the people of that country*. Accra, Govt. Printer, 1932. 266 pp.
Chief Census Officer, A. W. Cardinall.

1861 —— *The Gold Coast: census of population, 1948. Report and tables*. Crown Agents, 1950. 422 pp.

1862 HILTON, THOMAS ERIC. *Ghana population atlas: the distribution and density of population in the Gold Coast and Togoland under United Kingdom Trusteeship*. Published on behalf of the University College of Ghana by Nelson, 1960. 40 pp.
Based on the census of 1948.

1863 KUCZYNSKI, R. R. *The Cameroons and Togoland: a demographic study*. O.U.P., 1939. 580 pp.

1864   KUCZYNSKI, R. R. *A demographic survey of the British Colonial Empire. Vol 1: West Africa.* O.U.P., for the Royal Institute of International Affairs, 1948. 821 pp. 2 vols.

1865   —— *Population movements.* O.U.P., 1936.

1866   LORIMER, FRANK, AND OTHERS. *Culture and human fertility*, by Frank Lorimer, K. A. Busia, Audrey I. Richards, Priscilla Reining and Giorgio Mortara. Unesco, 1954.

1867   OMABOE, E. N. 'Counting the people in Ghana.' *Econ. bull.*, **3**, 2, Feb. 1959.
　　　Author is Government Statistician.

1868   —— 'Estimating the population in Ghana.' *Econ. bull.*, **3**, 3, 1959: 3–12.

1869   STEEL, ROBERT W. 'The population of Ashanti: a geographical analysis.' *Geog. J.*, July–Sept. 1948: 64–76.

1870   —— 'Some problems of population in British West Africa.' (in STEEL, R. W., AND FISHER, C. A. Eds. *Geographical essays on British tropical lands*, 1956: 19–50).

See also nos. 842, 843, 844, 944, 1001, 1009, 1091, 1907, 2307, 2552.

Social Surveys

1871 ACQUAH, IONÉ. *Accra survey: a social survey of the capital of Ghana, formerly called the Gold Coast, undertaken for the West African Institute of Social and Economic Research, 1953–6.* U.L.P., 1958. 176 pp.

1872 BUSIA, KOFI ABREFA. *Report on a social survey of Sekondi-Takoradi.* Crown Agents, 1950. 164 pp.

See also no. 337.

1873 DOXIADIS ASSOCIATES. *Proposed planning and consulting services for the development of the Accra-Tema region.* Athens, Doxiadis Associates, 1959. 14 pp. (Typescript.)

1874 DRAKE, ST. CLAIR. 'Social surveys in Ghana.' *Advance,* **29,** July 1959: 5–18.

1875 GOLD COAST. BROADCASTING COMMISSION. *A survey of the listeners and of listening habits in the towns of Accra, Swedru, Winneba and Keta, March to October, 1955.* Accra, Govt. Printer, 1956. 7 pp.

1876 GOLD COAST. TOWN PLANNING DEPT. *Report on a preliminary social survey of Kete-Krachi.* Accra, Govt. Printer, 1956. 43 pp.

1877 GOLD COAST. UNIVERSITY COLLEGE. DEPT. OF EXTRA-MURAL STUDIES. *Report of the Tongu rural survey.* Accra, University College, 1953. 58 pp. (Typescript.)

1878 GHANA. MINISTRY OF HOUSING. *Accra: a plan for the town.* Accra, Govt. Printer, 1958. 137 pp.

1879 GHANA. UNIVERSITY COLLEGE. *Preliminary report of a social survey of Egya I: 1959–60.* Accra, University College, 1961. 118 pp.

1880 MUNGER, EDWIN S. 'L'usage du terrain à Accra.' *Zaire,* **8, 9,** nov. 1954: 911–919.

1881 TEMA DEVELOPMENT CORPORATION. *Social and economic survey of Tema,* by I. NEUSTADT AND E. N. OMABOE. Accra, Govt. Statistician's Office, 1959. 90 pp.

1882 TETTEH, P. A. *A plan for Nungua village. Part 1: Social survey; Part 2: Planning report.* Accra, Govt. Printer, 1955. 63 pp.

Economics, Trade and Finance

1883 ADDAE, G. 'The retailing of imported textiles in the Accra market.' *W. Afr. Inst. Soc. Econ. Res. Third Annual Conference, Proceedings, 1956:* 51–56.

1884 ADY, P. *The future of the sterling area: Ghana.* Oxford, Institute of Commonwealth Studies, 1960. 12 pp.

1885 'The African trader.' *Econ. bull.,* **2/3,** 1957: 2–6, 4–7.

1886 AJIBOLA, J. O. *Economic development of West Africa.* West African Society, 1949.

1887 APEADU, K. K. *The co-operative movement.* Bureau of Current Affairs, 1951. 15 pp. (West African affairs pamphlets, no. 12.)

1888 BANK OF BRITISH WEST AFRICA, LTD. *British West Africa: a promising market.* 1947. 52 pp.

1889 BANKS, A. L. *The development of tropical and sub-tropical countries with particular reference to Africa.* E. Arnold, 1954.

1890 BARCLAYS BANK, D. C. O. *The Gold Coast: an economic survey.* 1955. 20 pp.

1891 —— *Ghana: an economic survey.* 1960. 32 pp.

1892 BARLTHROP, E. W. 'Labour in West Africa.' *Corona,* **I,** 6, July 1949: 11–13.

1893 BATTEN, T. R. *Problems of African development.* 2nd ed. O.U.P., 1954. 2 vols.

1894 BAUER, P. T. *West African trade: a study of competition, oligopoly and monopoly in a changing economy.* C.U.P., 1954.

1895 BEVIN, H. J. 'The Gold Coast economy about 1880.' *Trans. Gold Coast & Togoland Hist. Soc.,* **2,** 1956: 73–86.

1896 BIRMINGHAM, W. B. 'An index of real wages of the unskilled labourer in Accra.' *Econ. bull.,* **4,** 2, 1960.

1897 BOLTON, F. P. *Report of the special mission to Africa, south and east of the Sahara.* Washington, D.C., Govt. Printing Office, 1956. 151 pp.

1898   BREWSTER, S. P. *Gold Coast income tax.* Takoradi, the author, 1954. 60 pp.

1899   —— *Gold Coast income tax in a nutshell.* Accra, Methodist Book Depot, [1956]. 12 pp.

1900   CENTRE DE DOCUMENTATION ÉCONOMIQUE ET SOCIALE AFRICAINE. *Contribution à l'étude de la progression économique de l'Afrique.* Brussels, CEDESA, 1960. 216 pp.

1901   CHAPMAN, DANIEL A. 'The natural resources of the Gold Coast. (Part of an address delivered at the Youth Conference, Akropong, on 24th March 1940.) Achimota, Achimota Press, (1940). 17 pp.

1902   'Controlled cocoa sales and imports.' *West Africa,* 10 March 1962: 259. (Economic planning in Ghana—2.)

1903   'Controlling Ghana's imports.' *West Africa,* 9 Dec. 1961: 1351.

1904   COX-GEORGE, N. A. *Finance and development in West Africa.* Dobson, 1961. 333 pp.

1905   —— 'Studies in finance and development: the Gold Coast experience, 1914–18. *Public finance,* 13, 2, 1958: 146–177.

1906   DAVISON, R. B. 'Labor relations in Ghana.' *Ann. Amer. Acad. pol. & soc. Sci.,* 310, March 1957: 133–141.

1907   —— *Migrant labour in the Gold Coast.* Achimota, University College of Ghana, 1954. 41 pp. (Typescript.)

1908   DE GRAFT JOHNSON, J. C. *African experiment: co-operative agriculture and banking in British West Africa.* Watts, 1958. 198 pp.

1909   —— *An introduction to the African economy.* Delhi, Asia Publishing House, 1959. 115 pp.

1910   'Economic developments in West Africa: some recent developments in the independent Commonwealth countries.' *Commonwealth survey,* Nov. 1961: 1154–1158.

1911   'Economics of independence.' *West Africa,* 2337, 17 March 1962: 293.

1912   'Exchanging cocoa for factories.' *West Africa,* 2335, 3 March 1962: 227. (Economic planning in Ghana—1.)

1913   FRANKEL, S. H. *Capital investment in Africa.* O.U.P., 1938.

1914   GAMBRAH, BERNARD. *A guide to savings.* Accra, the author, 1962. 15 pp.

1915   GARLICK, PETER CYRIL. *African business enterprise: a study of a group of traders in Kumasi*. Achimota, University College of Ghana, 1958. 68 pp. (Economic Research Division, monograph no. 1.)

1916   —— 'African-owned private-enterprise company formation in Ghana.' *Econ. bull.*, **4,** 2, Feb. 1960: 1–10.

1917   —— *African traders in Kumasi*. Accra, University College of Ghana, Economic Research Division, 1960. 115 pp. (African business series, no. 1.)
        Survey confined to traders with permanent premises; effects of traditional custom on business.

1918   —— 'The French trade with Kumasi.' *Econ. bull.*, **2,** 6, 1958: 5–10.

1919   —— 'The Gaos in Kumasi.' *Econ. bull.*, **2,** 11, 1958: 3–9.

1920   GHANA. DEPT. OF RECRUITMENT AND TRAINING. *Careers in the Civil Service for boys and girls leaving secondary schools*. Accra, Govt. Printer, 1957. 37 pp.

1921   GHANA ASSOCIATION FOR THE ADVANCEMENT OF MANAGEMENT. *Ghana's women workers*. Accra, the Association, [1962]. [8] pp. (General publication, no. 1.)

1922   *Le Ghana*. Supplement to *Bull. commercial belge*, Feb. 1960. 16 pp.

1923   GOLD COAST. MINISTRY OF FINANCE. *A survey of some economic matters*. Accra, Govt. Printer, 1952. 31 pp.

1924   GOLD COAST. MINISTRY OF TRADE AND LABOUR. *Report of the Gold Coast Mines Board of Inquiry, 1956*. Accra, Govt. Printer, 1956.

1925   GREAT BRITAIN. BOARD OF TRADE. *British West Africa: economic and commercial conditions in the territories of Nigeria, Gold Coast, Sierra Leone and the Gambia*, by Aubrey R. Starck. H.M.S.O., 1949. 51 pp.

1926   —— *Hints to business men visiting Ghana*. Board of Trade, [1962]. 28 pp.

1927   —— *Report of the United Kingdom Trade and Industrial Mission to Ghana*. H.M.S.O., 1959. 60 pp.

1928   HANCE, W. A. *African economic development*. O.U.P., 1958. 307 pp. Refers to the Volta River Project.

1929   HANNA, M. 'The Lebanese in West Africa.' *West Africa*, **2140–2145,** 1958: 369+

1930   HAUSER, A. 'A note on some labour problems in Ghana.' *Int. Afr. Labour Inst. Bull.*, **4,** 6, Nov. 1957: 76–83.

1931 HAZLEWOOD, ARTHUR D. *Ghana's finances.* Oxford, Institute of Commonwealth Studies, 1957. 12 pp.

1932 —— 'How poor is Ghana?' *West Africa,* 30 March 1957: 295–296.

1933 HEIGHAM, J. B. 'Industrial relations in the Gold Coast.' *Bull. inter-Afr. labour Inst.,* Nov. 1955: 8–24.

1934 HOLT, JOHN & CO. (LIVERPOOL) LTD. *Merchant adventure.* [1951]. 80 pp.

1935 HUTCHINSON, J. B., AND PEARSON, E. O. *Report on a visit to the Gold Coast 10th–23rd December, 1947.* Empire Cotton Growing Corporation, 1948. 18 pp.

1936 INTERNATIONAL LABOUR OFFICE. *African labour survey.* I.L.O., 1958. xiv, 712 pp.

1937 ITALY. ISTITUTO PER IL COMMERCIO ESTERO. *Ghana.* Roma, 1960. 184 pp.

1938 JOHNSTON, BRUCE F. *The staple food economies of western tropical Africa.* Stanford U.P., 1958. 305 pp.

1939 KATHOLIEKE UNIVERSITEIT TE LEUVEN, INSTITUUT VOOR TEOGEPASTE EKONOMISCHE WETENSCHAPPEN. *Ghana: ekonomische struktuur en modelijkheden.* 1960. 191 pp. (Typescript.)

1940 LAWSON, ROWENA M. *The economics of village life on the lower Volta.* (Unpublished thesis, University of South Africa, 1958. 122 pp.)

1941 —— *Elements of commerce in West Africa.* Revised ed. Longmans, 1961. 136 pp. First published 1957.

1942 ——'Ghana in economic transition.' *South Afr. J. Econ.,* **25,** 2, 1957: 103–114.

1943 LEVERHULME TRUST. *The West Africa Commission, 1938–1939: technical reports.* 1943: 86 pp.

1944 LEWIS, WILLIAM ARTHUR. *Problems of economic development.* [Zaria, Norla, 1955]. 13 pp.

1945 MCCALL, DANIEL F. 'Trade and the role of the wife in a modern West African town' [Koforidua] (in SOUTHALL, A., ED. *Social change in modern Africa,* 1961).

1946 MACDONALD, G. *Report on conditions of mining labour in the Northern Territories of the Gold Coast.* The Ross Institute, 1952.

1947   MCPHEE, A. *The economic revolution in British West Africa.* Routledge, 1926.

1948   'Les Municipalités de Gold Coast et leurs ressources.' *Bull. Association de l'Etude des Problèmes de l'Union Française,* **101,** juin. 1956: 19–25.

1949   NEWLYN, W. T., AND ROWAN, D. C. *Money and banking in British colonial Africa.* O.U.P., 1954. 301 pp.

1950   'New trade unionism in Ghana.' *West Africa,* **2179,** Jan. 1959: 57; **2180,** 83–84.

1951   NKRUMAH, KWAME. *Speech delivered to the Commission for Technical Co-operation in Africa South of the Sahara (C.C.T.A.), 19th February, 1958.* Accra, Govt. Printer, 1958. 3 pp.

1952   —— *Statement on development, 20th February, 1958.* Accra, Govt. Printer, 1958. 13 pp.

1953   NYPAN, ASTRID. *Market trade: a sample survey of market traders in Accra.* Accra, University College of Ghana, Economic Research Division, 1960. 78 pp.

1954   —— 'Market trade in Accra.' *Econ. bull.,* **4,** 3, March 1960: 7–16.

1955   OBU. *Commerce in West Africa: a lecture entitled "West African economics in relation to world economics", delivered on Friday the 11th November 1939 at 5.30 p.m. at the Oguaa School Hall, Kawanupandu, Cape Coast.* Cape Coast, Mfantsiman Press, [1939?]. 15 pp.

1956   PANOFSKY, HANS E. *The significance of labour migration for the economic growth of Ghana* (Unpublished thesis, N.Y., Cornell University, 1958. 138 pp.)

1957   —— 'The significance of labour migration for the economic welfare of Ghana and the Voltaic Republic.' *Bull. inter-Afr. labour Inst.,* **7,** 4, July 1960: 30–44.

1958   PETCH, GEORGE ALLAN. *Economic development and modern West Africa.* U.L.P., 1961. 224 pp.

1959   PIM, SIR ALAN WILLIAM. *The financial and economic history of African tropical territories.* Oxford, Clarendon Press, 1940. vii, 234 pp.

1960   POLEMAN, T. T. 'The food economies of urban middle Africa: the case of Ghana.' Reprinted from *Food Res. Inst. Studies,* **2,** 2, May 1961: 121–175.

1961   RAEBURN, J. R. *Report on a preliminary economic survey of the Northern Territories of the Gold Coast.* H.M.S.O., 1950. 47 pp.

1962 'Recent economic developments in Ghana.' *Commonwealth Survey*, **7**, 6, 14 March 1961: 281–285.

1963 ROPER, J. I. *Labour problems of West Africa.* Penguin Books, 1958. 112 pp.

1964 ROPER, J. I., AND DAVISON, R. B. *The labour and trade union ordinances of the Gold Coast.* Bureau of Current Affairs, [1951?]. 19 pp. (West African affairs pamphlets, no. 15.)

1965 ROYAL EMPIRE SOCIETY. EMPIRE INFORMATION BUREAU. *Notes on conditions in Nigeria and the Gold Coast.* 1947. 4 pp. (Information papers, nos. 7 & 9.)

1966 —— *Notes on conditions in Ghana.* Revised ed. 1957. 8 pp.

1967 SEERS, D., AND ROSS, C. R. *Report on financial and physical problems of development in the Gold Coast.* Accra, Office of the Govt. Statistician, 1952. 172, 63 pp.

1968 SENCHIREY, A. K. 'The Ghana co-operative movement.' *African Eagle*, **I**, 1, May 1960: 5–7.

1969 'State trading and marketing.' *West Africa*, **2337**, 17 March 1962: 296. (Economic planning in Ghana—3.)

1970 STOCKDALE, F. A. *Report on a visit to Nigeria, Gold Coast and Sierra Leone, 1935–6.* Colonial Office, 1936. 125 pp.

1971 TETTEGAH, J. K. *A new chapter for Ghana labour.* Accra, Ghana T.U.C., 1958. 51 pp.

1972 THOMAS, BENJAMIN E. *Trade routes of Algeria and the Sahara.* California U.P., 1957.

1973 TOKUNBOH, M. A. *Problems of trade unions.* Bureau of Current Affairs, 1955. 17 pp. (West African affairs pamphlets, no. 20.)

1974 'Tourist trade for Ghana.' *W. Afr. Rev.*, May 1959: 330–332.

1975 UNITED AFRICA COMPANY. 'Merchandise trading in British West Africa.' *Statistical & Econ. Rev.*, **5**, March 1950: 1–36.

1976 —— 'Surf port operations in the Gold Coast.' *Statistical & Econ. Rev.*, **5**, March 1950: 45–52.

1977 —— *Unicorn pie.* Accra, U.A.C., [1957?]. 41 pp.

1978 UNITED NATIONS. DEPT. OF ECONOMIC AND SOCIAL AFFAIRS. *Economic survey of Africa since 1950.* N.Y., United Nations, 1959. 247 pp.

1979 WANNER, GUSTAF ADOLF. *Die Basler Handels-Gesellschaft A.G., 1859–1959.* Basel, Basler Handels-Gesellschaft, A.G., 1959. 677 pp. [Privately printed.]
    History of the Basel Trading Co. (U.T.C.) in Ghana.

1980 WEST AFRICAN INSTITUTE OF SOCIAL AND ECONOMIC RESEARCH. *Annual conference, Economics Section, Achimota, April 1953.* [Proceedings.] Ibadan, University College, 1953. 176 pp.

1981 WHITE H. P. 'Internal exchange of staple foods in the Gold Coast.' *Econ. Geog.*, **32,** 2, April 1956: 115–125.

1982 WILLIAMS, DAVID. 'Women traders in West African markets.' *Times Brit. Colonies Rev.*, **36,** 1959: 11.

1983 WILLIAMS, J. W. 'State banking in the Gold Coast.' *Banker*, **107,** 374, 1957: 171–175.

1984 WILLS, COLIN. 'The surf-boats of Accra.' *Progress*, **46,** 256, Autumn 1957: 69–73.

1985 WITTMAN, G. H. INC. *The Ghana report: economic development and investment opportunities.* N. Y., Wittman, 1959. 236 pp.
    An analysis of the problems likely to confront the foreign investor.

1986 WOOD, R., AND OTHERS. *Report on trade and investment opportunities in the Gold Coast.* Revised ed. N., Richardson Wood & Co., Accra, Ministry of Trade and Labour, 1956. 105 pp.

See also nos. 5, 12, 205, 206, 1051, 2353, 2433.

Industries and Transport

1987 AKWAWUAH, K. A. *Prelude to Ghana's industrialisation.* Mitre Press, [1959]. 96 pp.

1988 ALCOCK, A. E. S. 'A new town in the Gold Coast.' [Tema.] *Colonial Building Notes,* **32,** 1955: 11–14.

1989 AMEGBE. 'Triumph of the akpeteshi industry.' *Evening News,* 14 Feb. 1962: 7.

1990 BALDWIN, K. *New industries.* Bureau of Current Affairs, [1954?]. (West African affairs pamphlets, no. 3.)

1991 BONAVIA, M. R. *Report on transport in the Gold Coast.* Accra, Govt. Printer, 1951. (Typescript.)

1992 BROWN, G. N. 'Clio as a working girl in Ghana.' *Trans. Hist. Soc. Ghana,* **4,** 2, 1960: 3–13.

1993 DICKSON, K. B. 'The development of road transport in southern Ghana and Ashanti since about 1850.' *Trans. Hist. Soc. Ghana,* **5,** 1, 1961: 33–42.

1994 GHANA. MINISTRY OF INFORMATION. *Ghana's new town and harbour: Tema.* Accra, Ghana Information Services, 1961. 52 pp.

1995 —— *Port of Tema: official handbook.* Accra, Ghana Information Services, 1962. 24 pp.

1996 GHANA. MINISTRY OF TRADE AND INDUSTRIES. *Industrial promotion in Ghana.* Accra, Govt. Printer, 1959. 12 pp.

1997 GHANA. MINISTRY OF TRANSPORT AND COMMUNICATIONS. *Report of investigation into the control, organization and development of the ports of Ghana.* Accra, Govt. Printer, 1960. 24 pp.

1998 GOULD, PETER R. *The development of the transportation pattern in Ghana.* Northwestern University, Dept. of Geography, 1960. x, 165 pp. (Studies in geography, no. 5.)

1999 GRIFFITHS, SIR P., AND WATT, M. J., *Report on a visit to Nigeria and the Gold Coast, March to May 1955.* Federation of British Industries, 1955. 46 pp.

2000   HALCROW, SIR WILLIAM AND PARTNERS. *Report on the origin and destination of traffic approaching Accra in January 1957.* Accra, the authors, 1957. 30 pp.

2001   LEWIS, WILLIAM ARTHUR. *Report on industrialisation in the Gold Coast.* Accra, Govt. Printer, 1953. viii, 24 pp.

2002   NKRUMAH, KWAME. *Address at the opening ceremony of the Nzima Oil Mills (I.D.C.) at Esiama, 11th February, 1961.* Accra, Govt. Printer, 1961. 5 pp.

2003   —— *Gateway to Ghana: speech on the occasion of the official opening of the Tema Harbour on Saturday, 10th February, 1962.* Accra, Govt. Printer, 1962. 5 pp.

2004   —— *The opening of the Canadian Trade Fair: a speech.* Accra, Govt. Printer, 1962. 4 pp.

2005   —— *Strengthening the bonds of industry: speech when opening the United States Small Industries Exhibition in Accra on 27th November, 1961.* Accra, Govt. Printer, 1961. 4 pp.

2006   'Tema: a shop window of Ghana.' *New Ashanti Times*, **3**, 27, 7 April, 1962: 7.

2007   'Ten million Polish factories for Ghana.' *West Africa*, 30 Dec. 1961.

2008   WISE, C. G. *Notes on transport.* Achimota, Achimota Press, 1939. 48 pp.

2009   WORTHINGTON, E. B. *Science in the development of Africa: a review of the contribution of physical and biological knowledge south of the Sahara.* C.C.T.A., 1958. 462 pp.

Housing and Social Welfare

2010   *Achimota social service: a review and forecast.* Achimota, College Press, 1931. 31 pp.

2011   CHRISTIAN, A. 'The place of women in Ghana society.' *Afr. women*, **3**, 3, Dec. 1959: 57–59.

2012   DREW, J. B., AND OTHERS. *Village housing in the tropics, with special reference to West Africa.* Lund, Humphries, 1947. 134 pp.

2013   *Duke of Edinburgh's study conference on the human problems of industrial communities within the Commonwealth and Empire, 9–27 July, 1956.* O.U.P., 1957. 2 vols.

2014   DUPRIEZ, GÉRARD. 'Le Développement communautaire en milieu rural au Ghana.' *Probl. Afr. centr.*, **12**, 4, 1958: 154–159.

2015   GOLD COAST. DEPT. OF RECRUITMENT AND TRAINING. *Notes on training arrangements in departmental boarding institutions.* Accra, Govt. Printer, 1955. 17 pp.

2016   GOLD COAST. DEPT. OF SOCIAL WELFARE & COMMUNITY DEVELOPMENT. *Children and the cinema: a report of an enquiry into cinema going among juveniles.* Accra, 1954. 14 pp. (Typescript.)

2017   —— *Problem children of the Gold Coast.* Accra, 1955. 28 pp.

2018   GOLD COAST FILM UNIT. *Films from the Gold Coast, 1949–1953.* Accra, 1954. 16 pp.

2019   RICHARDS, J. M., Ed. *New buildings in the Commonwealth.* Architectural Press, 1962. 240 pp.
      Includes an essay on West African architecture, by Maxwell Fry.

2020   TOOTH, GEOFFREY. *A survey of juvenile delinquency in the Gold Coast.* Colonial Social Science Research Council, 1946. 27 pp. (Typescript.)

2021   UNITED NATIONS. TECHNICAL ASSISTANCE PROGRAMME. *Report on housing in the Gold Coast.* N.Y., United Nations, 1956. 174 pp.

2022   —— *Housing in Ghana.* N.Y., United Nations, 1957. 220 pp.

2023   VOLUNTARY WORKCAMPS ASSOCIATION. *Chichiwere: voluntary workcamps for West Africa.* Accra, Guinea Press, [1958?]. 144 pp.

2024   WEST AFRICAN BUILDING RESEARCH INSTITUTE. *Soil-cement blocks,* by R. SPERLING. ACCRA, 1961. 4 pp. (*Note no. 2.*)

2025   —— *Sandcrete blocks,* by R. G. TYLER. Accra, 1961. 6 pp. (*Note no. 4.*)

2026   —— *Factors governing school building programmes,* by G. C. HARRIS AND B. G. WHITE. Accra, 1961. 5 pp. (*Note no. 7.*)

2027   —— *The shape of a building in plan for which the cost of walls is a minimum,* by C. J. DAVIS AND B. G. WHITE. Accra, 1961. 5 pp. (*Note no. 9.*)

Mining

2028 ALLEN, G. K. *Gold mining in Ghana.* Institute of Mining and Metallurgy, 1957. 20 pp.

2029 BLAY, J. BENIBENGOR. *The Gold Coast Mines Employees' Union.* Ilfracombe, Stockwell, 1950. 297 pp.

2030 'Ghana's mineral wealth.' *W. Afr. Rev.*, **31**, 497, Dec. 1960: 65–67.

2031 GOLD COAST CHAMBER OF MINES. *Gold from the Gold Coast.* Accra, 1950. 43 pp.

2032 HENNESSY, M. N. 'Diamond mining by Gold Coast Africans.' *Crown Colonist*, **20**, 224. July 1950: 422–423.

2033 JOPP, KEIGH. *C.A.S.T. in Ghana.* Consolidated African Selection Trust, 1958.
Mines and mineral resources.

2034 SCHWARZ, W. 'Crisis in Ghana's gold mines.' *W. Afr. Rev.*, **32**, 402, June 1961: 5–9.

2035 SUTHERLAND, D. A. *The primitive uses of gold and methods of gold mining, with particular reference to the Gold Coast.* Accra, Govt. Printer, 1952. 22 pp.
Cover title: Gold through the ages.

2036 TAYLOR, H. *Handbook of West African gold mines.* Hutchinson, [1947]. 110 pp.

2037 TURNER, G. W. EATON. *Ashanti Goldfields Corporation, Ltd., 1897–1947: a short history.* London, the Corporation, 1947. 20 pp.

See also Geology and nos. 2309, 2352, 2395, 2398, 2464, 2498, 2519.

Volta River Project

2038 AGGREY, CHRISTIAN. 'The Volta River Project, the "giant of reconstruction".' *Ashanti Pioneer*, 5 March, 1962: 2.

2039 ANDERSON, J. G. C. *Volta river development: geological report and supplementary geological report.* London, Sir William Halcrow and Partners, 1951.

2040 BERNER, L. *Entomological report on development of the River Volta basin.* Gainesville, University of Florida, 1950. 83 pp. (Typescript.)

2041 BIRD, C. ST. J. *Volta River scheme. Vol 1: Report on investigations and findings. Vol 2: Details of scheme, quantities and estimated costs.* Accra, West African Aluminium Ltd., 1949. 2 vols.

2042 CARNEY, DAVID. *The Volta River scheme: its social and economic implications.* Accra, West Africa Graphic Co., 1952.

2043 DAVISON, R. B. 'The Volta River aluminium scheme.' *Political Quarterly*, **25**, 1, Jan.–March 1954: 55–66.

2044 DE GRAFT JOHNSON, J. C. *Background to the Volta River Project.* Kumasi, Abura Printing Works, [1955]. 41 pp.

2045 FAHLQUIST, F. E. *Final report on geologic investigations, Volta River dam project.* Aluminium Laboratories, Ltd., 1951.

2046 FOCUS DISCUSSION GROUP. ACHIMOTA. *Power in the Volta: a study of the Volta River, its waters and its power.* Achimota, Achimota Press, 1949. 11 pp.

2047 GOLD COAST. INFORMATION SERVICES. *The Volta River Project: what it means to you.* Accra, 1956. 32 pp.

2048 —— *Wealth from the Volta: an outline of the Volta River Project.* Accra, [1954]. 31 pp.

2049 GOLD COAST. GOVERNMENT. *The Volta River Project, 1914–1950: an account of the development of the mining of bauxite in the Gold Coast and the history of the Volta River Project.* Accra, Chief Secretary's Office, 1951.

2050 GOLD COAST. GOVERNMENT *Development of the Volta River basin: a statement by the Government of the Gold Coast on the Volta River Project and related matters.* Accra, Govt. Printer, 1952. 11 pp.

2051 GOLD COAST. LANDS DEPT. *Report on a preliminary survey of land tenure in the Volta River basin. Part 1.* Accra, Govt. Printer, 1955.

2052 GHANA. GEOLOGICAL SURVEY DEPT. *The geology of the Volta River Project, with geological plans, and sections,* by W. B. TEVENDALE. Accra, Govt. Printer, 1957.

2053 GHANA. GOVERNMENT. *The Volta River Project: statement by the Government of Ghana, 20th February, 1961.* Accra, Govt. Printer, 1961.

2054 —— *The Volta River Project: statement by the Government of Ghana: the finalizing of the plan and the arrangements for the consummation of the project.* Accra, Govt. Printer, 1961. 14 pp.

2055 GREAT BRITAIN. COLONIAL OFFICE. *Volta River aluminium scheme.* H.M.S.O., 1952. 22 pp. (Cmd. 8702.)

2056 HALCROW, SIR WILLIAM AND PARTNERS. *Preliminary and final report on development of the River Volta basin.* London, Halcrow, 1950–51. 2 vols.

2057 NKRUMAH, KWAME. *Speech on the Volta River Project and its bearing on African unity.* Accra, Govt. Printer, 1962. 9 pp.

2058 —— *The Volta River Project: a statement to the National Assembly, February 21, 1961.* Accra, Govt. Printer, 1961. 14 pp.

2059 'Russians on the Volta.' *West Africa,* **14,** Jan. 1961: 29.

2060 VOLTA RIVER PROJECT PREPARATORY COMMISSION. *The Volta River Project.* H.M.S.O., 1956. 3 vols. *Vol 1: Report of the Preparatory Commission. Vol 2: Appendices to the report. Vol 3: Engineering report.*

Travel

2061 ABRAHAMS, PETER. 'Gold Coast reflections.' *W. Afr. Rev.*, July 1954.

2062 ALMGREN, GERD. *Kakaokust.* Stockholm, Natur och Kultur, 1958. 262 pp.

2063 BAKER, RICHARD ST. BARBE. *Africa drums.* Drummond, 1943. 159 pp.

2064 BELL, SIR H. HESKETH. *Love in black.* E. Arnold, 1911.

2065 —— *Witches and fishes.* E. Arnold, 1948. 187 pp.

2066 BERNARD, J. *Black mistress.* Hodder & Stoughton, 1957. 224 pp. Reminiscences of the wife of a D.C. in the Northern Territories.

2067 BRAUN, RICHARD, AND BRAUN, GERTRUDE. *Letters from Ghana.* Philadelphia, Christian Education Press, 1959. 154 pp.

2068 CAMPBELL, ALEXANDER. *Heart of Africa.* Longmans, 1954.

2069 CHAPMAN, EDDIE. *Free agent; being the further adventures of Eddie Chapman.* Wingate, 1955. 223 pp. Includes references to personalities and events in the Gold Coast.

2070 CLOETE, STUART. *The African giant: the story of a journey.* Collins, 1956. 448 pp.

2071 CONE, VIRGINIA. *Africa—a world in progress: an American family in West Africa.* N.Y., Exposition Press, 1960. 99 pp. Life in Accra.

2072 ESKELUND, KARL. *Black man's country: a journey through Ghana.* Redman, 1958. 164 pp.

2073 GREEN, L. G. *White man's grave: the story of the West African coast, the cities, seaports and castles, white exiles and black magic.* Paul, 1954. 249 pp.

2074 HARDING, C. *Far bugles.* Simpkin Marshall, 1933. 229 pp.

2075 HELFRITZ HANS. *Schwarze Ritter zwischen Niger und Tschad: ein Reisebericht von Westafrika durch die Länder Liberia, Französisch-Guinea, Elfenbeinküste, Französischer-Sudan, Obervolta, Ghana,*

Togo, Dahomey und Nigeria. Berlin, Safari-Verlag, [1958]. 357 pp. (Die Welt von heut.)

2076   HOWE, R. W. *Black star rising: a journey through West Africa in transition.* Jenkins, 1958. 254 pp.

2077   HUXLEY, ELSPETH. *Four guineas: a journey through West Africa.* Chatto & Windus, 1953. 303 pp.

2078   INGRAMS, WILLIAM HAROLD. *Seven across the Sahara from Ash to Accra.* Murray, 1950. xvi, 231 pp.
Chief Commissioner, Northern Territories, 1947–1948.

2079   KILLMER, LOTHAR. *Die Freiheitstrommel von Accra: Reisenotizen aus Ghana.* Berlin, Neues Leben, 1962. 168 pp.

2080   KLAGES, J. *Navrongo: ein Afrikabuch mit 108 Aufnahmen.* Zürich, Rotapfel, 1953.
Northern Ghana, mainly photographs.

2081   KUKKAMAKI, ANNA-LIISA. *Rumpujen Afrikkaa.* Helsinki, Soderstrom, 1948.
A Finnish writer's description of the Gold Coast.

2082   LEITH-ROSS, SYLVIA. *Beyond the Niger.* Lutterworth Press, 1951. 123 pp.

2083   LEWIS, N. *The changing sky: travels of a novelist.* Cape, 1959. 254 pp.

2084   MALAVOY, J. 'Sur le Voltaien et l'Atacora, Togo et Dahomey.' *Notes Communiqués à l'Académie des Sciences,* **195,** 1933: 617–713.

2085   MEEKER, ODEN. *Report on Africa.* Chatto & Windus, 1955.

2086   METZGER, O. F. *Unsere alte Kolonie Togo.* Neudamm, Neumann, 1941. 295 pp.

2087   MITCHISON, NAOMI. *Other people's worlds.* Secker & Warburg, 1958. 160 pp.
Impressions of Ghana during the independence celebrations.

2088   MOSSLEY, N. *African switchback.* Weidenfeld & Nicholson, 1958. 224 pp.
A journey from Dakar to Lagos.

2089   REYNOLDS, ALEXANDER JACOB. *African passage.* Muller, 1935. 303 pp.

2090   —— *From the Ivory Coast to the Cameroons.* Knopf, 1929. 298 pp.

2091   ROUCH, JANE. *Le rire n'a pas de couleur.* Paris, Gallimard, 1956. 267 pp.
The Gold Coast before independence.

2092 RYAN, ISOBEL. *Black man's town* [Takoradi.] Cape, 1953. 249 pp.

2093 SCHMIDT-DANNERT, CHRISTA. *Als Hausfrau und Mutter in den Tropen: Erfahrungen und Erlebnisse einer deutschen Arztfrau.* Stuttgart, Hippokrates Verlag, 1942. 231 pp.
Experiences of a doctor's wife at Agogo.

2094 —— *Birgit im Busch: Erzählung von der Goldküste.* Stuttgart, Evang. Missionsverlag, 1955. 112 pp.

2095 SUTHERLAND, EFUA, AND BELL, WILLIS E. *Playtime in Africa;* text by Efua Sutherland, photographs by Willis E. Bell. Accra, the authors, 1960.
A picture book for children.

2096 —— *The roadmakers;* photographs by Willis E. Bell, planned and written by Efua Sutherland. Neame, 1961. 4, 63 pp.

2097 VANE, M. *Black magic and white medicine: a mine medical officer's experiences in South Africa, the Belgian Congo, Sierra Leone and the Gold Coast.* Chambers, 1957. 254 pp.

2098 WARNER, D. *Ghana and the new Africa.* Muller, 1960. 181 pp.

2099 WILLS, COLIN. *White traveller in black Africa.* Dobson, 1951. 207 pp.
Mainly West Africa.

2100 WRIGHT, RICHARD. *Black power: a record of reactions in a land of pathos.* N.Y., Harper, 1954. Dobson, 1956. 358 pp.

2101 —— *Puissance noire; traduit de l'Americain par Roger Giroux.* Paris, Chastel, 1955. 400 pp.

Arts and Crafts

2102 ABEL, H. 'Déchiffrement des poids à peser l'or en Côte d'Ivoire.' *J. Soc. Africanistes*, **22**, 1952: 95–114.

2103 ANTUBAM, KOFI. 'Arts of Ghana.' *United Asia*, **9**, 1, 1957: 61–70.

2104 BRINKWORTH, IAN. 'Ashanti art in London: the Wallace Collection.' *W. Afr. Rev.*, March 1960: 26–30.

2105 COLLINS, W. B. 'Rural industries in the Gold Coast.' *Empire forestry J.*, **26**, 2, 1947: 263–267.

2106 ELISOFON, E. *The sculpture of Africa;* text by William Fagg. Thames & Hudson, 1958. 256 pp.
Many examples from West Africa. Well illustrated.

2107 FAGG, WILLIAM. 'A golden ram head from Ashanti.' *Man*, **54**, 20, Feb. 1954: 17.

2108 'Little known examples of native art: art in the Gold Coast.' *W. Afr. Rev.*, July 1951: 761–764.

2109 FAHRENFORT, J. J. 'Negerrijken in Afrika.' *Geografisch T.* ['s-Gravenhage], **11**, 3 July 1958: 106–117.

2110 GHANA CRAFTS, LTD. *Ghanacraft.* Accra, [1960?]. [12] pp.
Advertising brochure, mainly illustrations.

2111 'Ghana's art in museum collections.' *W. Afr. Rev.*, Dec. 1957: 1183–1188.

2112 GLUCK, J. *Die Goldgewichte von Oberguinea.* Heidelberg, Winter, 1937. 132 pp.

2113 'Gold Coast architecture.' *W. Afr. Rev.*, **15**, 198, March 1944: 19–22.

2114 HIMMELHEBER, HANS. *Negerkunst und Negerkünstler.* Braunschweig, Klinkhardt & Biermann, 1960. 436 pp.

2115 HUBER, HUGO. 'Traditional crafts in a Ningo village.' *Anthropos*, **54**, 3/4, 1959: 574–576.

2116 KJERSMEIER, CARL. *African Negro sculptures*. Zwemmer, 1947. 86 pp.

2117 —— *Ashanti-Vaegtlodder*. [Ashantiweights.] Copenhagen, Gjeller-ups Forlag; Kegan Paul, 1948. 23 pp.

2118 KYEREMATEN, A. A. Y. *Asante Cultural Centre*. Accra, Guinea Press, 1959. 22 pp.
The Cultural Centre in Kumasi includes a museum, library and zoological gardens.

2119 —— *Regalia for an Ashanti Durbar: guide to Durbar in honour of Her Majesty Queen Elizabeth II at Kumasi on 14th November, 1961*. Kumasi, Kwame Nkrumah University of Science and Technology, 1961. 16 pp.

2120 LEONARD, A. G. K. 'Stamps of West Africa.' *W. Afr. Rev.*, July 1960: 12–16.

2121 LEUZINGER, ELEY. *Africa: the art of the Negro peoples*. Methuen, 1960. 247 pp.

2122 MELLANBY, JOHN. 'African stamp album: the old Gold Coast.' *Afr. Trade*, **8**, 4, 1961: 15–16.

2123 MEYEROWITZ, EVA L. R. 'Some gold, bronze and brass objects from Ashanti.' *Burlington Magazine*, **139**, 526, Jan. 1947: 18–21.

2124 'National Museum of the Gold Coast.' *W. Afr. Rev.*, May 1954: 406–408.

2125 'New stamps for old: first permanent Ghana issue.' *W. Afr. Rev.*, Dec. 1959: 837–839.

2126 PARSONS, H. ALEXANDER. *The colonial coinages of British Africa*. Spink, 1950. 94 pp.

2127 PLASS, MARGARET WEBSTER. 'Poids à l'or des Ashanti.' *Présence afr.*, **10/11**, 1951: 163–166.

2128 'Preserving Ashanti culture: Cultural Centre at Kumasi.' *W. Afr., Rev.*, **31**, 395, Oct. 1960: 43–45.

2129 SADLER, M. E. *Arts of West Africa (excluding music)*. O.U.P., 1935.
Published for the International Institute of African Languages and Cultures.

2130 SEGY, L. *African sculpture speaks*. Calder, 1955.

2131 SUTHERLAND, CAROL H. V. *Gold: its beauty, power and allure*. Thames & Hudson, 1959. 196 pp.

2132 SYDOW, ECKART VON. *Handbuch der westafrikanischen Plastik.* Berlin, Reimer, 1930. Bd. 1. xii, 494 pp.

2133 'Town of royal weavers' [Bonweri]. *West Africa*, 14 July 1956: 483.

2134 'The Treasures of Ghana: focus on the greatest artistic achievement of the Ashanti nation.' *W. Afr. Rev.*, March 1957: 297–302.

2135 TROWELL, M. *African design.* Faber, 1960. 79 pp.
Patterns on textiles, basketry, wood, pottery and metalwork.

2136 UNDERWOOD, LEON. *Bronzes of West Africa.* Tiranti, 1949. 32 pp.

2137 —— *Figures in wood of West Africa.* Tiranti, 1947. 49 pp.

2138 —— *Masks of West Africa.* Tiranti, 1948. 49 pp.

See also nos. 486, 850, 936.

Music

2139   AMU, E. 'How to study African rhythm.' *Teachers' J.*, **6**, 2, 1934: 121–124.

2140   —— *Three solo songs with pianoforte accompaniment.* Accra, Presbyterian Book Depot, 1961. 16 pp.
     Contents: Bonwere Kentenwene (Bonwere weaving); Akwaabadwom; Mawue naa me, Mawue tea me.

2141   —— *Twenty-five African songs in the Twi language. Music and words.* Sheldon Press, 1932. 91 pp.

2142   AZU, ENOCH. *Adangbe historical and proverbial songs.* Accra, Govt. Printer, 1929. vii, 136 pp.

2143   BOATENG, O. A. *Infant singing in African schools.* O.U.P., 1948. 29 pp.

2144   —— *Songs for infant schools (Twi).* O.U.P., 1948. 32 pp.
     A collection of Gold Coast Folk songs with melody and tonic sol-fa.

2145   CUDJOE, SETH D. 'The techniques of Ewe drumming and the social importance of music in Africa.' *Phylon [Atalanta]*, **14**, 3, 3, 1953: 280–291.

2146   GADZEKPO, B. SINEDZI. 'Making music in Eweland.' *W. Afr. Rev.*, Aug. 1952: 817–821.

2147   GBEHO, PHILIP. *Music of the Ghana National Anthem.* Accra, Govt. Printer, 1958.
     Piano score, with words.

2148   —— 'Music of the Gold Coast.' *Afr. Music*, **1**, 1954: 62–64.

2149   JONES, A. M. 'African rhythm.' *Africa*, **24**, 1, Jan. 1954: 26–47.

2150   —— *Studies in African music.* O.U.P., 1959. 2 vols. Published for the School of Oriental and African Studies. Contains extensive references to Ewe music, with transcriptions. A comment on this publication appears in *W. Afr. Rev.*, March 1961: 39+ (Philip Gbeho and Seth Cudjoe).

2151 NKETIA, J. H. KWABENA. 'African Gods and music.' *Universitas*, **4**, 1, 1959: 3–7.

2152 —— 'Changing traditions of folk music in Ghana.' *J. Int. Folk Music Council*, **11**, 1959: 31–36.

2153 —— 'The ideal in African folk music: a note on "klama".' *Universitas*, **3**, 2, 1958: 40–42.

2154 —— 'Modern trends in Ghana music.' *Afr. music*, **1**, 4, 1957: 13–17.

2155 —— *Monkamfo no: S.A.T.B.* Words and music by J. H. Kwabena Nketia. Accra, Arts Council of Ghana, 1961. 12 pp. (Choral series, no. 1.)

2156 —— 'The organisation of music in Adangme society.' *Universitas*, **3**, 1, 1957: 9–11.

2157 —— 'Possession dances in African societies.' *J. Int. Folk Music Council*, **9**, 1957: 4–9.

2158 —— 'The role of the drummer in Akan society.' *Afr. music*, **1**, 1954: 34–43.

2159 —— 'Traditional music of the Ga people.' *Universitas*, **3**, 3, 1958: 76–81.

2160 —— 'Yoruba musicians in Accra.' *Odù*, **6**, June 1958: 35–44.

2161 OSAFO, F. O. 'An African orchestra in Ghana.' *Afr. music*, **1**, 4, 1957: 11.

2162 OWUSU, HENRY. *Waltz: Kumasi.* [Piano score.] Kumasi, the author, 1926. 6 pp.

2163 RIVERSON, ISAAC D. *Akan songs*, collected and edited by Isaac D. Riverson. [New ed.] Cape Coast, Methodist Book Depot, 1954. vi, 56 pp.
  Piano score with tonic sol-fa. Previously published as *Songs of the Akan peoples*, 1939.

2164 —— 'The growth of music in the Gold Coast.' *Trans. Gold Coast & Togoland Hist. Soc.*, **1**, 1954: 121–132.

2165 ROBERTS, J. T. *A hymn of thanksgiving, and other songs.* Accra, High School, 1953. 10 pp.

2166 STEWART, J. L. 'Northern Gold Coast songs.' *Afr. Music Soc. Newsletter*, **1**, 65, June 1952: 39–42.

See also nos. 26, 370, 405, 448, 810, 890.

Literature

2167 ABEDI-BOAFO, J. *As I see it.* Aburi, the author, 1941. 57 pp.
Contributions from The African Morning Post.

2168 *Approaches to African literature.* Non-English writings, by Janheinz
Jahn, and English writings in West Africa, by John Ramsaran, with
reading lists. Ibadan U.P., 1959. 31 pp.

2169 GHANA. MINISTRY OF INFORMATION AND BROADCASTING. *Voices of
Ghana: literary contributions to the Ghana Broadcasting System,
1955–57;* edited by H. M. Swanzy. Accra, Govt. Printer, 1958.
266 pp.

2170 HUHES, L., Comp. *An African treasury: articles, essays, stories, poems by
black Africans.* Gollancz, 1961. 207 pp.

2171 JAHN, JANHEINZ. 'Non-English writings' (in *Approaches to African
literature,* 1959).

2172 KOMEY, ELLIS AYITEY. 'Wanted—creative writers.' *W. Afr. Rev.,*
Nov. 1961: 63.

2173 MCLEOD, A. L. ED. *The Commonwealth pen: an introduction to the
literature of the British Commonwealth.* N.Y., Cornell U.P., 1961.
243 pp.
West Africa, by K. E. SENANU: 167–184.

2174 NKETIA, J. H. KWABENA. 'Literatur und Dichtung in Ghana; trans.
by Johannes Stöckle.' *Mitt. Inst. Auslandsbeziehungen,* **9,** 4, Oct.–
Dec. 1959: 265–272.

2175 OFORI, JOHN PATRICK ("Prince of Larteh"). *Wales and Larteh, or
The wonder-portrait.* Nsawam, the author, 1943. 24 pp.
Published to commemorate the visit of the Prince of Wales to
the Gold Coast in 1925. Letters and verses.

2176 RAMSARAN, JOHN. 'English writings in West Africa' (in *Approaches
to African literature,* 1959).

2177 RUTHERFOORD, PEGGY, ED. *Darkness and light: an anthology of
African writing.* Faith Press, 1958. 208 pp.
American edition entitled *African voices,* Vanguard Press, 1960.

2178   SENANU, K. E. 'West Africa' (in MCLEOD, A. L., Ed. *The Common-wealth pen*, 1961: 167–184).

2179   STORCH, R. F. 'Writing in Ghana.' *Universitas*, **2**, 5, 1957: 148–151. *See also* no. 473.

Fiction

2180 ABBS, AKOSUA, PSEUD. (i.e. E. Nockolds). *Ashanti boy*. Collins, 1959. 256 pp.
A story for young people "of all ages".

2181 ABRAHAMS, PETER. *A wreath for Udomo*. Faber, 1956. 309 pp.

2182 ANNAN, K. 'Ding dong bell.' *Africa south*, **3**, 2, 1959: 117–124.
A short story about an Ashanti village.

2183 ASHTON, HELEN. *Letty Landon*. Collins, 1951. 320 pp.
A biography of L. E. L., the London-born journalist and poet who married Capt. George Maclean and died at Cape Coast castle.

2184 BEHN, APHRA. *Two tales: The royal slave, and The fair jilt*. Folio Society, 1953. 147 pp.
Oroonoko, or The history of the royal slave, 1688, is the first English novel referring to the Gold Coast.

2185 BLAY, J. BENIBENGOR. *Dr. Bengia wants a wife*. Blackheath Press, 1953. 23 pp.

2186 BROWN, J. *Boboh, and other stories*. Callam, 1955. 60 pp.

2187 CAUTE, DAVID *At fever pitch*. Deutsch, 1959. 283 pp.
An African state on the point of independence seen through the eyes of a young British subaltern.

2188 CONTON, WILLIAM F. *The African*. Heinemann, 1960. 213 pp.
A young mission-educated Hausa visits England and returns to West Africa to take up a brilliant political career. Author, a Sierra Leoneian, was Headmaster of Accra High School.

2189 DARKO, D. O. *Friends today, enemies tomorrow*. Akropong-Akwapim, Presbyterian Training College, 1959. 45 pp.

2190 DEFOE, DANIEL. *Life, adventures and piracies of the famous Captain Singleton, 1720*. Dent, [194–?].

2191 DESEWU, P. M. *The three brothers, and other stories*. Longmans, 1951. 87 pp.
Ewe traditional tales.

2192 EDU, JOHN E. *Cape Coast "cousin".* Accra, Bureau of Ghana Languages, 1958. 31 pp.

2193 —— *Makola market mysteries.* Accra, [United Press] 1953. 24 pp.

2194 ESKELUND, CARL, AND ESKELUND, K. *Bamburu, boy of Ghana, in West Africa.* Methuen, 1958. 46 pp.
Mainly illustrations. Translated from the Danish.

2195 FIELDING, ANN MARY. *Ashanti blood.* Heinemann, 1952. 246 pp.
The story of a mining disaster.

2196 FRESHFIELD, MARK, PSEUD. (i.e. M. J. Field). *The stormy dawn.* Faber, 1946. 191 pp.
Mission school education in the cocoa producing region of the Gold Coast.

2197 GAUNT, MARY, AND ESSEX, J. R. *Arm of the leopard: a West African story.* Richards, 1904. 306 pp.

2198 —— *The silent ones.* Laurie, [19—]. 344 pp.

2199 HAMBER, THOMAS RUMSEY. *The mine.* Cassell, 1953. 213 pp.
Operations of a gold mine syndicate in western Ghana.

2200 HAMILTON, ANTHONY. *The palm-oil ruffian.* Greening, 1907. 304 pp.

2201 HUXLEY, ELSPETH. *The walled city.* Chatto & Windus, 1947. 319 pp.
The conflict between two colonial civil servants in a West African protectorate.

2202 JOSLIN, MIKE. *Dschungel-Abenteuer: als Wagebauer an der Goldküste.* Wiesbaden, Eberhard, 1957. 190 pp.

2203 —— *Den Medizinmännern entronnen.* Wiesbaden, Eberhard, 1955. 187 pp.

2204 —— *Der Urwald lässt sich nicht besiegen: Weitere Dschungelabenteuer an der Goldküste.* Wiesbaden, Eberhard, 1958. 187 pp.

2205 KNIGHT, BRIGID. *I struggle and I rise.* Cassell, 1946. 432 pp.
Elizabethan maritime enterprise in the sixteenth century and the first landings at Elmina.

2206 LAMPTEY, JONAS. *The village in the trees.* Heinemann, 1955. 274 pp.
Experiences of a young mining engineer in Ashanti.

2207 LAURENCE, MARGARET. *This side Jordan.* Macmillan, 1960. 282 pp.
The Gold Coast some months before independence.

2208 LOADER, W. R. *The guinea stamp.* Cape. 1956. 224 pp.

2209 —— *No joy of Africa.* Cape, 1955. 220 pp.

2210 MUSKETT, NETTA. *Flame of the forest.* Hutchinson, 1958. 240 pp.

2211   NEVILLE, C. J. *Salifu the detective*. 2nd revised ed. Macmillan, 1957. 185 pp.
A book for children on the adventures of a boy in the north of the Gold Coast. First published 1950.

2212   OBENG, R. E. *Eighteenpence*. Birkenhead, Willmer Brothers, 1943. 167 pp.
Claimed to be the first full length novel by a Gold Coast author. See *W. Afr. Rev.*, April 1950: 393.

2213   OKAE, J. D. *Why so stories: Twi stories*, collected by J. D. Okae. Sheldon Press, 1947. 16 pp.

2214   RATTRAY, ROBERT SUTHERLAND. *The leopard priestess*. Butterworth, 1934.

2215   SAM, GILBERT A. *A Christmastide tragedy*. Kumasi, Gilisam Publishing Syndicate, [1956?]. 12 pp.

2216   —— *Love in the grave*. Kumasi, Gilisam Publishing Syndicate, [1959]. 46 pp.

2217   —— *Who killed Inspector Kwasi Minta?* A crime-love story. Kumasi, Gilisam Publishing Syndicate, [1956]. 26 pp.

2218   SKERTCHLY, J. A. *Melinda the caboceer, or, Sport in Ashanti: a tale of the Gold Coast*. Chapman & Hall, 1876. 358 pp.
The Gold Coast in the days of King Koffee Kalcalli.

2219   SOUTHON, ARTHUR E. *The whispering bush: true tales of West Africa*. Hodder & Stoughton, [192–]. 256 pp.

2220   STEEN, MARGUERITE. *The sun is my undoing*. Collins, 1941. 1015 pp.
Slave trading in the West Indies and West Africa.

2221   —— *Twilight on the Floods*. Collins, 1950. 704 pp.
Bristol and the Gold Coast in 1900.

2222   THOMAS, ELWYN. *Night of the Jassies*. Cape, 1959. 222 pp.
The Resident Commissioner faces a tribal uprising in West Guinea before independence.

2223   WELMAN, JOHN B. *A thorny wilderness*. Blackwood, 1952. 292 pp.
Short stories.

2224   WYLLIE, JOHN. *Riot*. Secker & Warburg, 1954. 256 pp.
A British West African colony before independence.

2225   YEULETT, M. *The graven image: West African stories*. Lane, 1939. 206 pp.

2226   YOUNG, CULLEN, Ed. *African new writing: short stories by African authors*. Lutterworth Press, [1947]. 126 pp.
Mainly West African authors.

Poetry

2227 AKO, O. DAZI. *The seductive coast: poems lyrical and descriptive from West Africa.* Ouseley, 1909. 164 pp.

2228 ARMATTOE, RAPHAEL ERNEST GRAIL. *"Between the forest and the sea": collected poems.* Londonderry, Lomeshire Research Centre, [1950]. 77 pp.
The poetry of Dr. R. E. G. Armattoe is discussed in the *W. Afr. Rev.*, March–May 1957. See also no. 2241.

2229 —— *Deep down the blackman's mind: poems.* Ilfracombe, Stockwell, [195–]. 112 pp.

2230 ASANTE, DAVID. 'Illusion' [poems]. *Afr. affairs*, **52**, 209, Oct. 1953: 334–336.

2231 BASSIR, OLUMBE, Comp. *An anthology of West African verse.* Ibadan U.P., 1957. xii, 68 pp.
Includes verses by Ghanaian writers: Efua Morgue, J. B. Danquah, Seth D. Cudjoe and R. E. G. Armattoe.

2232 BLAY, J. BENIBENGOR. *Thoughts of youth.* Aboso, Benibengor Book Agency, 1961. 130 pp.

2233 BORQUAYE, J. B. Y. *Songs of kings: a book of verse.* Ilfracombe, Stockwell, [193–]. 23 pp.

2234 DEI-ANANG, MICHAEL. *Africa speaks: a collection of original verse with an introduction on "Poetry in Africa".* Accra, Guinea Press, 1959. 99 pp.

2235 —— *Wayward lines from Africa.* United Society for Christian Literature, 1946. 48 pp. (Africa's own library, no. 15.)

2236 HEDGES, WALTER FREDERICK. *Christiansborg Castle, and other verse; with illustrations by the author.* Eastleigh (Hants.), Eastleigh Printing Works, 1924. 106 pp.

2237 KOMEY, ELLIS AYITEY. 'Africa: three poems on the African personality.' *W. Afr. Rev.*, April 1960: 47.

2238 KURANKYI-TAYLOR, D. *Reflected thoughts.* Ilfracombe, Stockwell, 1959. 39 pp.

2239 NICOL, DAVIDSON. *West African poetry*. Africa south in exile, April–June 1961: 115–122.
A short history of West African poetry and European influence.

2240 NKETIA, K. 'Akan poetry.' *Black Orpheus*, **3**, May 1958: 5–28.

2241 RAS KAN, PSEUD. (i.e. Amon Kotei). 'The poetry of Dr. R. E. G. Armattoe.' *Présence afr.*, fév.–mars 1957: 32–47.

2242 SITWELL, EDITH. *Gold Coast customs*. [Poems.] Duckworth, [1929]. 63 pp.

2243 STEWART, MACNEILL. *The ballad of the village girl*. Accra, Guinea Press, [196–]. 12 pp.

Plays

2244 DANQUAH, JOSEPH BOAKYE. *Nyankonsem*. Fables of the celestial. *Agoru bi a woakye abiesa*. A play in three acts, done entirely in the Twi language. Longmans, 1941. viii, 56 pp.

2245 —— *The third woman: a play in five acts*. United Society for Christian Literature, 1943. 151 pp.

2246 DEI–ANANG, MICHAEL. *Cocoa comes to Mampong: brief dramatic sketches based on the story of cocoa in the Gold Coast, and some occasional verses*. Cape Coast, Methodist Book Depot, 1949. 47 pp.

2247 —— *Okomfo Anokye's golden stool: a play in three acts*. Ilfracombe, Stockwell, 1960. 54 pp.
   Based on the traditional story of the Ashanti Golden Stool. Review: *W. Afr. Rev.*, May 1960: 67.

2248 FIAWOO, F. KWASI. *The fifth landing stage: a play in five acts*. Lutter-worth Press, 1943. 88 pp.
   An Ewe traditional story.

2249 ——'Die fünfte Lagune.' [The fifth landing stage.] Translated by Reinhold Schober. *Mitt. Ausland-Hochschule*, **40**, 1937: 1–127.

2250 SOUTHERNE, THOMAS. *Oroonoko: a tragedy*.
   Based on the novel by Aphra Behn. First published 1695.

See also no. 503.

Government Publications

Publications of the respective governments of the Gold Coast, Ghana and the United Kingdom are arranged in chronological order.

The Gold Coast

2251   GOLD COAST. GOVERNMENT, 1930. *Despatches relating to coast erosion in the neighbourhood of Keta.* (Sessional paper 15 of 1929–30.)

2252   —— 1930. *Report by the Special Commissioner for Anthropology, 1929–30.*

2253   —— 1930. *Correspondence relating to the revision of the initial rates of salary in the African Civil Service.* (Sessional paper 1 of 1930–31.)

2254   —— 1930. *Scheme for the re-organization of the Government Technical School, Accra.* (Sessional paper 2 of 1930–31.)

2255   —— 1930. *Despatch relating to the oil palm industry, with particular reference to a subsidy scheme for palm oil mills.* (Sessional paper 3 of 1930–31.)

2256   —— 1930. *Notes of evidence taken by the Commission of Enquiry regarding consumption of spirits in the Gold Coast.* (Sessional paper 4 of 1930–31.)

2257   —— 1930. *Report on the Gold Coast Government Commercial Intelligence Bureau for the year 1929.* (Sessional paper 5 of 1930–31.)

2258   —— 1930. *Report of the Standing Finance Committee of the Legislative Council held on the 14th May, 1930.* (Sessional paper 6 of 1930–31.)

2259   —— 1930. *Despatches relating to the Kumasi water supply (Owabi) scheme.* (Sessional paper 7 of 1930–31.)

2260   —— 1930. *Despatches relating to the estimates of revenue and expenditure, 1930–31.* (Sessional paper 8 of 1930–31.)

2261   —— 1930. *Further despatches relating to the scheme for the immunisation of cattle in the Northern Territories of the Gold Coast against rinderpest.* (Sessional paper 9 of 1930–31.)

2262 GOLD COAST. GOVERNMENT, 1930. *Correspondence relating to the proposed Western Province railway from Tarkwa to Bibianiha.* (Sessional paper 10 of 1930–31.)

2263 —— 1930. *Report of the Standing Finance Committee of the Legislative Council held on the 25th, 26th June, 1930.* (Sessional paper 11 of 1930–31.)

2264 —— 1930. *Report of the Standing Finance Committee of the Legislative Council held on the 25th September, 1930.* (Sessional paper 12 of 1930–31.)

2265 —— 1930. *Correspondence relating to the installation of an electric light and power plant at Cape Coast.* (Sessional paper 13 of 1930–31.)

2266 —— 1930. *Despatches relating to the Tamale Water Supply Scheme.* (Sessional paper 14 of 1930–31.)

2267 —— 1930. *Correspondence relating to a scheme for extending the system of village dispensaries and improving the training of the African nursing and dispensing staff.* (Sessional paper 15 of 1930–31.)

2268 —— 1930. *Despatches from the Secretary of State relating to the proposal to establish a Medical College in the Gold Coast, together with regulations and conditions for the award of Government scholarships to African students for the purpose of studying medicine in the United Kingdom.* (Sessional paper 16 of 1930–31.)

2269 —— 1930. *Despatches on the subject of the report of the Commission of Inquiry regarding the consumption of spirits in the Gold Coast.* [Continuation of no. 4 of 1930–31.] (Sessional paper 17 of 1930–31.)

2270 —— 1930. *Memorandum on the creation of a fund for improving the quality and marketing of cocoa.* (Sessional paper 18 of 1930–31.)

2271 —— 1930. *Enquiry under the Fires and Occurrences Inquiry Ordinance (Cap. 59) into the wounding of eight Africans at Prestea on 15th September, 1930.* (Sessional paper 19 of 1930–31.)

2272 —— 1930. *Further correspondence relating to the proposed Western Province railway, Tarkwa-Bebianiha.* (Sessional paper 20 of 1930-31.)

2273 —— 1930. *Report of the Standing Finance Committee of the Legislative Council held on the 6th December, 1931.* (Sessional paper 21 of 1930–31.)

2274 —— 1930. *Memorandum by Sir Albert Kitson, C.M.G., C.B.E., on the operations of the Geological Survey Department of the Gold Coast, 1913–30.* (Sessional paper 22 of 1930–31.)

2275 GOLD COAST. GOVERNMENT, 1930. *Papers relating to the organization of a unified Colonial Agricultural Service.* (Sessional paper 23 of 1930–31.)

2276 —— 1930. *Correspondence relating to the raising of a loan of £1,156,000.* (Sessional paper 24 of 1930–31.)

2277 —— 1930. *Report by Dr. M. B. D. Dixey, Medical Secretary, British Empire Leprosy Relief Association (Gold Coast Branch): leprosy in the Gold Coast.* (Sessional paper 25 of 1930–31.)

2278 —— 1930. *Correspondence relating to the rates of pensions paid to ex-members of the Gold Coast Regiment, Royal West African Frontier Force.* (Sessional paper 26 of 1930–31.)

2279 —— 1930. *Reports on the water supply of the coastal area of the Eastern Province of the Gold Coast Colony.* (Sessional paper 27 of 1930–31.)

2280 —— 1930. *Report of the Standing Finance Committee of the Legislative Council held on the 24th February, 1931.* (Sessional paper 28 of 1930–1931.)

2281 —— 1930. *Report of the Select Committee on the estimates for the financial year 1931–1932.* (Sessional paper 29 of 1930–31.)

2282 —— 1930. *Correspondence relating to the gift of £3,000 by Cadbury Brothers, Limited for the purpose of assisting the Government of the Gold Coast in the training of Practical Cacao Farmers. "Hunter Hostels."* (Sessional paper 30 of 1930–31.)

2283 —— 1930. *Report of a committee appointed by H. E. the Governor to consider the cost of education to Government and to the Missions, under the existing education rules.* (Chairman, R. A. Kelly.)

2284 —— 1930. *Address delivered by the Governor, Sir Ransford Slater, on the occasion of the opening of the 1930–31 session of the Legislative Council of the Gold Coast.*

2285 —— 1931. *Correspondence relating to the proposal to close down the Gold Coast Commercial Intelligence Bureau.* (Sessional paper 1 of 1931–32.)

2286 —— 1931. *Further correspondence relating to the revision of the initial rates of salary in the African Civil Service.* [Continuation of no. 1 of 1930–31.] (Sessional paper 2 of 1931–32.)

2287 —— 1931. *Report of the meeting of the Standing Finance Committee of the Legislative Council held on the 10th June, 1931.* (Sessional paper 3 of 1931–32.)

2288 —— 1931. *Cola survey of the Eastern Ashanti areas and a general review of the Gold Coast cola industry.* (Sessional paper 4 of 1931–32.)

2289   GOLD COAST. GOVERNMENT, 1931. *Despatches relating to the estimates of revenue & expenditure, 1931-32.* (Sessional paper 5 of 1931-32.)

2290   —— 1931. *Report on Keta lagoon,* by J. L. LONGBOTTOM. (Sessional paper 6 of 1931-32.)

2291   —— 1931. *Statement showing the area of land owned by the Government in each Province and District in the Gold Coast Colony relating to the total area thereof.* (Sessional paper 7 of 1931-32.)

2292   —— 1931. *Report of the meeting of the Standing Finance Committee of the Legislative Council held on the 23rd September, 1931.* (Sessional paper 8 of 1931-32.)

2293   —— 1931. *Report of the committee appointed to consider certain proposals to amend the Motor Traffic Ordinance.* (Sessional paper 9 of 1931-32.)

2294   —— 1931. *Report and recommendations of the Further Retrenchment Committee, 1931.* (Sessional paper 10 of 1931-32.)

2295   —— 1931. *Correspondence relating to the proposed imposition of a water rate in areas enjoying a pipe-born supply.* (Sessional paper 11 of 1931-32.)

2296   —— 1931. *The Asafu Organization of the Gold Coast.* (Sessional paper 12 of 1931-32.)

2297   —— 1931. *Railway Retrenchment Committee report and recommendations, 1931.* (Sessional paper 13 of 1931-32.)

2298   —— 1931. *Correspondence relating to the extension of Cape Coast water supply to Elmina, Saltpond and intermediate villages.* (Sessional paper 14 of 1931-32.)

2299   —— 1931. *Report of the Select Committee on the estimates, 1932-33.* (Sessional paper 15 of 1931-32.)

2300   —— 1931. *Reports on the water supply of the coastal area of the Eastern Province of the Gold Coast Colony,* by W. G. G. COOPER. (Sessional paper 27 of 1931.)

2301   —— 1931. *Address delivered by His Excellency the Acting Governor on the occasion of the opening of the 1931-2 session of the Legislative Council.*

2302   —— 1932. *Report and recommendations of the Committee on Educational Expenditure.* (Sessional paper 1 of 1932.)

2303   —— 1932. *Report of the meeting of the Standing Finance Committee of the Legislative Council held on the 7th March, 1932.* (Sessional paper 2 of 1932-33.)

2304 GOLD COAST. GOVERNMENT, 1932. *Report of the Railway Revenue Committee (road v. rail).* (Sessional paper 3 of 1932–33.)

2305 ——— 1932. *Despatches relating to the estimates of revenue & expenditure, 1932–33.* (Sessional paper 4 of 1932–33.)

2306 ——— 1932. *Report of the meeting of the Standing Finance Committee of the Legislative Council held on the 16th September, 1932.* (Sessional paper 5 of 1932–33.)

2307 ——— 1932. *The Gold Coast, 1931: appendices containing comparative and general statistics of the 1931 census.* 246 pp.

2308 ——— 1932. *Address delivered by His Excellency the Governor on the occasion of the opening of the 1932–33 session of the Legislative Council 1st March 1932.*

2309 ——— 1933. *The gold and other mineral resources of the Gold Coast and Sierra Leone: an address delivered in London on the 12th October, 1932 by N. R. Junner, Director of the Geological Survey.* (Sessional paper 1 of 1933.)

2310 ——— 1933. *Report of the meeting of the Standing Finance Committee of the Legislative Council held on 24th March, 1933.* (Sessional paper 2 of 1933.)

2311 ——— 1933. *Report of the Select Committee on the estimates for 1933–34.* (Sessional paper 3 of 1933.)

2312 ——— 1933. *Joint Conference on the Provincial Councils: memorial and Governor's reply.* (Sessional paper 4 of 1933).

2313 ——— 1933. *Despatches relating to the estimates of revenue & expenditure, 1933–34.* (Sessional paper 5 of 1933.)

2314 ——— 1934. *Report on the commercial possibilities and development of the forests of the Gold Coast.* (Sessional paper 1 of 1934.)

2315 ——— 1934. *Report of the Cocoa Exportation Committee.* (Sessional paper 2 of 1934.)

2316 ——— 1934. *Cocoa memorandum by His Majesty's Government of the United Kingdom.* (Sessional paper 3 of 1934.)

2317 ——— 1934. *Report of the meeting of the Standing Finance Committee of the Legislative Council held on the 14th March, 1934.* (Sessional paper 4 of 1934.)

2318 ——— 1934. *Report of the Select Committee on the estimates for 1934–35.* (Sessional paper 5 of 1934.)

2319   GOLD COAST. GOVERNMENT, 1934. *Report of the meeting of the Standing Finance Committee of the Legislative Council held on the 12th June, 1934.* (Sessional paper 7 of 1934.)

2320   —— 1934. *Report of the Advisory Committee on Education in the colonies on the educational functions of local bodies in the tropical African dependencies.* (Sessional paper 8 of 1934.)

2321   —— 1934. *Despatches relating to the estimates of revenue & expenditure 1934–35.* (Sessional paper 9 of 1934.)

2322   —— 1934. *Papers relating to the petition of the delegation from the Gold Coast Colony and Ashanti.* (Sessional paper 11 of 1934.)

2323   —— 1934. *Report of the committee appointed to investigate the possibility of establishing a permanent Bureau of African Industries.* (Sessional paper 12 of 1934.)

2324   —— 1935. *Papers relating to the accident which occurred on the 5th June, 1934 at the Prestea Mine, in which forty-one persons were killed.* (Sessional paper 1 of 1935.)

2325   —— 1935. *Report of the Select Committee on the estimates for 1935–1936.* (Sessional paper 2 of 1935.)

2326   —— 1935. *Despatches relating to the estimates of revenue & expenditure, 1935–36.* (Sessional paper 4 of 1935.)

2327   —— 1935. *Report of the development of the live-stock industry of the Eastern Province,* by A. FULTON. (Sessional paper 5 of 1935.)

2328   —— 1935. *Memorandum on the revision of salaries and other conditions of service of European officers in West Africa.* (Sessional paper 6 of 1935.)

2329   —— 1935. *Report of the committee on human trypanosomiasis.* 29 pp. (Chairman, F. W. F. Jackson.)

2330   —— 1935. *Papers relating to the restoration of the Ashanti Confederacy.* 115 pp.

2331   —— 1936. *Report on the economics of peasant agriculture in the Gold Coast,* by C. Y. SHEPHARD. (Sessional paper 1 of 1936.)

2332   —— 1936. *Report of the Select Committee on the estimates for 1936–37.* (Sessional paper 2 of 1936.)

2333   —— 1936. *Despatches relating to the estimates of revenue & expenditure, 1936–37.* (Sessional paper 3 of 1936.)

2334   —— 1936. *New leave and passage regulations framed by the Secretary of State for the Colonies in respect of the British West African Colonies.* (Sessional paper 4 of 1936.)

2335 GOLD COAST. GOVERNMENT, 1936. *Financial organization of the Government of the Gold Coast.* (Sessional paper 5 of 1936.)

2336 —— 1937. *Report on the eradication of tsetse fly (of the G. Palpalis group) from the Pong-Tamale area, Northern Territories, Gold Coast.* (Sessional paper 1 of 1937.)

2337 —— 1937. *Papers regarding the proposed establishment of a Technical School at Takoradi.* (Sessional paper 2 of 1937.)

2338 —— 1937. *Report of the Select Committee on the estimates, 1937–38.* (Sessional paper 3 of 1937.)

2339 —— 1937. *Despatches relating to the estimates of revenue & expenditure, 1937–38.* (Sessional paper 4 of 1937.)

2340 —— 1937. *Swollen shoot of cacao: report on Mr. H. A. Dade's visit to the Gold Coast.* 15 pp. (Sessional paper 5 of 1937.)

2341 —— 1938. *Report of the Select Committee on the estimates for 1938–39.* (Sessional paper 1 of 1938.)

2342 1938. *Despatches relating to the estimates of revenue & expenditure, 1938–1939.* (Sessional paper 2 of 1938.)

2343 —— 1939. *Report of the Select Committee on the estimates for 1939–40.* (Sessional paper 1 of 1939.)

2344 —— 1939. *Despatches relating to the estimates of revenue & expenditure. 1939–40.* (Sessional paper 2 of 1939.)

2345 —— 1939. *Preliminary report on the earthquake of 22nd June, 1939.* 5 pp.

2346 —— 1939. *Report on the draft collective marketing scheme framed by the Commission on the Marketing of West African Cocoa.* 191 pp. (Chairman, A. C. Duncan-Johnstone.)

2347 —— 1939. *Report of the Ashanti Advisory Committee on the recommendations of the Cocoa Commission.* 70 pp. (Chairman, J. C. Warrington.)

2348 —— 1939. *Notes for the guidance of Europeans arriving in the Gold Coast.* 6 pp.

2349 —— 1940. *Report of the Select Committee on the estimates for 1940–41.* (Sessional paper 1 of 1940.)

2350 —— 1940. *Report of the Accra Earthquake Rehousing Committee.* (Chairman, E. Norton Jones.)

2351 GOLD COAST. GOVERNMENT, 1941. *Report of the Select Committee on the estimates for 1941–42.* (Sessional paper 1 of 1941.)

2352 —— 1941. *An interim report on the prevalence of silicosis and tuberculosis among mine workers in the Gold Coast.* 17 pp. (Medical Officer, A. J. Murray.)

2353 —— 1942. *Report on the enquiry into the cost of living in the Gold Coast held in January, 1942.* 12 pp. (Chairman, R. O. Ramage.)

2354 —— 1943. *Developmental schemes.* (Sessional paper 1 of 1943.)

2355 —— 1943. *Report of the Native Tribunals Committee of Enquiry.* 29 pp.

2356 —— 1943. *Report of the Committee of Enquiry into the distribution and prices of essential imported goods.* 14 pp.

2357 —— 1944. *Statement on government's policy regarding the appointment of African candidates to the senior posts of the various Government departments.* (Sessional paper 1 of 1944.)

2358 —— 1944. *General plan for development in the Gold Coast.* (Sessional paper 2 of 1944.)

2359 —— 1944. *Water supply schemes for towns.* (Sessional paper 3 of 1944.)

2360 —— 1944. *Electric light and power schemes.* (Sessional paper 4 of 1944.)

2361 —— 1944. *Educational development plans: schemes for immediate expansion of staff.* (Sessional paper 5 of 1944.)

2362 —— 1944. *Technical Training School of the Posts and Telegraphs Department.* (Sessional paper 6 of 1944.)

2363 —— 1944. *The development of the Gold Coast fishery industry.* (Sessional paper 7 of 1944.)

2364 —— 1944. *Firewood reserves.* (Sessional paper 8 of 1944.)

2365 —— 1944. *Report by a Select Committee of the Legislative Council appointed to investigate an allegation made by the Hon. P. Barrow against the Hon. A. W. Kojo Thompson.* (Sessional paper 9 of 1944.)

2366 —— 1944. *Report of the committee appointed by the Resident Minister, West Africa, on the organisation of air transport in West Africa, 1943–1944.* 84 pp.

2367 —— 1944. *Address delivered by His Excellency the Governor, Sir Alan Cuthbert Maxwell Burns, K.C.M.G., on the occasion of the opening of the 1944 session of the Legislative Council, 13th March, 1944.* 38 pp.

2368   GOLD COAST. GOVERNMENT, 1944. *General plan for development in the Gold Coast.* 11 pp.

2369   —— 1944. *Report of the Gold Coast Commission on the distribution and prices of essential imported goods.*

2370   —— 1945. *The development of co-operation in the Gold Coast, 1944–45.* (Sessional paper 1 of 1945.)

2371   —— 1945. *Report of the Select Committee of the Legislative Council appointed to consider the Draft Estimates, 1945–46.* (Sessional paper 2 of 1945.)

2372   —— 1945. *Forestry in the Northern Territories of the Gold Coast,* by R. C. MARSHALL, Chief Conservator of Forests. (Sessional paper 3 of 1945.)

2373   —— 1945. *Further proposals for the development of education in the Gold Coast.* (Sessional paper 4 of 1945.)

2374   —— 1945. *Demobilisation and resettlement of Gold Coast Africans in the armed forces.* (Sessional paper 5 of 1945.)

2375   —— 1945. *Report of the Road-Rail Transport Committee.* (Sessional paper 6 of 1945.)

2376   —— 1945. *Address delivered by His Excellency the Governor, Sir Alan Cuthbert Maxwell Burns, K.C.M.G., on the occasion of the opening of the 1945 session of the Legislative Council, 6th March, 1945.* 38 pp.

2377   —— 1945. *Report on the service malaria control scheme at Accra and Takoradi.*

2378   —— 1945. *Report of the Commission of Inquiry into expenses incurred by litigants in the courts of the Gold Coast, and indebtedness caused thereby.* 47 pp. (Chairman, C. R. Havers.)

2379   —— 1946. *Despatches relating to the separation of the accounts of the Gold Coast Railway, Takoradi Harbour and the Railway Electricity Supply from those of the Colony.* (Sessional paper 1 of 1946.)

2380   —— 1946. *Report of the Select Committee on the estimates, 1946–47.* (Sessional paper 2 of 1946.)

2381   —— 1946. *Report on the control of malaria in the Accra, Takoradi and Sekondi area,* by DR. BRUCE WILSON. (Sessional paper 3 of 1946.)

2382   —— 1946. *Despatch on higher education in West Africa,* by the Secretary of State for the Colonies. (Sessional paper 4 of 1946.)

2383 GOLD COAST. GOVERNMENT, 1946. *Trusteeship proposals for territories under United Kingdom Mandate.* (Sessional paper 5 of 1946.)

2384 —— 1946. *Report of the Committee on Higher Education, August-November, 1946.* 26 pp. (Sessional paper 7 of 1946.) (Chairman, K. Bradley.)

2385 —— 1946. *A brief account of the Gold Coast, prepared for the use of visitors.* 21 pp.

2386 —— 1946. *Progress report on the ten-year plan of development and welfare.*

2387 —— 1947. *Revised conditions of service for the Gold Coast civil service, 1946.* 72 pp. (Sessional paper 1 of 1947.)

2388 —— 1947. *Despatch on development of trades unions in the Gold Coast.* 4 pp. (Sessional paper 2 of 1947.)

2389 —— 1947. *Report of the Select Committee on the estimates, 1947–48.* (Sessional paper 3 of 1947.)

2390 —— 1947. *The training of nurses in the Gold Coast.* (Sessional paper 4 of 1947.)

2391 —— 1947. *Report of the committee on the unestablished and daily-paid subordinate staff of the Central Government of the Gold Coast.* (Sessional paper 5 of 1947.)

2392 —— 1947. *Report of the committee on the scale of emoluments applicable to teachers in non-Government institutions.* 20 pp. (Sessional paper 6 of 1947.)

2393 —— 1947. *Report by a Select Committee of the Legislative Council appointed to examine the question of the abandonment of the criterion of past performances and the substitution therefor of a suitable alternative system.* 4 pp. (Sessional paper 7 of 1947.)

2394 —— 1947. *Correspondence relating to representations of the Gold Coast Railway Employees Union, Post Office Employees Union and P.W.D. Employees Union in regard to wages and conditions of service.* (Sessional paper 8 of 1947.)

2395 —— 1947. *Memorandum on colonial mining policy.* (Sessional paper 9 of 1947.)

2396 —— 1947. *Town and country planning in the Gold Coast.* 16 pp.

2397 —— 1947. *Report of the Committee of Enquiry into the conduct and management of the Supplies and Customs Departments.* 51 pp.

13

2398   GOLD COAST. GOVERNMENT, 1947. *Trade dispute between the Gold Coast Mines Employees Union and the Gold Coast Chamber of Mines: award of Arbitrator.* 83 pp. (Arbitrator, William Gorman.)

2399   —— 1948. *Interim report of the Committee of Enquiry to review legislation for the treatment of the swollen shoot disease of cocoa.* (Sessional paper 1 of 1948.) (Chairman, W. H. Beeton.)

2400   —— 1948. *Concluding report of the Committee of Enquiry to review legislation for the treatment of swollen shoot disease of cocoa.* (Sessional paper 2 of 1948.)

2401   —— 1948. *Report of the Select Committee of the Legislative Council of the Gold Coast on the Draft Estimates, 1948–49 as adopted at the meeting of the Legislative Council held on the 7th May, 1948.* (Sessional paper 3 of 1948.)

2402   —— 1948. *Supplement to the report of the Select Committee on the estimates, 1948–49.* (Sessional paper 4 of 1948.)

2403   —— 1948. *Report of a conference on the Cape Coast Secondary School.* 7 pp. (Sessional paper 5 of 1948.)

2404   —— 1948. *Financial devolution.* (Sessional paper 6 of 1948.)

2405   —— 1948. *Report of the Committee of Enquiry into the representations made repudiating allegations in the report of the committee of enquiry into the conduct and management of the Supplies and Customs Departments.* 144 pp.

2406   —— 1948. *Progress reports for the period ended 31st December 1947 on the draft ten-year plan of development and welfare.* 14 pp.

2407   —— 1949. *Report of the Select Committee of the Legislative Council of the Gold Coast on the draft estimates of revenue and expenditure of the Gold Coast for 1949–50.* (Sessional paper 1 of 1949.)

2408   —— 1949. *Supplement to the report of the Select Committee on the draft estimates for the financial year 1949–50.* (Sessional paper 2 of 1949.)

2409   —— 1949. *Revenue and expenditure of native authority in the Colony, Ashanti and the Northern Territories for the year ending 31st March 1948.* (Sessional paper 3 of 1949.)

2410   —— 1949. *Award in the matter of a trade dispute between employers and workmen of the Gold Coast Railway.* 9 pp. (Arbitrator, L. E. V. M'Carthy.)

2411   GOLD COAST. GOVERNMENT, 1949. *The application of nomograms to the purification by chemical treatment of tropical waters,* by J. S. DUNN. 17 pp.

2412   —— 1949. *Official statement on the report of the Committee on Constitutional Reform and the Secretary of State's despatch.* 2 pp.

2413   —— 1949. *The Gold Coast: a brief description for presentation at the Gold Coast stand, British Industries Fair, 1949: topography, climate, population, history, agriculture, forestry statistics.* 32 pp.

2414   —— 1950. *Report of the Select Committee on Africanization of the Public Service.* 45 pp. (Sessional paper 1 of 1950.)

2415   —— 1950. *Report of the Select Committee of the Legislative Council of the Gold Coast on the draft estimates of revenue and expenditure of the Gold Coast for 1950–51.* (Sessional paper 2 of 1950.)

2416   —— 1950. *Supplement to the report of the Select Committee on the draft estimates for the year 1950–51.* (Sessional paper 3 of 1950.)

2417   —— 1950. *Supplement to the report of the Select Committee of the Legislative Council on the Africanization of the Public Service.* (Sessional paper 4 of 1950.)

2418   —— 1950. *Report of the Select Committee appointed to examine the questions of elections and constituencies.* 43 pp. (Sessional paper 5 of 1950.) (Chairman, F. K. Ewart.)

2419   —— 1950. *Revenue and expenditure of local governments in the Colony, Ashanti and the Northern Territories for the year ending 31st March, 1949.* (Sessional paper 6 of 1950.)

2420   —— 1950. *Report of the committee appointed to examine the grant-in-aid system for educational institutions.* (Sessional paper 7 of 1950.)

2421   —— 1950. *Address delivered by His Excellency the Governor, Sir Charles Noble Arden-Clarke, K.C.M.G., on the occasion of the opening of the 1950 budget meeting of the Legislative Council on the 28th February, 1950.* 58 pp.

2422   —— 1950. *The new consititution in outline.* 11 pp.

2423   —— 1950. *A handbook for departmental training officers.* Dept. of Recruitment and Training. 28 pp.

2424   —— 1950. *Report to the Secretary of State for the Colonies by Dr. G. B. Jeffery, F.R.S. on a visit to West Africa, December 1949 to March 1950.* 15 pp.
       Recommendations for the creation of a "West African Examinations Council".

2425   GOLD COAST. GOVERNMENT, 1950. *Report of the committee of the Legislature appointed to consider and report on certain questions arising from the effect of the cost of living on the civil service.* 22 pp. (Chairman, Sir Tsibu Darku.)

2426   —— 1950. *Supplementary report of the committee of the Legislature appointed to consider and report on certain questions arising from the effect of the cost of living on the civil service.* 8 pp.

2427   —— 1950. *Ashanti native authority finance, 1949–1950.* Public Relations Dept. 30 pp.

2428   —— 1950. *The Coussey Report in outline.* Public Relations Dept. 14 pp.

2429   —— 1950. *General elections for the new Legislative Assembly. Part 1: How to register as an elector.* Public Relations Dept. 16 pp.

2430   —— 1951. *Memorandum on the Gold Coast estimates for the financial year.* (Sessional paper 1 of 1951.)

2431   —— 1951. *Report on local government finance, 1950.* (Sessional paper 2 of 1951.)

2432   —— 1951. *Report of the Committee on Prisons.* (Sessional paper 3 of 1951.)

2433   —— 1951. *Report on banking conditions in the Gold Coast and on the question of setting up a National Bank.* (Chairman, Sir Cecil Trevor.)

2434   —— 1951. *Regional administration: report of the Commissioner (Sir S. Phillipson).* 219 pp.

2435   —— 1951. *Report of the Commission on Native Courts.* 43 pp. (Chairman, K. A. Korsah.)

2436   —— 1951. *Report of the Committee of Enquiry into rentals.*

2437   —— 1951. *The Development Plan, 1951.* 34 pp.

2438   —— 1951. *Report of the Committee of Enquiry into the existing organisation and methods for the control of swollen shoot disease by the compulsory cutting out of infected cocoa trees.* 26 pp. (Chairman, K. A. Korsah.)

2439   —— 1951. *Report by a Select Committee on local government (Colony), 1950.* (Chairman, A. J. Loveridge.)

2440   —— 1951. *Report of a Select Committee appointed to make recommendations concerning local government in Ashanti.* 64 pp.

2441 GOLD COAST. GOVERNMENT, 1951. *A report of a committee on the territorial council of the Northern Territories appointed to make recommendations concerning local government in the Northern Territories.* (Chairmen, G. N. Burden and E. Norton-Jones.)

2442 —— 1951. *Report of the Commission on the civil service of the Gold Coast, 1950–51.* 2 vols. (Chairman, Sir David Lidbury.)

2443 —— 1951. *Statement of the Gold Coast Government on the report of the Commission on the civil service of the Gold Coast, 1950–1.* 9 pp.

2444 —— *Letters Patent, Orders in Council, and Royal Instructions.* 56 pp.

2445 —— 1951. *Achievement in the Gold Coast: aspects of development in the British West African territory.* Public Relations Dept. 96 pp.

2446 —— 1951. *The Gold Coast: a brief description for presentation at the Gold Coast stand, British Industries Fair, 1951.*

2447 —— 1951. *Local government reform in outline, being a summary of the three reports on local government reform and of the related proposals concerning regional administration.* Public Relations Dept. 41 pp.

2448 —— 1952. *Memorandum on the Gold Coast estimates for the financial year.* (Sessional paper 1 of 1952.)

2449 —— 1952. *Report on local government finance.* (Sessional paper 2 of 1952.)

2450 —— 1952. *Report of the Select Committee on the Lidbury Report.* (Sessional paper 3 of 1952.)

2451 —— 1952. *Report of the committee set up to review the salaries and conditions of service of non-Government teachers.* 27 pp. (Sessional paper 4 of 1952.) (Erzuah Report.)

2452 —— 1952. *Report of the Commission of Enquiry into the health needs of the Gold Coast.* (Sessional paper 5 of 1952.)

2453 —— 1952. *Statement of the Government on the report of Commission of Enquiry into the health needs of the Gold Coast.*

2454 —— 1952. *A report upon the Gold Coast police,* by A. E. YOUNG.

2455 —— 1952. *Statement of the Gold Coast Government on the report upon the Gold Coast police,* by A. E. YOUNG.

2456 —— 1952. *Report on the Vernacular Literature Bureau, April 1951–March 1952.* 5 pp.

2457 —— 1952. *A survey of some economic matters.* 31 pp.

2458 GOLD COAST. GOVERNMENT, 1952. *First report of the Select Committee of the Legislative Assembly appointed to consider and advise on plans for a new legislative building.* 10 pp.

2459 —— 1952. *Second report of the Select Committee of the Legislative Assembly appointed to consider and advise on plans for a new legislative building.* 10 pp. 11 plans.

2460 —— 1952. *The new local government: urban, local and district councils explained.* Public Relations Dept. 23 pp.

2461 —— 1953. *Report of the Commission of Enquiry into representational and electoral reform.* (Sessional paper 1 of 1953.) (Chairman, Mr. Justice Van Lare.)

2462 —— 1953. *Report of the Northern Territories Transport Committee.*

2463 —— 1953. *Report on finance and physical problems of development in the Gold Coast.*

2464 —— 1953. *Report of the Mines Labour Enquiry Committee.* 641 pp. (Typescript.)

2465 —— 1953. *The Government's proposals for constitutional reform.* 74 pp.

2466 —— 1953. *The Governor's speech at the prorogation of the Legislative Assembly, 1953 session.* 3 pp.

2467 —— 1953. *Report on the disturbances which took place at Elmina on 9th May, 1953.* 8 pp.

2468 —— 1953. *Handbook for native courts in Ashanti.* 62 pp.

2469 —— 1953. *Final report of the working party to review the Africanisation programme.* 45 pp.

2470 —— 1953. *Appendices to the final report of the working party to review the Africanisation programme.* 171 pp.

2471 —— 1953. *Report of the Broadcasting Commission appointed by the Government of the Gold Coast.* 36 pp. (Chairman, J. Grenfell Williams.)

2472 —— 1953. *Agricultural statistical survey of south-east Akim Abuakwa, 1952-3.* 40 pp. (Statistical and economic papers, no. 1.)

2473 —— 1953. *Accra survey of household budgets, 1953.* 62 pp. (Statistical and economic papers, no. 2.)

2474 —— 1954. *Statement on the programme of the Africanisation of the Public Service.* 76 pp.

2475 GOLD COAST. GOVERNMENT, 1954. *Development progress report for the financial year 1st April 1953–31st March 1954.* 21 pp.

2476 —— 1954. *The Establishment of Building Societies in the Gold Coast:* report by CHARLES GARRATT-HOLDEN. 12 pp.

2477 —— 1954. *Report of the Commission of Enquiry into Mr. Braimah's resignation and allegations arising therefrom.* 46 pp.

2478 —— 1954. *T.V.T. local enterprise, 1952–1954.* 60 pp.

2479 —— 1954. *Report of the Northern Territories Council on general development in the Northern Territories.* Tamale, Govt. Printer, 1954.

2480 —— 1955. *Feeder roads in Trans-Volta Togoland.*

2481 —— 1955. *Your government: the story of the Gold Coast general elections of 1954.* 64 pp.

2482 —— 1955. *Gold Coast Industrial Development Corporation.* 48 pp.

2483 —— 1955. *Report on enquiry with regard to Friendly and Mutual Benefit Groups in the Gold Coast, 1954.* 16 pp.

2484 —— 1955. *Report of the Constitutional Adviser.* [Sir Frederick C. Bourne.] 8 pp.

2485 —— 1955. *Report from the Select Committee on federal system of Government and second chamber for the Gold Coast.* 198 pp. (Chairman, C. H. Chapman.)

2486 —— 1955. *Report of the Committee on Ashanti-Brong dispute.* 8 pp. (Chairman, Azzu Mate-Kole.)

2487 —— 1955. *Record of the 21st session of the Northern Territories Council held at Tamale from 24th to 27th May, 1955.* Tamale, Govt. Printer, 1955. 59 pp.

2488 —— 1955. *1954 Akuse survey of household budgets.* 24 pp. (Statistical and economic papers, no. 3.)

2489 —— 1956. *Part 1: Government proposals in regard to the future constitution and control of Statutory Boards and Corporations in the Gold Coast. Part 2: Report of the Commission of Enquiry into the affairs of the Cocoa Purchasing Company Limited.* 73 pp. (Part 2: Chairman, O. Jibowu.)

2490 —— 1956. *Constitutional proposals for Gold Coast independence and statement on the report of the Constitutional Adviser and the report of the Achimota Conference.* 8 pp.

2491 GOLD COAST. GOVERNMENT, 1956. *Report of the Achimota Conference.* 20 pp.
Conference considered the recommendations of the Constitutional Adviser, Sir Frederick C. Bourne.

2492 —— 1956. *The Government's revised constitutional proposals for Gold Coast independence.* 18 pp.

2493 —— 1956. *Development progress report, 1955.* 46 pp.
Review of the First Development Plan, 1951–55.

2494 —— 1956. *Notes on Government finance.* 41 pp.

2495 —— 1956. *Report of the enquiry into the proposal to set up three district councils in place of the Mamprusi District Council.* 28 pp.

2496 —— 1956. *Report on the Northern Territories, 1955.* Tamale, Govt. Press, 1956. 120 pp.

2497 —— 1956. *Record of the 25th (emergency) meeting held at Tamale on the 17th March, 1956.* Tamale, Northern Territories Council, 1956. 13 pp.

2498 —— 1956. *Report of the Gold Coast Mines Board of Enquiry.*

2499 —— 1956. *Kumasi survey of population and household budgets, 1955.* 51 pp. (Statistical and economic papers no. 5.)

2500 —— 1956. *Sekondi Takoradi survey of population and household budgets, 1955.* 47 pp. (Statistical and economic papers, no. 4.)

2501 GOLD COAST. LANDS DEPARTMENT. *Gold Coast land tenure,* by R. J. H. Pogucki. Accra, Govt. Printer, 1955–57. 6 vols.
Vol 1: A survey of land tenure in customary law of the Protectorate of the Northern Territories. 60 pp.
Vol 2: Report on land tenure in Adangme customary law. 57 pp.
Vol 3: Land tenure in Ga customary law. 52 pp.
Vol 4: Land tenure in Ga customary law. Map supplement, Accra, 1826–1954. 11 maps.
Vol 5: A handbook of main principles of rural land tenure in the Gold Coast. 40 pp.
Vol 6: General principles of land tenure in Ghana. 79 pp.

2502 GOLD COAST. STATUTES. *Laws of the Gold Coast.* Revised ed. Accra, Govt. Printer, 1951. 5 vols.

2503 —— *Laws of the Gold Coast.* Revised ed. Sub legislation. Accra, Govt. Printer, 1954. Vols. 6–9.

2504 —— *Laws of the Gold Coast.* Supplement. Accra, Govt. Printer, 1952–54. 2 vols.

Ghana

2505 GHANA. GOVERNMENT. 1957. *Ghana is born, 6th March 1957*, by L. BIRCH. Ghana Information Services; Neame. 108 pp.

2506 —— 1957. *The speech from the throne delivered at the opening of the first session of the Parliament of Ghana by H.R.H. the Duchess of Kent on 6th March, 1957*. 2 pp.

2507 —— 1957. *National Workers' Brigade.* 7 pp.

2508 —— 1957. *Report of the Commission appointed to enquire into salaries and wages of the civil service and non-Government teaching service, 1957.*

2509 —— 1957. *Government proposals on the report of the Salaries and Wages Commission, 1957.*

2510 —— 1957. *Report of the Commissioner for Local Government Enquiries, June 1957.* (Commissioner, A. F. Greenwood.)

2511 —— 1957. *Ghana, 1957*, by KEITH JOPP. Ghana Information Services. 48 pp.

2512 —— 1957. *A new broadcasting house: the story of Radio Ghana.* 20 pp.

2513 —— 1957. *Civil aviation statistics, 1954–56.* 31 pp.

2514 —— 1958. *Government proposals regarding State lotteries.* 11 pp.

2515 —— 1958. *Regional Assemblies report to His Excellency the Governor-General, by the Regional Constitutional Commission.* viii, 227 pp. (Chairman, Mr. Justice Van Lare.)

2516 —— 1958. *Statement by the Ghana Government on the Regional Constitution Commission.* 4 pp.

2517 —— 1958. *Report of the Commission appointed to enquire into the affairs of the Akim Abuakwa State.* 52 pp. (Commissioner, J. Jackson.)

2518 —— 1958. *Report of the Commission appointed to enquire into the affairs of the Kumasi State Council and the Asanteman Council*, by MR. JUSTICE SARKODEE–ADOO.

2519 —— 1958. *An examination of the need for Government assistance to the gold mining industry in Ghana.* [40] pp.

2520 —— 1958. *Proposed scheme for the international service of the Ghana Broadcasting System*, by A. L. PIDGEON AND J. L. MARSHALL.
   A report by two officers of the Canadian Broadcasting Corporation.

2521   GHANA. GOVERNMENT. 1958. *Report of the expert adviser in pharmaceutical matters, Dr. H. Davis.* [30] pp.

2522   —— 1958. *Ghana and India.* Ghana Information Services. 24 pp.

2523   —— 1958. *Ghana and the United Nations.* Ghana Information Services. 24 pp.

2524   —— 1958. *Migration statistics, 1953–1957.* 85 pp.

2525   —— 1958. *Survey of population and budgets of cocoa producing families in the Oda-Swedru-Asamankese area, 1955–1956.* 105 pp. (Statistical and economic papers, no. 6.)

2526   —— 1958. *Education statistics.* 41 pp. (Statistical report series 1, no 5.)

2527   —— 1958. *Labour statistics, 1957.* 24 pp. (Statistical report series 3, no. 2.)

2528   —— 1958. *Local government financial statistics, 1955–56.* 50 pp.

2529   —— 1959. *Joint declaration and communiqué by the Governments of Liberia, Ghana and Guinea.* 16 pp.
       Formation of the Community of Independent African States.

2530   —— 1959. *Enquiry into matters disclosed at the trial of Captain Benjamin Awhaitey. . . 20th and 21st January 1959, before a court-martial convened at Giffard Camp,* Accra. 54 pp. (Chairman, G. Granville Sharp.)

2531   —— 1959. *Proceedings and report of the Commission appointed to enquire into the matters disclosed at the trial of Captain Benjamin Awhaitey before a court-martial and the surrounding circumstances, with the minutes of evidence taken before the Commission, January–March, 1959.* (Chairman, G. Granville Sharp.)

2532   —— 1959. *Report of the Commission appointed under the Commissions of Enquiry Ordinance (Cap. 249).* (Chairman, G. Granville Sharp.)

2533   —— 1959. *Statement by the Government on the report of the Commissioners appointed to enquire into the matters disclosed at the trial of Captain Benjamin Awhaitey before a court-martial and the surrounding circumstances.* 50 pp.

2534   —— 1959. *Interim report of the Commission of Enquiry into the working and administration of the present company law of Ghana.* (Commissioner, L. C. B. Gower.)

2535   —— 1959. *Second Development Plan, 1959–64.* 124 pp.

2536 GHANA. GOVERNMENT. 1959. *Preko Board of Enquiry: report on the proceedings of the Board appointed by the Minister of Transport and Communications to investigate level-crossing accidents.* 27 pp.

2537 —— 1959. *Labour statistics, 1958.* 28 pp.

2538 —— 1960. *Government proposals for a Republican constitution.* 16 pp.

2539 —— 1960. *Draft constitution of the Republic of Ghana.* 8 pp.

2540 —— 1960. *Ghana today: a new charter for the civil service.* 12 pp.

2541 —— 1960. *The Governor-General's speech on the prorogation of Parliament, 30th June, 1960.* 3 pp.

2542 —— 1960. *Information paper prepared by the Government of Ghana in relation to apartheid laws applying in the mandated territory of South West Africa and the Union of South Africa.* 14 pp.

2543 —— 1960. *Recommendations on the establishment of a television service in Ghana,* by R. D. CAHOON AND S. R. KENNEDY. 25 pp.

2544 —— 1960. *Government statement on the report on a television service, by Messrs. R. D. Cahoon and S. R. Kennedy of the Canadian Broadcasting Corporation.*

2545 —— 1960. *Survey of high-level manpower in Ghana.* 62 pp.

2546 —— 1960. *Report of the working party on the executive structure within the civil service.* 19 pp.

2547 —— 1960. *Report of the working party on the need for accounting qualifications in Government service.* 11 pp.

2548 —— 1960. *Report of investigation into the control, organization and development of the ports of Ghana.* 24 pp.

2549 —— 1960. *Ghana, ten great years, 1951–1960* [by KEITH JOPP]. 56 pp.

2550 —— 1960. *The Duke in Ghana: a pictorial record of the visit to Ghana of His Royal Highness the Prince Philip, Duke of Edinburgh, in 1959.* 36 pp.

2551 —— 1960. *Ghana as a republic: your questions answered.* Information Services.

2552 —— 1960. *Knowing ourselves: the 1960 Ghana population census.* 16 pp.

2553 —— 1960. *Survey of cocoa producing families in Ashanti, 1956–57.* xi, 112 pp. (Statistical and economic papers, no. 7.)

2554   GHANA. GOVERNMENT. 1960. *Directory of enterprises.* Office of the Government Statistician. 54 pp.

2555   —— 1961. *Joint-communiqué issued during Osagyefo's tour of Eastern European countries.* 28 pp.

2556   —— 1961. *White paper on marriage, divorce and inheritance.* 7 pp. (W/P no. 3/61.)

2557   —— 1961. *Report of the Commission of Enquiry into concessions.* 87 pp.

2558   —— 1961. *Report of the Commission of Enquiry into the insolvency law of Ghana.* 272 pp.

2559   —— 1961. *Report of the Commission on University education, December 1960–January 1961.* 43 pp. (Chairman, Kojo Botsio.)

2560   —— 1961. *Statement by the Government on the report of the Commission on University education, December 1960—January 1961.* 7 pp.

2561   —— 1961. *Report of the Committee on the education, rehabilitation and employment of disabled people in Ghana.* 23 pp.

2562   —— 1961. *Miscellaneous information, 1961–1962.* Ministry of Information. 225 pp. (Typescript.)

2563   —— 1961. *A brief guide to Ghana.* Ministry of Information. 71 pp.

2564   —— 1961. *The budget and you.* Ministry of Information. 10 pp.

2565   —— 1961. *Visit to Ghana by His Imperial Majesty Haile Selassie I, Emperor of Ethiopia, December 1-5, 1960.* 16 pp.

2566   —— 1961. *Statement by the President concerning properties and business connections of Ministers and Ministerial Secretaries.* 9 pp.

2567   —— 1961. *Statement by the Government on the recent conspiracy.* 41 pp.

2568   —— 1961. *Budget statement, 1961-62, by the Minister of Finance* (F. K. D. Goka). 14 pp.

2569   —— 1961. *Progress report, National Food & Nutrition Board, 1st Oct. 1960—April 1961.* 17 pp.

2570   —— 1961. *Field survey work in the Ghana Statistics Office.* 95 pp. (Statistical and economic papers, no. 8.)

2571   GHANA. STATUTES. *Ordinances and Acts of Ghana.* Accra, Govt. Printer, 1957+

Great Britain

2572 GREAT BRITAIN. CENTRAL OFFICE OF INFORMATION. 1947. *Local self-government in British West Africa.* 17 pp. (Typescript.)

2573 —— 1951. *Constitutional progress in the Gold Coast.* 9 pp.

2574 —— 1957. *Facts about the Gold Coast.* 5 pp.

2575 —— 1957. *The making of Ghana.* 46 pp.

2576 GREAT BRITAIN. COLONIAL OFFICE. 1936. *Report of a committee on pensions to widows and orphans of officers in the Colonial Service and on Colonial Provident Funds.* 63 pp. (Cmd. 5219.) (Chairman, A. W. Watson.)

2577 —— 1938. *Report of the Commission on the marketing of West African cocoa.* 221 pp. (Cmd. 5845). (Chairman, William Nowell.)

2578 —— 1940. *Native administration and political development in British tropical Africa:* report by LORD HAILEY. 1940–42. 293 pp.

2579 —— 1941. *Report by Major G. St. J. Orde-Browne, O.B.E., on labour conditions in West Africa.* (Cmd. 6277.)

2580 —— 1944. *Report on cocoa control in West Africa, 1939–1943, and statement on future policy.* 16 pp. (Cmd. 6554.)

2581 —— 1945. *Report of the Commission on higher education in West Africa.* 190 pp. (Cmd. 6655.)

2582 —— 1946. *Statement on future marketing of West African cocoa.* 12 pp. (Cmd. 6950).

2583 —— 1947. *Report of the Commission on the civil services of British West Africa, 1945–46,* by SIR WALTER HARRAGIN. 189 pp.

2584 —— 1947. *Togoland under United Kingdom Trusteeship: text of Trusteeship agreement as approved by the General Assembly of the United Nations.* 7 pp. (Treaty series, no. 21.)

2585 —— 1947. *Report by H.M. Government to the General Assembly of the United Nations on the administration of Togoland.*

2586 —— 1947. *Report of the mission appointed to enquire into the production and transport of vegetable oils and oil seeds produced in the West African colonies.* 76 pp. (Col. no. 211.)

2587 —— 1948. *Report of West African oilseeds mission.* 60 pp.

2588 —— 1948. *Report of the Commission of Enquiry into disturbances in the Gold Coast, 1948.* 103 pp. (Watson Report.)

2589   GREAT BRITAIN. COLONIAL OFFICE. 1948. *Statement by H.M. Government on the report of the Commission of Enquiry into the disturbances in the Gold Coast, 1948.* 19 pp.

2590   —— 1948. *Report of the Commission of Enquiry into the swollen shoot disease of cacao in the Gold Coast.* 10 pp.

2591   —— 1949. *Gold Coast: report to His Excellency the Governor by the Committee on constitutional reform.* (Chairman, J. H. Coussey.)

2592   —— 1952. *An economic survey of the Colonial territories. Vol 3: The Gambia, the Gold Coast, Nigeria and Sierra Leone, and St. Helena* 103 pp.

2593   —— 1954. *Dispatches on the Gold Coast Government's proposals for constitutional reform exchanged between the Secretary of State for the Colonies and H. E. the Governor, 24 August, 1953 to 15 April, 1954.* 15 pp.

2594   —— 1956. *Introducing West Africa.* 3rd ed. 79 pp.

2595   —— 1956. *Report to the General Assembly of the United Nations on Togoland under United Kingdom administration for the year 1955.* 198 pp.

2596   —— 1957. *Public Officers agreement between the Government of the United Kingdom and the Government of Ghana.* 4 pp.

2597   —— 1957. *Britain and the Gold Coast: the dawn of Ghana.* 41 pp.

2598   —— 1957. *Gold Coast becomes Ghana.* [Set of 12 plates.]

2599   —— 1957. *The proposed constitution of Ghana.* 10 pp. (Cmnd. 71).

2600   —— 1958. *Agreement between the United Kingdom and Ghana for air services between and beyond their respective territories.* 9 pp. (Cmnd. 567.)

2601   GREAT BRITAIN. DIRECTORATE OF OVERSEAS SURVEYS. *Gold Coast* (General topographical series), 1952–3. Scale 1:50,000. Preliminary plots covering the proposed Volta River Project reservoir area.

2602   —— *Volta delta, Gold Coast.* Scale 1:5,000. 1947. 8 sheets.

2603   —— *Volta river area, Gold Coast.* Scale 1:50,000. 1948. 22 sheets covering the proposed Volta River Project dam area.

2604   GREAT BRITAIN. STATUTES. 1950. *No. 2094. The Gold Coast (Constitution) Order-in-Council, 1950.*

2605   —— 1954. *No. 551. The Gold Coast (Constitution) Order-in-Council, 1954.*

2606   GREAT BRITAIN. STATUTES. 1957. *No. 277. The Ghana (Constitution) Order-in-Council, 1957.*

2607   —— 1957. *Ghana Independence Act, 1957, 5 & 6 Eliz. 2. Ch. 6.* 7 pp.

2608   —— 1960. *An Act to make provision. . . in view of Ghana's becoming a Republic while remaining a member of the Commonwealth.* 2 pp.

Index